Palgrave Studies in Globalization, Culture and Society

Series Editors
Jeroen de Kloet
Centre for Globalisation Studies
University of Amsterdam
Amsterdam, The Netherlands

Esther Peeren
Literary and Cultural Analysis
University of Amsterdam
Amsterdam, The Netherlands

Palgrave Studies in Globalization, Culture and Society traverses the boundaries between the humanities and the social sciences to critically explore the cultural and social dimensions of contemporary globalization processes. This entails looking at the way globalization unfolds through and within cultural and social practices, and identifying and understanding how it effects cultural and social change across the world. The series asks what, in its different guises and unequal diffusion, globalization is taken to be and do in and across specific locations, and what social, political and cultural forms and imaginations this makes possible or renders obsolete. A particular focus is the vital contribution made by different forms of the imagination (social, cultural, popular) to the conception, experience and critique of contemporary globalization. Palgrave Studies in Globalization, Culture and Society is committed to addressing globalization across cultural contexts (western and non-western) through interdisciplinary, theoretically driven scholarship that is empirically grounded in detailed case studies and close analyses. Within the scope outlined above, we invite junior and senior scholars to submit proposals for monographs, edited volumes and the Palgrave Pivot format. Please contact the series editors for more information: b.j.dekloet@uva.nl/e.peeren@uva.nl

More information about this series at
http://www.palgrave.com/gp/series/15109

David Craig • Jian Lin
Stuart Cunningham

Wanghong as Social Media Entertainment in China

palgrave
macmillan

David Craig
USC Annenberg School for
Communication and Journalism
Los Angeles, CA, USA

Jian Lin
Centre for Media and Journalism
Studies, University of Groningen
Groningen, The Netherlands

Stuart Cunningham
Digital Media Research Centre
Queensland University of Technology
Brisbane, QLD, Australia

ISSN 2730-9282 ISSN 2730-9290 (electronic)
Palgrave Studies in Globalization, Culture and Society
ISBN 978-3-030-65375-0 ISBN 978-3-030-65376-7 (eBook)
https://doi.org/10.1007/978-3-030-65376-7

© The Editor(s) (if applicable) and The Author(s), under exclusive licence to Springer Nature Switzerland AG 2021
This work is subject to copyright. All rights are solely and exclusively licensed by the Publisher, whether the whole or part of the material is concerned, specifically the rights of translation, reprinting, reuse of illustrations, recitation, broadcasting, reproduction on microfilms or in any other physical way, and transmission or information storage and retrieval, electronic adaptation, computer software, or by similar or dissimilar methodology now known or hereafter developed.
The use of general descriptive names, registered names, trademarks, service marks, etc. in this publication does not imply, even in the absence of a specific statement, that such names are exempt from the relevant protective laws and regulations and therefore free for general use.
The publisher, the authors and the editors are safe to assume that the advice and information in this book are believed to be true and accurate at the date of publication. Neither the publisher nor the authors or the editors give a warranty, expressed or implied, with respect to the material contained herein or for any errors or omissions that may have been made. The publisher remains neutral with regard to jurisdictional claims in published maps and institutional affiliations.

Cover illustration: Alex Linch / shutterstock.com
Cover design: eStudioCalamar

This Palgrave Macmillan imprint is published by the registered company Springer Nature Switzerland AG.
The registered company address is: Gewerbestrasse 11, 6330 Cham, Switzerland

Acknowledgments

David Craig received funding support from Shanghai Jiao Tong University's USC-SJTU Institute of Cultural and Creative Industry, and from Zizhu National High-Tech Industrial Development Zone, via the Zizhu New Media Management Research Center. This book is an output from the Australian Research Council (ARC) Discovery Project 160100086 "The New Screen Ecology and Opportunities for Innovation in Production and Distribution" for 2016–2018 awarded to Stuart Cunningham.

We take this opportunity to thank Dr. Adam Swift, who has worked (again) with us on this project and has contributed meticulous editorial oversight.

For David Craig, the Annenberg School for Communication and Journalism at the University of Southern California has provided tremendous support as have his mentors and colleagues, including Dean Willow Bay, Henry Jenkins, Sarah Banet-Weiser, Josh Kun, Hector Amaya, Ben Lee, Junyi Lv, Francois Bar, Nicholas Cull, Hernan Galperin, Colin Maclay, and Patti Riley.

From Jian Lin, a heartfelt thanks to Jeroen de Kloet and Esther Peeren for their firm support of this project and the invaluable coaching received from them in the past years. He appreciates the University of Groningen for allotting research time for writing and his superb colleagues at the Department of Media Studies and Journalism for their kind encouragement and friendship. The previous research experience at the Department of Media Studies and Amsterdam School for Cultural Analysis at the

University of Amsterdam has proven to be tremendously inspiring. Deepest thanks to Grace for her love and companionship, especially at the time of pandemic.

For Stuart Cunningham, the Digital Media Research Centre in the Creative Industries Faculty at Queensland University of Technology has been an enormously stimulating environment. He wishes to thank Jo, Vivien, Hugo, Ben, Brooke, Belle, and Billie for their sustaining love.

We use the hanyu pinyin system for Chinese terms although these are not italicized. Family names are listed first for Chinese scholars and journalists, unless listed in another order in English-language texts.

Contents

1 Introduction   1

2 Policy and Governance   29

3 Platforms   59

4 Creators   105

5 Culture   135

6 Global Wanghong   161

Index   189

List of Figures

Fig. 2.1	The growth of the Chinese digital economy 2008–2019. (Source: CAICT 2020)	37
Fig. 3.1	Chinese and United States internet users and penetration 2009–2018	64
Fig. 3.2	Percent of Chinese internet users who are mobile 2013–2020. (Source: CNNIC 2020)	65
Fig. 3.3	China's digital economy 2016–2018	65
Fig. 3.4	Li Jiaqi promoting a lipstick in livestreaming	87
Fig. 4.1	Wanghong labor	111
Fig. 5.1	Taxonomy of Wanghong content	138
Fig. 5.2	The main genres of content	139
Fig. 5.3	Liu Suliang and his bamboo rat	142
Fig. 5.4	One episode of *Zhu Yidan's boring life*	144
Fig. 5.5	Shougong Geng and his robotic washing machine	147
Fig. 5.6	Xiao Xiangge eating a light bulb lollipop	149
Fig. 6.1	Webpages of TikTok and Kwai (captured on 13-July-2020)	169
Fig. 6.2	Li Ziqi making food in her video	178

CHAPTER 1

Introduction

In 2016, co-author David Craig visited Suzhou University to deliver a lecture in the communication school. He had been invited to present ongoing research into an emerging industry of amateur entrepreneurs harnessing social media platforms to carve out quite new career opportunities which became *Social Media Entertainment: The New Intersection of Hollywood and Silicon Valley* (Cunningham and Craig 2019). In transit to the lecture, Craig inquired whether there were local enterprises of this sort. Jumping on WeChat, his student escort sent out a general request to friends who recommended a possible contact—Wei Kan. When contacted, Wei Kan agreed to participate in a Q&A after the lecture.

When the time came, Kan revealed himself as the COO of The Best of Soochow, a firm comprised of local vloggers and bloggers using Chinese social media platforms to recommend local restaurants, bars, and activities. Kan then presented his investor deck, showing Best of Soochow had secured multiple rounds of investment and expanded into seven cities in just 18 months. Toward the end of the Q&A, Kan mentioned that he was still a college student—in fact, a junior right there, at Suzhou University, in the Dental School. When the assembled communication scholars asked him why he wasn't in their school, he said, "what are you going to teach me?" Checking back a few years later when this book was being prepared, we found that Best of Soochow no longer exists and Kan is working in the banking industry.

© The Author(s), under exclusive license to Springer Nature Switzerland AG 2021
D. Craig et al., *Wanghong as Social Media Entertainment in China*, Palgrave Studies in Globalization, Culture and Society, https://doi.org/10.1007/978-3-030-65376-7_1

The story tells us a lot in miniature about the wanghong phenomenon—at once cultural, social, industrial, and ultimately highly political—that has emerged, evolved, and embedded throughout Chinese society at remarkable speed. Like much of what has happened in the evolution of China since Deng Xiaoping started the process of economic modernization in the 1980s, this phenomenon has left both Chinese and Western scholars struggling to keep pace.

A vernacular term, wanghong is a contraction of wangluo hongren (Chinese for "people who have gone viral on the internet" or, literally, "red internet"), wanghong refers to online celebrities, or micro-celebrities (Tse et al. 2018; Han 2020). Comparable terms offered slight variations in connotation and reference: there were KOLs (key opinion leaders) and zhubo (showroom hosts), as well as explicitly pejorative uses of the term to describe how female livestreamers appealing to lonely Chinese men operated within what Aynne Kokas calls a "virtual girlfriends industry" (cited in Kaiman and Meyers 2017). Over time, wanghong came to be increasingly defined "by their acute ability to convert internet viewer traffic to money with diverse economic models in its contemporary context of wanghong economy" (Han 2020).

Wanghong, the term, is thus wildly polysemic. It means "popular online", "internet famous", and can refer to celebrification as a problematic process or an entire industry. The latter use is seen increasingly frequently in the Chinese media, industry reports, and recent scholarship. In this book, we use it to refer to both the creators themselves and to the wider industry. The wanghong industry, as we understand it, refers to social media entrepreneurs and platform and intermediary media professionals working within a highly competitive platform landscape, incubated through regulatory protection, fueled by a rising middle class and responding to the demographic challenges of the urban-rural divide, and which offers potentially more lucrative opportunities for creators than their Western counterparts.

How did this happen—essentially since 2015—and with what consequences? This book engages with these questions from a critical media industries perspective, combining insights from media industry and cultural studies, and social media and platform studies. It explores the conditions of emergence of wanghong with historical, industrial, and policy-minded, as well as cultural, social, and political, lenses.

When it comes to making claims about new media industries, veteran television scholar Horace Newcomb (2009) encourages us to be precise about "who" and "what" we are discussing when writing about "the industry". Nitin Govil (2013) responds, challenging the "obviousness of the object" and arguing that the process of industrial emergence is often "achieved rather than presumed, processual than preordained" (p. 176). These conditions apply to the protean status or formalized designation of new industries. In addition to *what* is an industry, *when* is it designated? For Sheilagh Ogilvie and Markus Cerman (1996), in their study of European proto-industrialization, the recognition of the shape of new industries emerges as a process through media attention, macro-economic analysis, and evidence of state-based policy interventions. As two of us argue in *Creator Culture* (Cunningham and Craig 2021), a wave of scholarship and research around these phenomena further support the assignation of social media entertainment and wanghong as industry and a cross-disciplinary subfield of study. We now introduce the wanghong phenomenon by drawing on these kinds of sources as well as the scholarship that has pioneered in the field.

A Soupçon of Wanghong: Scope, Scale, and Significance

Media and cultural studies analysis (Zhang and de Seta 2018; Xu and Zhao 2019) has identified internet celebrification (wangluo hongren) that dates from the 1990s. Xiaofei Han (2020) warns against using

> wanghong interchangeably with the term internet celebrities (Zhang and Hjorth 2019 2017, Li 2018). ... while interrelated, they have become distinct since the mid-2010s. The Chinese term for internet celebrities is 'wangluo mingren' ('mingren' literally meaning 'famous people'), and comprises a wide spectrum of participants, such as writers, grassroots activists, public intellectuals, opinion leaders, and memes. The term 'wangluo hongren' is more specific ('hongren' meaning people who are 'red', connoting people who have become viral/popular often within a short period). In the late 1990s and 2000s, use of the term wanghong still largely overlapped with 'internet celebrities' and the patterns and/or value chains for monetising such online fame—which is arguably one of the defining characteristics of contemporary wanghong since the mid- 2010s—were yet to emerge. The meaning of the term 'wanghong' changed significantly between 2015 and 2016 due to the construction of 'wanghong economy', which diverges from the term 'internet celebrities'. (p. 2)

This reminds us there is a wide variety of online practitioners; Han's critical distinction corresponds to the distinction we will make between cultural on the one hand and creative and social on the other.

The emerging cultural trend became "officially" an economic phenomenon from Alibaba's Wanghong Economy seminar held in 2015 to boost its social e-commerce business strategy (Chen 2016; Han 2020). From then, and with Papi Jiang's breakout success seeing 2016 named "Year One of Wanghong" across Chinese media outlets, the Chinese pinyin term *wanghong* became one of the top watchwords in China (Jing 2016). Since 2016, Chinese business consultant Yuan Guabao has written multiple editions of *The Wanghong Economy* (2016) that mapped the dimensions of this industry and best practices by industry professionals. Chinese industry websites like CBNData publish annual industry reports about the "wanghong economy" that are used in research by management scholars (Prud'homme et al. 2020). Referring to wanghong as the "internet celebrity economy", the China Business Industry Research Institute (2020) lays out "an economic phenomenon born in the Internet era. It means that Internet celebrities gather traffic and popularity on social media, market a huge fan base, and convert fans' attention to them into purchasing power, thereby turning a business model for monetizing traffic".

Estimates and comparative accounts of the economic size and scale of the wanghong industry signal high growth rates. However, these accounts vary wildly and demand close scrutiny of what boundaries are put around the industry, the accounting methods used, and reliability of the source. In 2016, a BBC journalist claimed the industry was in the order of USD 8.5 billion and had just surpassed China's box office (Tsoi 2016). Four years later, according to scholar Xinyuan Wang (2020), the industry was "32 times" China's box office, citing a government propaganda source from 2018 that offered unsubstantiated and inconceivable claims that the wanghong economy was worth nearly USD 300 billion (Beijing Review 2019).

Sober scholarly assessment is nevertheless expansive; the wanghong industry is now "considered the next economic growth pole for the Chinese internet" (Han 2020, p. 1). The most recent (in late 2020) and more reliable accounts come from Chinese platform owners, business consultants, and industry analysts. In the wake of the COVID-19 crisis, a Chinese business consultancy claimed the industry has tripled in size from USD 15 billion in 2019 to USD 44 billion in 2020 (1421.com 2020). This number was confirmed by leading industry reports by TopKlout published on CBNData (2020). Other business reports attribute said growth to the rise of 5G with industry estimates closer to USD 50 billion (China Business Industry Research Institute 2020).

Industry and press accounts of the revenue generated by wanghong creators also demand careful scrutiny. According to Bytedance China CEO Kelly Zhang, on Douyin (China's version of TikTok), 22 million wanghong creators made over USD 6 billion in 2019 with revenue expected to double in 2020 (Choudhury 2020). This estimate, however, is limited to those revenue streams for creators across a single platform in an environment populated by hundreds of platforms, as we detail in Chap. 3. In Chap. 4, we discuss how these creators harness these platforms to develop a diverse portfolio of business models and revenue streams. While most wanghong creators are by no means rich, and many struggles to generate sustainable incomes, in 2019, the top wanghong creator earned USD 67 million that year by "turning fans into customers" in an industry "you've never heard of" (Youmshajekian 2019).

The social dynamics of wanghong deserve close attention—for a greater level of detail, see Chaps. 4 and 5. Platforms specializing in wanghong content and performers operate nationally, but are socially "tiered". Platforms like Douyin are designed to appeal to urban and cosmopolitan users in Tier 1 and 2 cities. Other platforms like Kuaishou target lower-tier, rural, grassroots (caogen) users (McDonald 2016). These lower-tier cities also drove the rise of China's e-commerce platforms, like Taobao and T-mall (Perez 2016). There is solid evidence that economic and creative opportunity has been provided for rural, less-educated, and lower classes of wanghong entrepreneurs—what Jian Lin and Jeroen de Kloet (2019) refer to as "unlikely" creators. There are popular media accounts of this, such as the tale of a pig farmer turned livestreamer who is "making millions" (Liu 2018). Alibaba's e-commerce platform, Taobao, launched its "village broadcasting plans" to help convert rural farmers and factory workers into wanghong (Schaefer 2019).

China's provincial governments and municipalities are sponsoring wanghong platforms and creators. Notably, many of these are outside the more affluent and cosmopolitan coastal cities. With support by the Wuhan Municipal Committee, the Tencent-backed Douyu game streaming platform launched a festival in Wuhan. In 2019, the third year of the festival attracted nearly 410,000 fans along with 310 million viewers online while earning Wuhan the title of "live city" (Daily Economic News 2019). In partnership with a local investment firm, Wuhan built a "district" or "livestreaming base" to house over 100 livestreaming wanghong (Kun 2017) to live and stream all day. (Further research suggests that this venture may have been unsuccessful.) Located in southwest China, the Chongqing Institute of Engineering has offered wanghong courses since 2017 (Lianzhang 2017).

The disruptive emergence of wanghong has become the target of state-based interventions around cyber governance and internet control in Xi Jinping's China (Creemers 2015). Platform and cultural policies enacted by the Cyberspace Administration have led to the suspension of wanghong platforms and fines, warnings and even incarceration of violating wanghong (Huang 2018; Low 2018). State demands to moderate and censor content on platforms means the employment of tens of thousands of humans, in addition to algorithms, as content moderators. The vast majority of these are Party members deemed more "stable" and "men hailing from rural areas" with the exception of "moderators from a specific ethnic group", referring to Uyghur people (Yu and Xie 2018).

And well might the party-state concern itself. In 2016, a research department at Tencent, one of China's and the world's largest tech conglomerates, conducted a study of 13,000 Chinese college students. Fifty percent aspire to become wanghong (Marketing to China 2017). More recently, university research studies placed that number at 42 percent (Roxburgh 2018). These surveys became self-fulfilling prophecies accompanied by official recognition. As of mid-2020, "China has expanded the definition of 'employed' for 8.7 million fresh college graduates to cover those that open online shops, play competitive online games or have blogs" (Leng 2020). More than state-based acclamation to boost employment data, these classifications signal the future of Chinese gig and digital—but more accurately termed—social media labor.

One of the most recent trends in wanghong's short, accelerative history, one which is bringing platforms such as TikTok and WeChat to center stage in international politics in 2020, is the way wanghong platforms have achieved what no earlier efforts for China to "go out" had—to export its culture successfully. In 2019, Beijing-based Bytedance had become "the world's most valuable startup" (Chen and Wang 2019). In 2018, their app *Douyin* became the fastest growing platform in China (Lee 2018) as has TikTok, their alternative non-Chinese platform, which is outpacing Facebook, YouTube, and Instagram (Perez 2018). Concurrently, these parallel platforms have also launched a new wave of wanghong inside and outside of the country (Kharpal 2019). Yet, these platforms, users, and wanghong have also run afoul of cultural norms and policies, with entire platforms banned in Pakistan (Jahangir 2020) and India (Singh 2020). In the United States, Chinese platforms TikTok and WeChat were targeted by the Trump administration as threats to national security, threatening the livelihoods of Western-based creators operating across these platforms (Lorenz 2020) and, more profoundly, severing essential means for communication between Chinese immigrants and their families back home (Wakabayashi et al. 2020). The contested cultural politics of globalizing wanghong platforms are treated in Chap. 6.

Wanghong vis-à-vis Social Media Entertainment (SME)

The industry based on wanghong is a major variant of what Stuart Cunningham and David Craig (2019) call social media entertainment and flourishes inside China's digital economy, a "parallel universe" in so many ways to those seen in Western countries. SME is an emerging, distinct industry based on previously amateur creators professionalizing and monetizing their content across multiple social media platforms to build global fan communities and incubate their own media brands. SME comprises an industry ecology of platforms, creators, intermediary firms, and fan communities operating interdependently, and disruptively, alongside legacy media industries as well as VOD portals, down the middle of Madison Avenue (the advertising industry), and across global media cultures. These platforms include first-generation platforms like YouTube, Twitter, and Facebook competing against—and sometimes acquiring—later-generation platforms like Twitch, Instagram, and TikTok.

SME creators range from the more prominent—gameplayers like Ninja and Markiplier; lifestyle and beauty vloggers like Huda Beauty and Michelle Phan; personality vloggers Lily Singh and the Vlogbrothers; unboxers EvanTube and Ryans Toys Review—to mid-level creators and early career aspirationals. SME intermediaries, or as YouTube refers to them, "creative services" firms, include acquired divisions of media corporations (Disney's Maker Studios, RTL's Yohobo and Stylehaul), multi-channel networks (BroadbandTV, Brave Bison), influencer advertising and talent management agencies (ViralNation, Fullscreen), and data providers (Tubefilter, SocialBlade).

Like the wanghong industry, SME is native to social media platforms, including but not limited to YouTube, Facebook, Twitch, Twitter, and Instagram. Like wanghong, social media entertainment creators have been dubbed many things: influencers, micro-celebrities, YouTubers, vloggers, livestreamers, and gameplay commentators. Similar to wanghong, creators harness these platforms to engage and aggregate massive fan communities which they have found the means to convert into cultural and commercial value. Both wanghong and SME creators have been the targets of backlashes around their scandalous behavior and illicit business practices. Vloggers Jake and Logan Paul and PewDiePie are repeatedly penalized by both their platforms and communities for breaches of decorum, as has leading Chinese beauty wanghong Zhang Dayi for the appearance of backdoor dealing and affairs with platform executives. In both industries, the rapid and rising cultural influence of creators perceived as role models has been cause for critical concern from parents and politicians.

While mindful of and careful to note these continuities, we stress the differences between wanghong and SME. While operating on United States-based platforms, SME is a global phenomenon. Chinese platforms featuring wanghong creators have quite recently been successful in "going out", but are now, in 2020, the subject of major pushback. Wanghong has come to be considered a critical part of China's high-level policy and planning and to be a leader in the digital economy and the social as well as economic benefits it may confer on such leaders (Chaps. 2 and 4). Wanghong sports a wider range of content genre, especially noting the degree to which official state participation appears to be embedded. (We explore this aspect in Chaps. 4 and 5.) Wanghong is facilitated by a mix of technological advances and business model innovations that make it more lucrative on a per capita basis than SME (Chap. 3). While both industries exhibit endemic precariousness and highly problematic labor conditions for creators, wanghong have the onerous weight of dealing with the always-on surveillance of the party-state and its always-readiness to intervene, censor and not irregularly close down wanghong platforms.

We will throughout the book note quite systematically differences and similarities between the wanghong industry and SME. We do this mindful of, and seeking to address, long-standing concerns voiced by scholars about Western-centric analyses of Chinese media industries. Leading communication scholar Guobin Yang (2014) warns that we need to move beyond Chinese exceptionalism: "distinctively Chinese characteristics are the beginning, not the end, of analysis" (p. 136), which means any declaration of distinction demands further explication. These studies are often problematic for their binary "either/or" frameworks (Huang 2016) or "sweeping and dichotomous analytic frameworks" (Yang 2014, p. 136). Wilfred Wang and Ramon Lobato (2019) posit that scholars ought to reevaluate the degree to which implicit western centrism in media and social media studies theory and frameworks may have inhibited a fuller understanding of Chinese strategy and achievement in the screen industries. In our comparative account of both industries, we take up the charge posed by de Kloet et al. (2019) to "explore overlaps and similarities, alongside differences, and to zoom in on contradictions, ambivalences, and connections rendering it urgent to commit to detailed, locally specific, and empirical analyses" (p. 250).

CRITICAL MEDIA INDUSTRIES PERSPECTIVES

The critical media industries approach we adopt in this book seeks to analyze the dynamic relations of culture, media, technology and political power and policy. Douglas Kellner's (2003) critical cultural studies agenda recommended a three-fold project of analyzing the production and political economy of culture, cultural texts, and the audiences and reception of these texts and their effects. This approach "avoids too narrowly focusing on one dimension of the project to the exclusion of others" (2003, p. 4). Horace Newcomb (2009) advocated for "synthetic media industry research", proposing a balanced approach to the power, structure, and agency of media industries and workers. In his standard work on *The Cultural Industries* (2019), David Hesmondhalgh brings together "a combination of political economy, critical sociology and cultural studies of media industries and media production" (p. 77).

Building on these advances, critical media industry studies (CMIS) (Havens et al. 2009; Herbert et al. 2020), seeks to bring the concerns and focus of political economy and cultural studies closer together. To do this, however, it is necessary to critique both. CMIS pays close attention to the political, economic, and social dimensions of popular culture and its production practices. What political economy and cultural studies often see as mass culture fatally compromised by commercialism, CMIS regards as a major focus for representation and contestation, often around marginalized and emerging groups. "Ignoring the logic of representational practices in entertainment production works to reinforce the relative invisibility or misrepresentation of those who often have the least power in the public sphere" (Havens et al. 2009, p. 250).

Cultural studies inform CMIS' focus on "the complex and ambivalent operations of power as exercised through the struggle for hegemony" (Havens et al. 2009, p. 235). But serious, sustained attention to the industrial processes of digitization and globalization differentiates CMIS from cultural studies. On the other hand, the tendency in political economy to focus on news media means that CMIS often differentiates in its focus on entertainment—where pursuing the implications of power needs to be more nuanced: "If and when popular culture is considered within a political-economic analysis, there is a reductionist tendency to treat it as yet another form of commodified culture operating only according to the interests of capital. There is little room to consider the moments of creativity and struggles over representational practices from that vantage point" (Havens et al. 2009, p. 236).

To give an adequate account of creator or wanghong agency as more than "yet another form of commodified culture operating only according to the interests of capital [or party-state]", we need to address the question of commercialism and brand culture. Dealing with these questions across a wide range of contemporary online commercial and not-for-profit culture, Henry Jenkins, Sam Ford, and Joshua Green (2018) are clear that the kind of participatory culture exemplified in SME and wanghong practices cannot be reduced to "consumptive behavior by a different name":

> [I]f we see participatory culture, though, as a vital step toward the realization of a century-long struggle for grassroots communities to gain greater control over the means of cultural production and circulation—if we see participation as the work of publics and not simply of markets and audiences—then opportunities to expand participation are struggles we must actively embrace through our work. (Jenkins et al. 2018, p. 193)

Sarah Banet-Weiser (2012) has produced an important account of commercial culture from a critical perspective. She rejects the binary logic that equates the commercial with inauthenticity, and the noncommercial with authenticity, as "too simple" (Banet-Weiser 2012, p. 11), just as she similarly refuses the narrative that a citizenship culture has been transformed or disintegrated into a consumerist culture (Banet-Weiser 2012, p. 133). Brand culture is first and foremost *culture*; it is foundational, rather than the epiphenomenon thrown up as the byproduct of a singular, supervening capitalist hegemony. As such, it is fundamentally productive yet ambivalent, holding out the "possibility for individual resistance and corporate hegemony simultaneously" (Banet-Weiser 2012, p. 12). Deeming the anticonsumerist left critique to be "nostalgia for authenticity," Banet-Weiser recognizes that "individual resistance within consumer culture is defined and exercised within the parameters of that culture; to assume otherwise is to believe in a space outside consumerism that is somehow unfettered by profit motive and the political economy" (Banet-Weiser 2012, pp. 12–3).

Through vlogging, streaming, and tweeting alongside commenting, curating, and sharing, creators and wanghong enhance community engagement and, in turn, commercial viability. They generate alternative creator cultures distinct from what Kellner (1995) calls media culture. They foster fan communities built around their affinities, identities, and values, not necessarily in a critically progressive manner. Some of the most successful creators push cultural or social norms to secure the devotion of their fan communities.

Framing Themes: Cultural, Creative, Social

In addition to bedrock adherence to a form of cultural nationalism that has become progressively more bellicose under Xi Jinping, and investing hugely in reforms to shore up the growth of especially the digital creative industries, China has led the world in what we have come to dub "social" industries. To repeat, these concepts—cultural, creative, social industries—do not describe three separate phenomena; they are conceptual frameworks with which we seek to capture different aspects of China's wanghong's history and broader context.

Cultural Industries

The concept of cultural (or culture) industries has a decades-long history. (The best introduction is Hesmondhalgh's (2019) *The Cultural Industries*.) It also has an explicitly Marxist history—which may once have made it amenable to China's policy makers—dating back to Theodor Adorno and Max Horkheimer's attack on the capitalist industrialization of culture in the 1940s and the New Left's riffing on the theme in the 1960s, for example with Herbert Marcuse's critique of the one dimensionality of contemporary culture (Marcuse 1964). The term became more common from the 1970s, particularly as industry leaders and policy makers struggled with how to respond to both rapid deindustrialization and the emergence of world-leading popular music and broader popular culture in "Cool Britannia", turning to culture as a site for economic development strategies.

In Hesmondhalgh's (2019) *The Cultural Industries* we see a careful working out of the relationship between "core" cultural industries (television and radio, film, music, print and publishing, games, advertising and, marketing and public relations, and web design), and those that are "neighbouring", "peripheral", "borderline" or "problem" cases. This is helpful for underlining the relationships we are establishing across cultural, creative, and social themes in this book. On the one hand, Hesmondhalgh is critical that many accounts of the cultural industries and media industries fail to pay adequate attention to "neighbouring" sectors such as telecommunications, consumer electronics and the IT industry (pp. 17–9). On the other hand, he considers social media as a "borderline case" in even an open and inclusive treatment of cultural industries as "[social media industries'] basis is the commodification of ordinary sociality and communication, rather than of culture" (pp. 22–3).

"Cultural industries", says Michael Keane (2013, p. 23) in his detailed account of official Chinese state language use, "is the official national term emanating from Beijing". But the nuances are apparent when we consider that, according to Hesmondhalgh, "The cultural industries have usually been thought of as those institutions … which are most directly involved in the production of social meaning. … they deal with the industrial production and circulation of texts" (2019, pp. 14–5).

For the Chinese party-state, social cohesion, and "harmony" rests as much on a cultural base as on an economic one. And the "ultimate point of reference is China's pre-eminent civilization and the historical idea of the 'middle kingdom' (Zhongguo)" (Keane 2013, p. 27). This has meant that there has never been—despite all that has happened to turbocharge the Chinse digital and platform economy and its technological infrastructure—a fundamental move away from this historical term cultural industries and we will see how the attempt to persuade or enforce adherence to normative cultural precepts and norms plays out throughout succeeding chapters.

Creative Industries

The concept of creative industries has a shorter, twenty-plus year history. It was also incubated in the UK, developed by a mixture of industry leaders and policy makers seeking to contemporize the scope of cultural activity and maximize the export opportunities for British creative output. The original UK Government Department for Culture, Media and Sport (DCMS) definition describes the creative industries as "those industries which have their origin in individual creativity, skill and talent and which have a potential for wealth and job creation through the generation and exploitation of intellectual property" (DCMS 2001, p. 4). Sociologists Scott Lash and John Urry double down on the IP aspect of the category, arguing that each of the creative industries has an "irreducible core" concerned with "the exchange of finance for rights in intellectual property" (Lash and Urry 1994, p. 117).

What are the deeper drivers of this newer concept? These can be understood as long-term, structural changes in economy and society, summed up in the notion of "culturization". Fundamental economic trends underpin the process, such as rising affluence, which shifts aggregate expenditure towards cultural consumption; the related rise in human capital, which permits greater specialization; growth in ICT, which is the technology base of the creative industries; and globalization, as access to global markets both in demand and factor mobility (Potts and Cunningham 2008). Such economic indicators correlate with notions of the "creative" or "experience" economy and reflect the attempt to grasp the increasing proportion of activity that is occurring to meet what Abraham Maslow, with his concept of a hierarchy of needs, famously called the "higher-order" needs (social needs, esteem needs, and self-actualization) (see Cunningham 2014).

It was Lash and Urry (1994) who coined the term culturization of the economy. This marks a sharp break from the critique of the industrialization of culture—Adorno and Horkheimer's original dystopian version of the culture industry. Instead of culture being suborned by the industrial age, what Lash and Urry observed was "ordinary manufacturing industry ... becoming more and more like the production of culture" (p. 123). Creative industries is a term that captures the fact that cultural products and services are growing as a proportion of whole economies, but also that design and business models derived from the creative sector are infusing contemporary social and business practice.

In China, there has always been a cautious and skeptical approach to the adoption of the concept of creative industries. It exudes highly suspect Western ideals of individualism, self-expression, and creative freedom. In the early days of China's project to adopt and adapt this concept, United States-based China scholar Jin Wang (2004) noted that the "least problematic" idea in a western liberal democracy, that of creativity, might be the "most problematic" in China. But investing hugely in reforms to grow especially the digital economy and infrastructure has meant that China cannot avoid managing into public policy and programs such a concept. Thus, the slogan "from made in China to created in China" became a rallying cry for reform in the early 2000s (Keane 2013, p. 6).

These terms often get joined up, in terminology such as "cultural creative industries" and "cultural and creative industries", in a process of pragmatic inclusivity. There has often been a distinction made between the definition of the cultural/culture industries as those that have core propaganda functions such as the traditional big industrial media of broadcasting and print and those which belong in the light entertainment and small-medium business domains which can be allocated to the creative industries part of the field (Hartley et al. 2013). There are also the pragmatics of cultural industries remaining the preferred terminology in national policy statements while municipal and local governments will often use creative industries or the hybrid cultural creative industries (Keane 2013, p. 42). Chapter 2 goes further into these terminological nuances.

Social Industries

The centrality of the performance of authentic interpersonal communication and of the relational labor of sociality has been a strong theme in our previous work on SME and online creative labor (Cunningham and Craig 2019; Lin and de Kloet 2019). In Cunningham and Craig's previous work on the subject, we say that "[v]ital to grasping the significance of SME is understanding how social media entertainment platforms operated as both content delivery systems and networked communication technology" (Cunningham and Craig 2019, p. 32). SME creator culture is being developed and practiced at the intersection of the digital and the social, the interpersonal and the mass; SME is *both* a content *and* a communication industry and creators *both* produce and distribute content *and* manage through relational labor their communities.

Early scholarly accounts of "social industries" and "social media industries" looked at new markets created by public-service and non-profit social service providers (Freyens 2011). In his edited volume *The Social Media Industries* (2013), Alan Albarran and his contributors articulate the emerging market conditions for industries dependent on the network effects of social media platforms. Disruptive of legacy and even digital advertising, social marketing and advertising refer to strategies and practices derived from the information generated by widespread consumer engagement with platforms (Li and Bernoff 2008; Bakshy et al. 2012). Social marketing and advertising use the term "social video" for video circulated across social media platforms designed to drive engagement, rather than more traditional calculations of impressions. According to an industry website, "Every social video aims to drive social actions such as shares, comments, and likes. Those acts of engagement are what bring your content organically into the feeds of potential new followers and new audiences" (Wochit 2019). Fullscreen, one of the prominent firms in SME, promotes the term *social entertainment* (Nizan 2019).

Social games are based around social platforms "providing users with an identity and also can provide the backbone for simple forms of communication (such as notifications and so forth)" (O'Neill 2008). This concept has been featured in recent scholarship around the gaming industry, most notably in Asian markets where videogame practices are more advanced than in the West. Mirko Ernkvist (2016) described the formation of the new social game industry in Japan dating back to 2011 that "emerged from the entrepreneurial conditions of the mobile Internet-service sector rather than the established video-game industries" (p. 93).

Extending beyond advertising and entertainment discourses, the concept of social journalism varies from those practices by journalists on social media to a "hybrid model of content from professional journalists, paid and unpaid contributors and readers" (Sussman 2014). The term has been advanced by journalism scholars including Jeff Jarvis (2014), who launched a master's degree in social journalism at the Graduate School of Journalism at City University of New York. These developments accompanied the rise of digital-first news organizations like Daily Beast and Buzzfeed harnessing social media platforms for reach, and anticipated the rise of social publishing platforms like Medium and Substack (Botticello 2020).

For over a decade, social media studies (SMS) and platform studies scholars have advanced new concepts and research agendas to identify their fields as discrete objects of study (Montfort and Bogost 2009;

Fordyce and Apperley 2016). Nancy Baym's (2002) field-setting work around computer-mediated communication anticipates how social media allows users to foster online identities. danah boyd and Nicole Ellison (2007) further defined these platforms by their ability to allow users to construct public profiles, list their own connections, and view those connections with others. Jose van Dijck and Thomas Poell (2013) differentiate the logics of social media from those of mass media through the four principles of programmability, popularity, connectivity, and datafication. Peter Ballon (2014) further differentiated social media platforms from digital media portals such as video streaming services Netflix and Amazon Prime Video. The former, he argues, depend upon open access, user affinities, peer-to-peer connectivity, and empowerment. Van Dijck (2013) divided social media platforms into networking, content generation, and trading and marketing platforms, noting blurred lines "as part of the continuous battle to dominate a segment of online sociality" (2013, p. 8).

Recent work around the platformization of the internet and rise of the "platform society" (Helmond 2015; van Dijck et al. 2018) have placed greater focus and awareness of how social networking sites have become the primary means for users to harness the technological features of the internet, effectively turning the internet into the social web. David Nieborg and Thomas Poell (2018) further advanced this concept of platformization for "the penetration of economic, governmental, and infrastructural extensions of digital platforms into the web and app ecosystems" (p. 4276). These conceptual frameworks provide diagnostic tools for better understanding China's digital economy, as in the case of the growth of "superapps" like WeChat, which provide vital infrastructure upon which all forms of economic, social, and cultural activities transpire (Plantin and de Seta 2019).

The commercialization practices by creators who trade in these social dynamics are not fundamentally different to established media business models. Both SME creators and wanghong secure traditional advertising, subscription, and transactional revenue, as well as fees for live performance from platforms and in traditional media. However, these industries have introduced "social business models" including programmatic advertising, influencer marketing (branded content), and e-commerce integrations which are highly disruptive of the norms of media advertising as ROI is driven by the socialization and engagement practices by creators on these platforms. Crowd-funding and virtual goods comprise radically new forms of revenue generation built upon online engagement and interactivity.

What distinguishes wanghong industries from SME, however, is that Chinese social media platforms have developed world-leading integration of social features and monetizing affordances (exemplified by their social business models such as social video, social tipping, and social commerce). Haiqing Yu (2019, n.p.) argues that Chinese social media platforms have pioneered in advancing the so-called "social plus business model", which "combines social networking and entertainment in the context of e-commerce transactions".

The sociality of production on these platforms on the one hand echoes Jenkins' account of participatory culture on the western platforms: "the web has become a site of consumer participation" (2006, p. 137). In his political economy of networks, Yochai Benkler (2006) described how "social production in general and peer production in particular present new sources of competition to incumbents that produce information goods for which there are now socially-produced substitutes" (p. 122). Axel Bruns' neologism "produsers" captured the new opportunities on social media platforms (2008) and Burgess and Green's account of vernacular creativity across YouTube (2018) signals the industrialization of the social. On the other hand, rather than trading in traditional media intellectual property, for example, films or television, books or movies, many creators work to foster "social content", which aim at not only facilitating platform engagement and interactivity (through comments, likes, sharing, and curation), but also branding and e-commerce.

This particular feature of Chinese platforms demonstrates the wide integration of "social presence" in their interfaces and affordances. Though first introduced by western computer scientists in the 1970s (Short et al. 1976), Chinese computer scientists and media and communication scholars have deepened our understanding of the concept of social presence in their analysis of the socio-technological affordances of virtual reality, social media, and livestreaming (Lu et al. 2016; Liu et al. 2020). As Wang and Lobato (2019) note, Chinese scholars' focus on social presence signals their awareness of the need to differentiate the ontology of China's platforms from those of the West.

Wanghong as a practice and an industry takes the dimension of sociality to a new level. This social dimension of wanghong industry not only resides in its provocative contents and relational creator labor, but also its transformative influence on Chinese society and social governance. As we illustrate in the following chapters, the governance of wanghong economy goes beyond China's existing policy agenda of commercializing and digitizing cultural production, but also fits into the state's aspiration to platformize the economy and embed mass entrepreneurship as a step change in employment. The inclusive nature of wanghong employment promises to contribute to the state's agenda of poverty alleviation and rural regeneration (see Chap. 2). In practice, the wanghong economy invites and enables various Chinese individuals, especially those relatively marginal populations such as farmers, migrant workers, and housewives, to become entrepreneurial creators, forming the so-called "unlikely creative class" (Lin and de Kloet 2019). Alongside these "unlikely" creators are their similarly "unlikely aesthetics" as bodied forth in their contents, which originate from and resonate with the mundane lives lived by the majority of Chinese individuals. Chapter 5 profiles wanghong culture, through such aesthetic "unlikeliness" and its highly communicative features, light-heartedly reframing mundane everyday life and established Chinese screen culture, both of which can be experienced as "boring" within the Chinese hierarchical social, cultural, and economic order.

It is this intensification and extensification of the social dimension that distinguishes wanghong industry from both established media industries in general and from SME outside China, and justifies devoting some more space to this emerging concept—social industries—rather than the previous two well-established concepts. As earlier argued, the way the emerging shape of new industries may be evidenced is through the accumulation of popular journalistic and academic accounts, the adumbration of new data, and advent of policy interventions. We see evidence in these indictors for "social industries" as an emerging concept. Subsequent chapters contain our detailed discussion of the relevant policy (Chap. 2) and data (Chaps. 3, 4, and 5).

The Shape of the Book to Come

Chapter 2 concerns itself with policy and governance. The concept of governance captures more than state policy and regulation; '[g]overnance refers … to all processes of governing, whether undertaken by a government, market, or network, whether over a family, tribe, formal or informal organization, or territory, and whether through laws, norms, power or language' (Bevir 2012). *The governance of China*—the title of Xi Jinping's collected speeches (2014, 2017, 2020)—involves more than the development and implementation of state policy. As Wang and Lobato (2019) argue, in contrast to the "essentially liberal values" of free speech and free markets, which are the constitutive conditions underlying much of Silicon

Valley business practice, approaches to the governance of the Chinese internet do not see communication technologies as being outside the state's political domain. Instead, media and communication technologies have always been conceptualized as part of the state's political apparatus. China's platform evolution reflects this, requiring as it does constant realignment in the wake of ongoing policy shifts. For example, these developments have exposed ongoing policy tensions between protection of China's traditional cultural heritage and the pressure to keep their platform economy growing at rapid pace. The chapter builds on our core themes of the cultural, the creative and the social by demonstrating how policies embodying distinctive Chinese interpretations of western concepts of cultural industries and creative industries have been deployed, exemplifying how China has maintained its vestigial Marxist principles, alongside its more assertive cultural nationalism, while at the same time embracing the industrial modernization offered by creative industries policies including IP rectification and growing global brands. But it is China's pivotal embrace of the full potential of digital platformization of economy and society that marks Chinese policy and governance as world leading—both for its integration of social amelioration objectives as well as the concerning level of social surveillance.

Chapter 3 is a study of Chinese platforms on which the wanghong economy is built. We contrast these to the SME platform landscape, using the concepts of hyperplatformization, interplatformization, portalization, and the affordances of social presence. Hyperplatformization refers to the accelerated rate of adoption of ICT and mobile consumer technologies and the underlying material conditions for China's platform economy that makes it arguably a more competitive business environment than that on which SME is built. There are of course exceptions—platforms seek to secure monopolistic advantages (Tencent most particularly). But if the environment is more competitive, it is also more collaborative—perhaps because of such competitive pressures. Interplatformization is our term for this more collaborative environment, in which platforms engage in greater interoperability than their Western counterparts.

The chapter also analyses portalization as the process by which entertainment IP content is now increasingly curated and delivered by "portals"—Amanda Lotz's (2017) term for streaming professional video content services such as Netflix and Amazon Prime Video. Another distinctive feature of the Chinese online landscape is that the stand-off in Western online content delivery systems between platforms and portals—between SME and SVOD—is blurred in China. This is another sign of the dynamism and adaptability of the Chinese ecology but it produces both opportunity and threat for wanghong. We use the concept of social presence to build out our exposition of the social industries in this, current, chapter. In Chap. 3, the wanghong platform landscape is shown to be cultivated by technological innovations that allow for social commentary, social streaming, and social video. These affordances, in turn, enhance wanghong platform and creator viability through the near frictionless ability to engage in social tipping and social commerce, the latter two phenomena part of a "social+" business model. These developments have underpinned strong growth in the industry, and differentiate wanghong further from SME.

In Chap. 4, we examine the conditions of wanghong labor in the context of state surveillance, competitive pressures, algorithmic culture, and the role of intermediary management enterprises—multichannel networks (MCNs). The strength of our cultural, creative, and social explanatory categories is tested in their application to the socioeconomic and practice backgrounds of wanghong. There are "cultural" wanghong—the most successful referred to as "Big V" or KOLs. Cultural wanghong are typically media professionals and experts, for example, authors or actors, who use wanghong platforms to extend their celebrity status or advance their expertise. A number of these creators were previously employed by legacy media organizations in television, news media, and film. "Creative" wanghong are professionalizing amateur creators native to social media platforms generating content built around lifestyles and affinities. Creative wanghong range from urban-based university-educated young hipsters through to rural peasants and migrant workers and bear closest similarities to typical SME creators. "Social" wanghong have emerged on social streaming and social video platforms and have cultivated followers and revenue less by their content practices than through mediated social interaction, their cultivation of social presence. The affordances on later generation platforms such as Douyin and Kwai have nurtured the rise of business models including social tipping and social commerce. Combined, these socio-technological features and commercial business models further distinguish this landscape from its SME counterparts.

Chapter 5 delves into the paradoxes and dilemmas of wanghong culture. It firstly locates wanghong in the trajectory of cultural history in contemporary China, asking how distant it may be from the rebellious youth of the May Fourth movement and the revolutionary era as well as those Red Guard youth active during the Cultural Revolution in the

1970s. Wanghong presents as hypercommercialized, deeply depoliticized and non-revolutionary, defined by individualism and consumerism. But it also sits at the center of China's high-level policy pivot to building the world's most advanced digital economy and a robust domestic consumer economy rather than relying on cheap exports, to say nothing of the social amelioration entrusted by Chinese policy makers to vernacular creativity. And, to deepen the paradoxes, if wanghong's consumerism and commodified entertainment culture are degrading and apolitical, why is it also dangerous and disruptive to such an extent that the party-state becomes so wary and censorially intervenes so often? Chapter 5 continues to build on the book's themes of cultural, creative, and social by developing a taxonomy of their relationships illustrated by representative and leading wanghong. The dizzying range of genres and styles of wanghong content testifies again to differences compared with SME genre. The "unlikely" aesthetics and their inherent sociality, we argue, contributes to the authenticity of wanghong culture, serving as "light-hearted resistance" which does not challenge the social and political order, but teases, refuses, and disrupts everyday lives that have been made "boring" in a real-world of hierarchy, constraint, and conservatism.

Finally, Chap. 6 considers how the wanghong industry is "going out" transnationally, regionally, or globally. Our analysis also revisits the key arguments addressed throughout the book regarding wanghong governance, platforms, labor and management, and culture. Wanghong platforms, we argue, represent the most successful of many attempts for Chinese culture to go out, and thus compete against the United States-driven social media entertainment industry and the platforms it operates on. But the backlash against the take-up of particularly TikTok signals rising platform nationalism, and undermines the possibility of a global creator culture that transcends national borders, geography, and cultural differences. It is the wanghong industry, having produced a successful proof of concept for Chinese cultural going out, that now sits at the leading edge of concerns for the future prospects of globalizing popular culture.

REFERENCES

1421. (2020, June 24). The Influencer Economy in China. Retrieved September 15, 2020, from https://www.1421.consulting/2020/06/influencer-economy-in-china/.

Albarran, A. (Ed.). (2013). *The Social Media Industries*. London and New York: Routledge.

Bakshy, E., Eckles, D., Yan, R., & Rosenn, I. (2012). Social Influence in Social Advertising: Evidence from Field Experiments. In *Proceedings of the 13th ACM Conference on Electronic Commerce* (pp. 146–161).
Ballon, P. (2014). Old and New Issues in Media Economics. In K. Donders, C. Pauwels, & J. Loisen (Eds.), *The Palgrave Handbook of European Media Policy* (pp. 70–95). Basingstoke: Palgrave.
Banet-Weiser, S. (2012). *AuthenticTM: The Politics of Ambivalence in a Brand Culture*. New York: NYU press.
Baym, N. (2002). Interpersonal Life Online. In L. Lievrouw & S. Livingstone (Eds.), *The Handbook of New Media* (pp. 35–54). London: Sage.
Beijing Review. (2019, August 26). Internet Celebrity Economy. *Beijing Review*. Retrieved October 8, 2020, from http://www.bjreview.com/Nation/201908/t20190826_800176806.html.
Benkler, Y. (2006). *The Wealth of Networks: How Social Production Transforms Markets and Freedom*. New Haven: Yale University Press.
Bevir, M. (2012). *Governance: A Very Short Introduction*. Oxford: Oxford University Press.
Botticello, C. (2020, April 2). Substack vs Medium. *Medium*. Retrieved October 6, 2020, from https://medium.com/substack-writing/substack-vs-medium-dd3761bf3c34.
boyd, d., & Ellison, N. (2007). Social Network Sites: Definition, History, and Scholarship. *Journal of Computer-Mediated Communication, 13*(1), 210–230.
Bruns, A. (2008). *Blogs, Wikipedia, Second Life and Beyond: From Production to Produsage*. New York: Peter Lang.
Burgess, J., & Green, J. (2018). *YouTube: Online Video and Participatory Culture* (2nd ed.). Cambridge: Polity Press.
CBNData. (2020). White Paper on the Development of Wanghong E-commerce Ecology 2019 [2019网红电商生态发展白皮书]. Retrieved October 6, 2020, from https://www.cbndata.com/report/1861/detail?isReading=report&page=17.
Chen, X. (2016, September 8). Chinese Wanghong Industry Research Report 2016 [中国网红产业专题研究报告2016]. *Read01.com*. Retrieved July 3, 2020, from https://read01.com/4J8dnO.html#.XST0jZNKiXU.
Chen, L., & Wang, S. (2019, January 15). Bytedance Hits Lower-End of Sales Goal Amid Slowdown. *Bloomberg*. Retrieved July 3, 2020, from https://www.bloomberg.com/news/articles/2019-01-15/bytedance-is-said-to-hit-lower-end-of-sales-goal-amid-slowdown.
China Business Industry Research Institute. (2020). *2020 China Internet Celebrity Economic Market Prospects and Investment Research Report*. Retrieved October 8, 2020, from https://zhuanlan.zhihu.com/p/112871415.
Choudhury, S. (2020, September 15). Bytedance Douyin Has 600 Million Daily Active Users. *CNBC*. Retrieved October 8, 2020, from https://www.cnbc.

com/2020/09/15/bytedance-douyin-has-600-million-daily-active-users.html.
Creemers, R. (2015). Never the Twain Shall Meet? Rethinking China's Public Diplomacy Policy. *Chinese Journal of Communication, 8*(3), 306–322.
Cunningham, S. (2014). *Hidden Innovation: Policy, Industry and the Creative Sector.* St Lucia: University of Queensland Press.
Cunningham, S., & Craig, D. (2019). *Social Media Entertainment: The New Intersection of Hollywood and Silicon Valley.* New York: NYU Press.
Cunningham, S., & Craig, D. (Eds.). (2021). *Creator Culture: An Introduction to Social Media Entertainment.* New York: NYU Press.
Daily Economic News. (2019, June 23). 2019 Douyu Livestreaming Festival [2019斗鱼直播节完美落幕]. *Baidu.com.* Retrieved July 3, 2020, from https://baijiahao.baidu.com/s?id=1637059886188348162&wfr=spider&for=pc&ivk_sa=1023197a&isFailFlag=1.
de Kloet, J., Poell, T., Guohua, Z., & Yiu Fai, C. (2019). The Platformization of Chinese Society: Infrastructure, Governance, and Practice. *Chinese Journal of Communication, 12*(3), 249–256.
Department for Culture, Media and Sport. (2001, April 9). *Creative Industries Mapping Documents 2001.* Retrieved October 8, 2020, from https://www.gov.uk/government/publications/creative-industries-mapping-documents-2001.
Ernkvist, M. (2016). The Role of Dual Institutional- and Technological Entrepreneurship in the Formation of the Japanese Social-Game Industry. In A. Fung (Ed.), *Global Game Industries and Cultural Policy* (pp. 91–124). Cham: Palgrave Macmillan.
Fordyce, R., & Apperley, T. (2016). Introduction: Special Section on Platform Studies. *Digital Culture & Education, 8*(2), 170–172.
Freyens, B. (2011). The Mesoeconomics of Social Industries. In S. Mann (Ed.), *Sectors Matter! Exploring Mesoeconomics* (pp. 219–238). Berlin: Springer.
Govil, N. (2013). Recognizing 'Industry'. *Cinema Journal, 52*(3), 172–176.
Guabao, Y. (2016). 网红经济: 移动互联网时代的千亿红利市场 [Wanghong Economy: 100 Billion Dividend Market in the Era of Mobile Internet.] 企业管理出版社.
Han, X. (2020). Historicising Wanghong Economy: Connecting Platforms Through Wanghong and Wanghong Incubators. *Celebrity Studies.* https://doi.org/10.1080/19392397.2020.1737196.
Hartley, J., Potts, J., Cunningham, S., Flew, T., Keane, M., & Banks, J. (2013). *Key Concepts in Creative Industries.* London: Sage.
Havens, T., Lotz, A., & Tinic, S. (2009). Critical Media Industry Studies: A Research Approach. *Communication, Culture & Critique, 2*(2), 234–253.

Helmond, A. (2015). The Platformization of the Web: Making Web Data Platform Ready. *Social Media+ Society*, *1*(2). https://doi.org/10.1177/2056305115603080.

Herbert, D., Lotz, A., & Punathambekar, A. (2020). *Media Industry Studies*. London: Polity.

Hesmondhalgh, D. (2019). *The Cultural Industries* (4th ed.). London: Sage.

Huang, P. (2016). Our Sense of Problem: Rethinking China Studies in the United States. *Modern China*, *42*(2), 115–161.

Huang, E. (2018, January 5). China's Social Media Giants Want Their Users to Help Out with the Crushing Burden of Censorship. *Quartz*. Retrieved July 3, 2020, from https://qz.com/1172536/chinas-social-media-giants-tencent-toutiao-weibo-want-their-users-to-help-out-with-censorship/.

Jahangir, R. (2020, July 21). Live Streaming App Bigo Banned in Pakistan. *Dawn*. Retrieved October 6, 2020, from https://www.dawn.com/news/1570250.

Jarvis, J. (2014, April 26). A Degree in Social Journalism. *BuzzMachine*. Retrieved July 3, 2020, from https://buzzmachine.com/2014/04/26/degree-social-journalism/.

Jenkins, H. (2006). *Fans, Bloggers, and Gamers: Exploring Participatory Culture*. New York: NYU Press.

Jenkins, H., Ford, S., & Green, J. (2018). *Spreadable Media: Creating Value and Meaning in a Networked Culture*. New York: NYU Press.

Jing, J. (2016, January 21). 'In' Words. *Beijing Review*. Retrieved July 3, 2020, from http://www.bjreview.com/Lifestyle/201605/t20160527_800057979.html.

Kaiman, J., & Meyers, J. (2017, June 24). Chinese Authorities Put the Brakes on a Surge in Live Streaming. *Los Angeles Times*. Retrieved July 15, 2020, from https://www.latimes.com/world/asia/la-fg-china-live-streaming-crackdown-20170624-story.html.

Keane, M. (2013). *Creative Industries in China: Art, Design and Media*. New Jersey: John Wiley & Sons.

Kellner, D. (1995). *Media Culture: Cultural Studies, Identity, and Politics Between the Modern and the Postmodern*. London and New York: Routledge.

Kellner, D. (2003). Cultural Studies, Multiculturalism, and Media Culture. In G. Dines & J. Humez (Eds.), *Gender, Race, and Class in Media* (pp. 9–20). Thousand Oaks: Sage.

Kharpal, A. (2019, May 29). TikTok Owner ByteDance Is a $75 Billion Chinese Tech Giant – Here's What You Need to Know About It. *CNBC*. https://www.cnbc.com/2019/05/30/tiktok-owner-bytedance-what-to-know-about-the-chinese-tech-giant.html.

Kun, L. (2017, September 27). Wuhan to Open Livestreaming Base. *Chinadaily.com.cn*. Retrieved July 3, 2020, from http://www.chinadaily.com.cn/china/2017-09/27/content_32538318.htm.

Lash, S., & Urry, J. (1994). *Economies of Signs and Space*. London: Sage.

Lee, M. (2018, September 19). Short Video Apps Like Douyin (TikTok) Are Dominating Chinese Screen. *CNBC.com*. Retrieved October 6, 2020, from https://www.cnbc.com/2018/09/19/short-video-apps-like-douyin-tiktok-are-dominating-chinese-screens.html.
Leng, S. (2020, July 6). Coronavirus: China Tweaks Graduate Employment Rate to Include Students Who Find 'Work' as Gamers, Bloggers. *South China Morning Post*. Retrieved October 6, 2020, from https://www.scmp.com/economy/china-economy/article/3092001/coronavirus-china-tweaks-graduate-employment-rate-include.
Li, C., & Bernoff, J. (2008). *Groundswell: Winning in a World Transformed by Social Technologies*. Brighton: Harvard Business Press.
Lianzhang, W. (2017, September21). University Opens Course for Aspiring Net Celebs. *Sixth Tone*. Retrieved July 3, 2020, from https://www.sixthtone.com/news/1000895/university-opens-course-for-aspiring-net-celebs.
Lin, J., & de Kloet, J. (2019). Platformization of the Unlikely Creative Class: Kuaishou and Chinese Digital Cultural Production. *Social Media+ Society*, 5(4). https://doi.org/10.1177/2056305119883430.
Liu, Y. (2018, October 29). The Chinese Farmer Who Live-Streamed Her Life and Made a Fortune. *The New Yorker*. Retrieved July 3, 2020, from https://www.newyorker.com/culture/culture-desk/the-chinese-farmer-who-live-streamed-her-life-and-made-a-fortune.
Liu, Z., Yang, J., & Ling, L. (2020). Exploring the Influence of Live Streaming in Mobile Commerce on Adoption Intention from a Social Presence Perspective. *International Journal of Mobile Human Computer Interaction*, 12(2), 53–71.
Lorenz, T. (2020, July 10). What If the U.S. Bans TikTok? *The New York Times*. Retrieved October 6, 2020, from https://www.nytimes.com/2020/07/10/style/tiktok-ban-us-users-influencers-taylor-lorenz.html.
Lotz, A. (2017). *Portals: A Treatise on Internet-Distributed Television*. Michigan Publishing, University of Michigan Library.
Low, Z. (2018, October 16). Fugitive Chinese Social Media Influencer and Husband Await Trial After Returning from South Korea. *South China Morning Post*. Retrieved October 6, 2020, from https://www.scmp.com/news/china/society/article/2168839/fugitive-chinese-social-media-influencer-and-husband-await-trial.
Lu, B., Fan, W., & Zhou, M. (2016). Social Presence, Trust, and Social Commerce Purchase Intention: An Empirical Research. *Computers in Human Behavior*, 56, 225–237.
Marcuse, H. (1964). *One Dimensional Man*. Boston: Beacon Press.
Marketing to China. (2017, April 13). Chinese Millennial Wants to Be an Online Celebrity. *Marketing to China*. Retrieved July 3, 2020, from https://www.marketingtochina.com/1-chinese-millennial-2-dreams-dream-online-celebrity/.

McDonald, T. (2016). *Social Media in Rural China*. London: UCL Press.
Montfort, N., & Bogost, I. (2009). *Racing the Beam: The Atari Video Computer System*. Cambridge: MIT Press.
Newcomb, H. (2009). Toward Synthetic Media Industry Research. In J. Holt & A. Perren (Eds.), *Media Industries. History, Theory, and Method* (pp. 264–270). Hoboken: Wiley-Blackwell.
Nieborg, D., & Poell, T. (2018). The Platformization of Cultural Production: Theorizing the Contingent Cultural Commodity. *New Media & Society, 20*(11), 4275–4292.
Nizan, A. (2019, June 17). Cusper Cohorts – Exploring the Fringe of Gen Z and Millennials. *Fullscreen*. Retrieved July 3, 2020, from https://fullscreen.com/2019/06/17/cusper-cohorts-exploring-the-fringe-of-gen-z-and-millennials/.
O'Neill, N. (2008, July 31). What Exactly Are Social Games? *Adweek.com*. Retrieved July 3, 2020, from https://www.adweek.com/digital/social-games/.
Ogilvie, S., & Cerman, M. (Eds.). (1996). *European Proto-Industrialization: An Introductory Handbook*. London: Cambridge University Press.
Perez, B. (2016, April 14). Smaller Cities in China Take the Lead in E-commerce. *South China Morning Post*. Retrieved July 3, 2020, from https://www.scmp.com/tech/china-tech/article/1936018/smaller-cities-china-take-lead-e-commerce.
Perez, S. (2018, November 2). TikTok Surpassed Facebook, Instagram, Snapchat & YouTube in Downloads Last Month. *Techcrunch*. Retrieved July 3, 2020, from https://techcrunch.com/2018/11/02/tiktok-surpassed-facebook-instagram-snapchat-youtube-in-downloads-last-month/.
Plantin, J., & de Seta, G. (2019). WeChat as Infrastructure: The Techno-Nationalist Shaping of Chinese Digital Platforms. *Chinese Journal of Communication, 12*(3), 257–273.
Potts, J., & Cunningham, S. (2008). Four Models of the Creative Industries. *International Journal of Cultural Policy, 14*(3), 233–247.
Prud'homme, D., Zhao, X., & Tong, T. (2020). The New "Wanghong" Economy: How to Strategically Engage with China's Relational Digital Ecosystem. *California Management Review, 62*(4). https://doi.org/10.2139/ssrn.3592078.
Roxburgh, H. (2018, June 4). Selling with Selfies: How China's Social Media Stars Get Rich? *CKGSB Knowledge*. Retrieved July 3, 2020, from http://knowledge.ckgsb.edu.cn/2018/06/04/digital-economy/wanghong-online-celebrities-making-big-money/.
Schaefer, K. (2019, April 3). "Village Live-streaming": China's Farmers Are Becoming Content Creators. *Trivium User Behavior*. Retrieved July 3, 2020, from http://ub.triviumchina.com/2019/04/village-live-streaming-chinas-farmers-are-becoming-content-creators/.

Short, W., Williams, E., & Christie, B. (1976). *The Social Psychology of Telecommunications*. London and New York: Wiley.

Singh, M. (2020, June 30). India Bans TikTok, Dozens of Other Chinese Apps. *Techcrunch*. Retrieved October 7, 2020, from https://techcrunch.com/2020/06/29/india-bans-tiktok-dozens-of-other-chinese-apps/.

Sussman, E. (2014, March 29). The New Rules of Social Journalism: A Proposal. *Pando*. Retrieved July 3, 2020, from https://pando.com/2014/03/29/the-new-rules-of-social-journalism-a-proposal/.

Tse, T., Leung, V., Cheng, K., & Chan, J. (2018). A Clown, a Political Messiah or a Punching Bag? Rethinking the Performative Identity Construction of Celebrity Through Social Media. *Global Media and China, 3*(3), 141–157.

Tsoi, G. (2016, August 1). Wang Hong: China's Online Stars Making Real Cash. *BBC News*. Retrieved July 3, 2020, from https://www.bbc.com/news/world-asia-china-36802769.

van Dijck, J. (2013). *The Culture of Connectivity: A Critical History of Social Media*. Oxford University Press.

van Dijck, J., & Poell, T. (2013). Understanding Social Media Logic. *Media and Communication, 1*(1), 2–14.

van Dijck, J., Poell, T., & de Waal, M. (2018). *The Platform Society: Public Values in a Connective World*. Oxford: Oxford University Press.

Wakabayashi, D., Kang, C., & Browning, K. (2020, September 18). 'It's So Essential': WeChat Ban Makes U.S.-China Standoff Personal. *The New York Times*. Retrieved October 7, 2020, from https://www.nytimes.com/2020/09/18/technology/wechat-ban-united-states-china.html.

Wang, J. (2004). The Global Reach of a New Discourse: How Far Can Creative Industries Travel? *International Journal of Cultural Studies, 7*(1), 9–19.

Wang, X. (2020, September 1). 'Eating for the Eyes' in the Age of Smartphones. *Anthropology of Smartphones and Smart Ageing Blog*. Retrieved October 8, 2020, from https://blogs.ucl.ac.uk/assa/tag/food-posts/.

Wang, W., & Lobato, R. (2019). Chinese Video Streaming Services in the Context of Global Platform Studies. *Chinese Journal of Communication, 12*(3), 356–371.

Wochit. (2019, March 8). What Is Social Video? Everything You Need to Know. *Wochit*. Retrieved October 7, 2020, from https://www.wochit.com/blog/so-what-is-a-social-video/.

Xu, J., & Zhao, X. (2019). Changing Platformativity of China's Female *Wanghong*: From Anni Baobei to Zhang Dayi. In S. Cai (Ed.), *Female Celebrities in Contemporary Chinese Society* (pp. 127–158). Singapore: Palgrave Macmillan.

Yang, G. (2014). Political Contestation in Chinese Digital Spaces: Deepening the Critical Inquiry. *China Information, 28*(2), 135–144.

Youmshajekian, L. (2019, June 21). The $24 Billion Chinese Industry You've Never Heard of. *UNSW Newsroom*. Retrieved July 3, 2020, from https://newsroom.unsw.edu.au/news/business-law/24-billion-chinese-industry-youve-never-heard.

Yu, H. (2019, June 27). China's 'Social+' Approach to Soft Power. *East Asia Forum*. Retrieved October 8, 2020, from https://www.eastasiaforum.org/2019/06/27/chinas-social-approach-to-soft-power/.

Yu, Z., & Xie, W. (2018, April 16). China's Huge Pool of Web Moderators Required to Have an Eagle Eye for Dangerous Content. *Global Times*. Retrieved July 3, 2020, from http://www.globaltimes.cn/content/1098173.shtml.

Zhang, G., & de Seta, G. (2018). Being 'Red' on the Internet. In C. Abidin & M. Brown (Eds.), *Microcelebrity Around the Globe* (pp. 57–67). Bingley: Emerald Publishing Limited.

CHAPTER 2

Policy and Governance

As we noted in Chap. 1, governance refers to not only state-based policy and regulations, but the larger system of control by multiple stakeholders in any system. Examples of governance in the SME and wanghong industries would include practices of self-regulation by platforms and creators, often in response to or threat of state regulation. Other stakeholders include legacy media and advertising as well as intermediary firms operating between platforms, creators, the state, and affiliated industries. In this chapter, we will historicize and contextualize governance that contributes to the development of the wanghong industry and its differences from the SME industries of the West.

We first focus on the evolution of formal state policy frameworks vital to our understanding of the governance of wanghong. We historicize the analysis as the base layer, conceptualized as "cultural industries", is accreted by the terminology of "cultural and creative industries" and then by "digital creative industries". But our social theme is also key to understanding the significance of both the pivotal thirteenth 5-year Plan and its use of digital platformization to address both social amelioration and the increased governance focus on social morality and social surveillance. We then compare critically in some detail western SME platform governance. In principle, there is a stark contrast between western ideas of "governing at a distance" (Rose and Miller 2010) and, as we noted in Chap. 1, core information media and communication that have always been conceptualized in Chinese principles of governance as part of the state's political apparatus, having the function of propaganda arms of the state and party. In practice, however, the two systems, when compared, are full of contradiction as well as difference in their response to similar themes of cultural, industrial, and social disruption.

Given the structure of China's polity, state-based interventions are far more direct, dramatic, and consequential both supporting and constraining the wanghong industry. According to Yu Hong and Eric Harwitt (2020), China's industrial policies help to protect and promote the tech sector, the growth of digital economy, and a competitive platform landscape. Increasingly, as well, policies have featured ever-increasing restraint that signals the return of social ideology to "guide" and mold online expression and behavior. As outlined in our case study of China's livestreaming sector later in the chapter, wanghong platforms and creators have become focal points in the increasing tensions between the cultural politics and economic ambitions of digital China.

What is the analytical status of policy documentation of the sort we encounter in some detail in this chapter? While, in general, there are no necessary guarantees in liberal systems that policy papers and even official government pronouncements can and will be enacted due to the always contestable nature of democratic politics and public administration, in China it is different. Official policy discourse, especially at the national level, has provenance as a much more likely guide to what will be implemented, as lower level actors vie with each other to interpret and enact what is announced.

"Cultural Industries", "Cultural and Creative Industries", "Digital Creative Industries"

With its core being the production of symbolic meaning and the dissemination of representations, the wanghong economy first of all falls into the governing framework of cultural industries. As outlined in Chap. 1, cultural industries have been regarded as a fundamental framework for understanding and supporting the established industries in this domain. Rather than the traditional Western cultural policy perspective that places the arts at the core of the cultural industries, the Chinese Communist Party places the broadcast and print information media at the core of China's cultural industries. The Chinese authorities have always tended, especially at the national and supreme Party level, to make a distinction between the cultural (or culture—invoking its Marxist heritage) industries—which are core propaganda outlets, and the creative industries (which are often characterized as small and medium enterprises typically outside the stateowned sector). There is also a distinction between an emphasis on cultural industries at the national and an allowance of the use of creative industries at the provincial level, especially in the Shanghai and southern China regions. Additionally, pragmatics dictates that the cover-all phrase cultural and creative industries is often used.

But, as we saw in Chap. 1, long-term, structural changes in economy and society, explicitly pursued at the highest level of economic and social policy in China, set the stage for a strategic adoption of the notion of creative industries—now that they can be tied much more closely to the digital economy—thus the "digital creative industries". This thoroughly blended use of concepts is definitely policy the Chinese way.

Cultural and media creativity (文化创意 wenhua chuangyi) and information technological innovation (科技创新 keji chuangxin) have both been integrated into the national agenda to transform the national economy "from made in China to created in China" (Keane 2007). The Chinese central government officially adopted the cultural industries as one of the national strategies for economic development in early 2000. Dozens of official promotional and planning policy documents have been issued in the follow decades. In 2003, the Ministry of Culture released *Opinions on Supporting and Promoting the Development of Cultural Industries* (Ministry of Culture 2003). This document defines the cultural industries as "the commercial sectors that produce cultural products and provide cultural services" (Ministry of Culture 2003). As commercial and market-driven sectors, the "cultural industries" (文化产业 wenhua chanye) are distinguished from the "cultural institutions" (文化事业 wenhua shiye) which are non-profit public enterprises and mostly financed by the government. Both the cultural industries and the cultural institutions are crucial constituents of Chinese socialist cultural development (文化建设 wenhua jianshe). Art and theatrical performance, the film and television industry, the audio-video industry, cultural entertainment, cultural tourism, the internet cultural industry, publishing, art education and artwork trading were identified as the primary sectors of Chinese cultural industries (Ministry of Culture 2003).

These documents also promoted enterprise reform in Chinese stateowned cultural entities, formulating a series of regulatory and preferential policies to incubate "competitive market entities" including not only the state-owned but also private cultural enterprises, which have been touted as an indispensable constituent of the Chinese cultural industries (The State Council 2005). Information and internet technology have been seen as a crucial driving force for the Chinese cultural economy. The new technologies, as one of the policies asserts, will not only transform and upgrade traditional cultural industries, but also give birth to cutting-edge industries such as platform and Artificial Intelligence (AI) economies, which can "develop high value-added cultural products that combine world-leading technologies and independent intellectual property with national characteristics" (The State Council 2009). Furthermore, the state has been eager to advance the export of Chinese cultural goods, the so-called "cultural going-out" (文化走出去wenhua zouchuqu). Local artworks, exhibitions, films, television dramas, animations, internet games, publications, folk music and dance, acrobatics and other cultural products that have "national characteristics" are specifically encouraged and supported for export and international trade.

However, what distinguishes the Chinese creative industries approach from other instances is that behind the economic and commercializing discourse there is a political agenda which aligns culture and media not only with economic policy, but also with ideological control and social governance. Despite the fact that the justification for the "cultural industries" is seen to lie in its potential to contribute to the restructuring of the Chinese national economy, its authorization is also premised on the Party-State's configuration of culture as tool for social governance, or, in the official language, "socialist advanced culture" or "social benefits".

According to Wang Yongzhang, the previous director of the Cultural Industries Division at the Ministry of Culture, creativity, "the least problematic in the Western context", becomes for the Chinese party-state the "thorniest question" due to its promise of "individualism" and "creative destruction" (Wang 2004, p. 13). This equivocal stance is evidenced by the state's reluctance to use terms like "creativity" and "creative industries" at the national level. In 2005, when "creative industries" (创意产业 chuangyi chanye) discourse travelled to China, the central government insisted on using the older term "cultural industries" (文化产业 wenhua chanye) in policy documents even while allowing provincial initiatives to go ahead under the creative industries banner. One crucial reason, according to Wang, for not using "creative industries" was that the cultural industries in China not only refer to economy and commodity, but also have an ideological character (意识形态属性 yishixingtai shuxing):

"creative industries" mainly focus on design and individual creativity… if we use "creative industries" in our policy documents, there would be a risk that certain cultural sectors would fall out of the state's ideological control. (Wang 2007)

Chinese officials and cultural traditionalists are suspicious of the "individualism", "change" and "creative destruction" promised by the "creativity" discourse (Wang 2004; Keane 2009). If in the West debates around the term "creative industries" are mainly about its latent neoliberalism and depoliticizing effects on culture and media (Galloway and Dunlop 2007; Lee 2016), "depoliticization" also troubles the Chinese authorities but in a different way. As Wang Yongzhang's remark illustrates, the creative industries discourse is thought to overlook the "ideological character" of the cultural industries and as potentially giving rise to the decline of the state's role in ideological regulation—for social stability, national identity, and moral order (Keane 2009; Tong and Hung 2012).

Along with the promotional policies on the cultural economy, the Chinese authorities thus continued to configure the cultural sectors "in terms of what ought to be state-owned and what could involve the private sector, and thus what sorts of content were 'safe' and what 'political'" (O'Connor and Gu 2006, p. 276). Media and communication, as pointed out by Yuezhi Zhao (1998), have always been regarded as part of the state apparatus, and the marketization and commercialization reform since the 1990s have been initiated by the state and constantly subject to the state monitoring and guidance (Keane 2013; Zhao 2017). For example, although in *Decisions of the State Council on the entry of non-public capital into the cultural industries* (The State Council 2005), non-state investment had been allowed and supported as part of the Chinese cultural and media economy, non-state capital is still not permitted to set up independent news agencies, publishing houses and broadcasting networks for radio and television, or to conduct the import of books, journals, film, television and other audio-video products that are regarded as being of ideological importance (The State Council 2005). These examples demonstrate that there is a very particular version of marketization reform in Chinese cultural and media sectors, known officially as the "reform of the cultural system" (文化体制改革 wenhua tizhi gaige). Within the Chinese policy framework of cultural and media industries, there is a "state discursive formation". As McGuigan (2006) states with reference to cultural policy worldwide, the state discursive formation emerges from the belief that "the modern nation-state should command the whole of society, regulate the economy and cultivate appropriate selves" and therefore cultural policy should function to "engineer the soul" of the public (McGuigan 2006, p. 36). For contemporary China, the promotion of a commercial cultural economy is intertwined with a set of regulatory policies which aim to shape the whole cultural industries in accordance with the role of developing a national culture assigned by the party-state.

Take, for example, the two recurring discourses of "soft power" and "cultural security". The party-state has been eager to promote its national imagery to wield Chinese "soft power" on the global stage on the one hand, while it expects a conforming culture that ensures social stability and national unity on the other. Coined by Joseph Nye (1990), soft power—the ability to influence the behavior or thinking of others through the power of attraction and ideas—has been a popular term in international diplomacy, and cultural export has been touted as its key element. This term was embraced by Chinese government in the last decade and soft power became one of the prime objectives of developing the cultural economy—through the "going-out of Chinese culture" (Keane 2010), especially the traditional Chinese culture represented by state-approved legacy media and cultural products. According to president Xi Jinping, building Chinese soft power constitutes the Chinese Dream as the great rejuvenation of the Chinese nation (Xi 2015). At the same time, joining the WTO officially opened up China's doors to foreign popular culture such as Hollywood movies, American pop music and Korean and Japanese music waves. This cultural globalization agitates Chinese cultural traditionalists. "Cultural security" becomes a watchword for those who fear the cultural invasion of the West and the loss of Chinese identity and traditional culture.

A crucial pivot in China's rapid evolution of policy thought and praxis was the *Thirteenth Five-Year Plan* (2016–2020). This, the quinquennial iteration of the highest-level, longer-term, policy framework, did not presage any dilution of the official, national-level, adherence to cultural industries, but it did show how integral the "digital creative industries" had become in policy development. According to the Communist Party of China (CCP) *Thirteenth Five-Year Plan of China* (Central Committee of the CCP 2016), the "digital creative industries", along with next generation information technology, new-energy vehicles, biotechnology, green and low-carbon technology, and high-end equipment and materials, have been recognized as strategic "emerging industries" (新兴产业xinxing chanye). Compared with the *Twelfth Five-Year Plan*, the development objective of the cultural industries has been renewed as "accelerating the development of modern cultural industries" (NDRC 2016, p. 130). Online audio-visual, mobile media, digital publishing and animation and games are emphasized as key sectors for promoting the digital creative industries and the integration of culture and technology (NDRC 2016, p. 130). One of the clear signs of a paradigm shift, as argued by Terry Flew, Xiang Ren and Yi Wang (2019), was that the Plan's emphasis on the "digital creative industries" has superseded in terms of investment importance the previous approach of "creative clusters" that aimed at converting disused industrial spaces in urban areas to creative uses of "traditional and arts-centered" cultural sectors (Flew et al. 2019, p. 167). The new policy is much more ambitious. It moves from repurposing legacy spaces to the goal "to build upon the clear strength in digital services industries" that can directly challenge the hegemony of the Silicon Valley internet giants. It begins to build a policy scaffolding around the plan that digital platformed, user-generated media entertainment can advance Chinese media culture "going-out" and thus dramatically shift the focus of soft power strategy.

This renewed focus on digital and platformed creative production has officially legitimized the booming wanghong economy. The affordances of wanghong platforms have allowed a great diversity of the Chinese population to become wanghong creators. (It has also, through the global penetration of Chinese platforms like TikTok, offered the wanghong experience to other-than-Chinese entertainers.) As Chaps. 5 and 6 will show, the overseas success of Chinese creators like Li Ziqi is distinguished from the previous unsuccessful going-out efforts of state-endorsed legacy media, forming an alternative path of wielding Chinese global soft power. However, as we explore in the following section, the "digital creative industries" approach does not grant immunity to wanghong industries from state regulation. The Chinese authorities have been extremely wary of the cultural disruptions that wanghong creativity might cause. As reiterated by state media, the key to a sustainable growth of wanghong economy "depends on the proper regulation of the industry" (Yang 2020)—which refers to an effective censorship and regulation of online culture.

Towards Social Governance: Internet +, Mass Entrepreneurship, and the Platform Economy

In her field-setting book, *Networking China*, Yu Hong (2017a, pp. 10–13) shows the Chinese government has pledged to place information and communication at the center of the national economic restructuring plan, using information and communication technology (ICT) as industries and infrastructure to transform traditional industrial sectors. In his annual speech at the Chinese national congress in March 2015, Premier Li Keqiang announced China's "Internet +" agenda. "Internet +" is the continuation of the state's economic restructuring plan as seen in the *Twelfth Five-Year Plan*, aiming to replace the unsustainable "export-driven", "investment-dependent" model with a "consumption-based" and "innovation-driven" economy. The new policy agenda puts the internet at the center, aiming to integrate network connectivity and the "disruptive business and managerial model" (of decentralized, private sector-focused, post-Fordist corporate management) with a wide range of traditional sectors, from manufacturing, agriculture, energy, finance and transportation to public services and education (The State Council 2015a; Hong 2017b).

The "Internet +" strategy pledges to propel a new digital economy that can foster and benefit small start-ups, entrepreneurship, and innovation. It dovetails with another policy agenda championed by the government under the name "Mass Entrepreneurship and Innovation" (大众创业万众创新 dazhong chuangxin, wanzhong chuangye) (The State Council 2015b). The official document lays out a policy to mobilize the creativity and innovative power of grassroots individuals for national economic growth and boost employment among the vast population. Similar to Internet +, Mass Entrepreneurship is designed to induce a step-change in the Chinese economy from the previous labor- and energy-intensive economy to an innovation-driven model, while it also promises to further boost employment especially among the vast population of migrant workers, college graduates, and retired soldiers (The State Council 2015b). "Internet +" thus complements the "Mass Entrepreneurship" strategy in the sense that the prosperous digital economy provides opportunities for grassroots individuals to find employment and become entrepreneurs.

Building on "Internet +" and "Mass Entrepreneurship and Innovation", the central government further specifies its policy measures in *Guidelines on Developing Digital Economies and Expanding Employment* issued in 2018 (The State Council 2018). In this document, employment has been given primary focus in developing digital economies, which are expected to create new employment opportunities through the new digital industries including e-commerce and the platform economy. At the same time, the convergence of traditional industries with digital technologies and platform services are believed to provide new and "better" opportunities of employment and entrepreneurship to the workforce in what are bluntly described as "outdated" sectors such as agricultural and manufacturing industries (The State Council 2018).

The national agenda of "Internet +" and "Mass Entrepreneurship" has given the green light to a surging digital and platform economy. According to *The 44th Survey Report—Statistical Report on Internet Development* (China Internet Network Information Centre 2019, p. 75), the economic output of the Chinese digital economy in 2018 was RMB 31,300 billion, constituting 34.8 percent of Chinese GDP Gross Domestic Product and creating 191 million job positions (Fig. 2.1). Among these, various digital platforms and apps such as Taobao (e-commerce), WeChat (social media), Didi (transportation), Eleme (food delivery) and Kuaishou (short video and livestreaming) create over 60 million jobs (People's Daily 2019, n.p.). The retail sales through e-commerce platforms in the first half of 2019

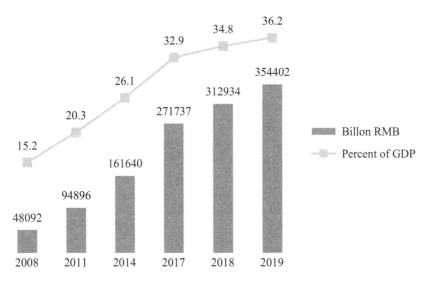

Fig. 2.1 The growth of the Chinese digital economy 2008–2019. (Source: CAICT 2020)

reached RMB 3810 billion, making up 20 percent of the total retail sales of consumer goods.

Geographically, this thriving digital economy is not necessarily limited to the urbanized east coast and other developed regions. As disclosed by the *White Paper on Chinese Digital Economy and Employment 2019* (CAICT 2019, p. 37), in 2018 there were over 9.8 million e-commerce companies located in Chinese rural areas, creating 28 million employment opportunities for local farmers. The online retail sales of agricultural products increased by 33.8 percent, to RMB 231 billion, in 2018. Less developed provinces like Anhui and Guizhou and non-coastal cities such as Chengdu, Nanjing and Wuhan have been lining up to promulgate incentive policies to promote digital industries and digital convergence. The digital economy, by state design, has the potential to break increasing spatialized disparity and inequality and contribute to a more balanced and diversified regional economic dynamic (China Internet Network Information Centre 2019, p. 74).

In 2019, the State Council issued *Guidance on Promoting and Regulating the Platform Economy*, the first policy issued by the central government dedicated to the promotion of the platform economy. The platform economy is celebrated as "the new productive force and momentum for economic development", believed to "optimize distribution of resources, stimulate industrial convergence, mass entrepreneurship and innovation, upgrade the industrial structure, expand the consumer market and, especially, boost employment" (The State Council 2019). According to the policy, the major tasks in developing the platform economy are to facilitate "private and social capital" in participating in the platformization of service industries, and to promote convergence between internet platforms and manufacturing and agricultural sectors. Innovation in technology and organization, participation of medium- and small-sized enterprises and development of internet infrastructure are viewed as crucial strategies.

In practice, resembling their western counterparts Google, Apple, Facebook, Amazon, and Microsoft, Chinese publicly-listed internet giants such as Alibaba, Tencent, Bytedance and Baidu, together with various private company platforms such as Taobao, Didi, WeChat, Jingdong, and Toutiao, have played a dominant role in the Chinese platform economy. Operating as business intermediaries or "multisided markets" (McIntyre and Srinivasan 2017; Nieborg and Poell 2018), these platforms facilitate a massive coming-together of stakeholders—for example, advertisers, service/product providers, end-users, and audience—into their online ecosystem, in which these platform companies hold the most dominant position. It is in this vast landscape that the wanghong economy finds itself positioned in the political economy of contemporary China. At the same time, the wanghong economy also falls into the existing policy framework of cultural and creative industries, for its immanent relations to media and culture, which often leads to great controversies around its culture and precarity in business and labor practice.

As a typical component of the platform economy, wanghong can appear to be a highly disruptive influence on media and cultural industries. According to the *White Paper* (CAICT 2019, p. 34), platformization has contributed to 55.5 percent of the total economic growth in broadcast, television, film and recording industries. Convergence is blurring the boundary between traditional media and the rapid growth of user-generated content production, which of course is the ground base of the wanghong industry. Short video platforms, such as TikTok and Kuaishou combined, for example, can boast a user base of over 648 million with an average usage rate at 78.2 percent (CAICT 2019, p. 35). Both traditional media companies and grassroots individuals are facilitated to start and expand their content and business on these new media platforms. Considering that the state has controlled for decades most of the traditional media sectors, the rise of the digital media platforms, especially regarding the user-centered nature of wanghong culture and economy, has the potential to impact the larger cultural market and the embedded dominance of state media and legacy cultural industries.

Moreover, enabled by the data-driven digital technologies and build-in affordances of advertising and e-commerce, the potential of the wanghong economy reaches beyond the realms of culture and technology. As we return to often in this book, wanghong phenomena have become social industries for their cultural value—symbolic meaning—but also their impact on existing social and economic relationships. First of all, the wanghong economy creates career and business opportunities for grassroots individuals to become online content producers. Wanghong creators are by no means limited to those who are educated, located in urban areas, and employed in legacy media and cultural sectors. By virtue of the integration of e-commerce and advertising affordances in video and livestreaming platforms, these diverse creators further bring financial and market opportunities to those working in the traditional sectors, such as farmers, craftsmen, and consumer goods manufacturers. Chinese livestreaming platforms, for example, have managed to attract over 500 million users in

2019 and achieved total transactions through e-commerce of over RMB 433 billion (Qianzhan 2020).

Together, platform companies, creators and diverse stakeholders form a platform-dominated network system—multisided markets in which places, localities, things, and people are connected in a commercial and dynamic online ecology. Within this ecology, the wanghong economy seems to have the capacity to transform various local places into mediaspaces (Couldry and McCarthy 2004), personalities and identities into cultural commodities, for the production, consumption as well as exploitation of wanghong culture. It not only fits into the state's agenda for cultural industries and digital creative industries, but also in a larger sense the framework of social governance, exemplified by the wanghong economy's contribution to employment promotion as well as the recent "poverty alleviation" agenda. For example, livestreaming has been widely used by rural wanghong creators to sell products on Chinese e-commerce platforms such as Taobao and Pinduoduo. In April 2020, hundreds of Chinese local county mayors even joined these livestreaming shows to help sell agricultural products, whose sales were heavily impacted by the COVID-19 (Wang and Xiong 2020). Meanwhile, given their infrastructural role in supporting the state-led Social Credit System (Liang et al. 2018), the immense popularity secures a maximum accumulation of individuals' online data and private information, which contribute to the state' digital surveillance of Chinese social and economic lives.

SME and Wanghong Governance Compared: SME

SME governance in the West has been historically shaped by United States liberal democratic dispositions and frameworks that celebrated American tech innovation and allowed the industry distinct freedoms. This is an extreme form of governing at a distance. The most fundamental United States disposition is the guarantee of free speech enshrined in the First Amendment. A crucial instrument of such governance is the DMCA rules of Safe Harbor in the 1996 *Telecommunication Act*, through which platforms were absolved of governance oversight of the content they carried, subject to minimum conditions. Key United States Federal agencies such as the Federal Communications Commission have therefore taken a studied hands-off approach to much online culture and practice. There has been a radical gap between tech affordance and growth and the social and cultural outcomes generated around such growth. Additionally, an equally hands-off approach to platform competition has resulted, through aggressive acquisition strategies, in United States platforms exercising unprecedented monopolistic or oligopolistic power. As we will see, especially in the next chapter, China's platform economy has a greater competitive dynamic than the supposed leading light of western capitalist achievement, the United States tech sector.

For a good part of the platform era, the United States liberal-innovation model has been adopted de facto or de jure in most western jurisdictions. But that has been changing with increasing intensity. Social media entertainment culture and creators, used to managing in a largely unregulated environment, have been neglected, overlooked, and often deeply damaged as a range of new concerns and a consequent threatened and actual "new regulatory era" (Cunningham and Craig 2019, pp. 266–287) has been visited upon them.

An increasing range of global critical concerns about the political and socio-cultural disruption wrought by tech, including the SME platforms, has resulted in a "techlash" (Smith 2018). Tech firms and owners have been rightfully criticized for their anti-trust violations, laissez faire attitudes towards self-regulation, and repeated but ineffectual apologies for their transgressive platforms practices in violation of socio-political norms. In addition to, and arguably as a direct consequence of, the consolidation of tech and platform power, an ever-multiplying array of concerns have emerged over privacy, data mining and algorithmic non-transparency, hate speech, cyber-bullying, and the promotion and monetization of extremist content, the failure of AI content moderation leading to the exploitation and psychological damage of human curators, and ongoing violations of children's regulatory policy. When you get an alignment of interests between notoriously conservative legacy media moguls like Rupert Murdoch and radically left-wing politicians like United States Senator Elizabeth Warren—both of which call on anti-trust policy initiatives to break up "big tech" (Stevens 2019)—you know you are in uncharted, tumultuous territory.

In the wake of the "techlash", United States platforms, including SME, have been faced with heightened, if often poorly conceived, regulatory scrutiny (Levy 2019). Numerous federal agencies have geared up to attend to public concerns but the cultural and commercial interests of creators have been ignored and their sustainability threatened by these policy interventions. While much of the United States state policy intervention has been too little, too late, SME platform governance has not, often leading to dire consequences for SME creators. YouTube's "adpocalypse" serves as one prime example. In response to press accounts of YouTube profiteering off extremist videos, the platform implemented crude filtering systems that amounted to a form of taxonomic tyranny. These filters led to the demonetization of responsible creators, most notably civic-minded, queer, and marginalized creators (Cunningham and Craig 2019, pp. 111–113). In this example, we understand how top-down governance operates directly, with platforms arguably overreacting to the peril of policy interventions from government and press scrutiny.

The techlash has also consisted of more than a decade of European Union and major European countries pushing back on United States light touch (de)regulatory frameworks and platform practices. These moves are cultural (seeking to advance European cultural expression against the perceived dominance of American influence), creative-industrial (Europe should develop a more robust creative digital economy) and social (privacy and identity theft, for example, have been top of European agendas for some time). The West is fractured at the top-most level. The European Union has advanced a series of policy interventions directing at curbing the cultural and economic influence of these United States-based platforms. Much like recent United States policy recommendations and platform self-regulatory policies, these European Union regulations have ignored the interests of creators, even those advancing their own cultural fare. The European Union's "Directive on Copyright in the Digital Single Market, otherwise known as Article 19, holds all web-based platforms responsible for the filtering out of all copyright infringement. "It's YouTube Content ID but for the entire Internet" (Jeong 2018), and full contradiction of the Safe Harbor provisions of the DMCA along with Fair Use provisions that have helped SME creators thrive. The unintended consequence is the inhibition of platform competition and further consolidation of platform power. These conditions further limit the options for creators engaging in multi-platform practices to manage risk and promote sustainability.

Other stakeholders in the governance of SME have emerged, particularly around concerns over the disruption of advertising norms by SME platforms and creators. These concerns involve "influencer marketing", a form of branded content advertising that has offered deep returns for brands and creators, as well as concern by users and consumers. The United States Federal Trade Commission (FTC) produced a set of Endorsement Guidelines directed towards creators to demand greater transparency of branded content deals (FTC 2017). These guidelines were subsequently adopted by the United Kingdom's Advertising Standards Authority (ASA) and Committee of Advertising Practice (CAP) (ASA-CAP 2018). Yet, while FTC regulation demands that online creators be transparent about sponsorship and branded content, influencers describe this practice as "as unfair and discriminatory because television shows, music videos, NBA stars and Kardashians get a pass for publishing the same content" (Glazer 2018). Industry experts accuse the FTC of double standards, applying weaker regulation in television around product placement than for individual influencers on these platforms (Guthrie 2019).

SME creators have relied in large part on the loyalty of their following communities, crowdfunding and their own entrepreneurial efforts to sustain their careers. Given that these efforts can be wiped out with an algorithmic tweak or threatened by blunt policy overreaction, creators have attempted to organize, or at least, align with traditional media and trade associations, guilds, and unions to secure greater protection and recognition as stakeholders in this industry. Hollywood unions and guilds, like the Screen Actors Guild, have made overtures to include creators in their ranks, while larger labor unions like the Teamsters and AFL-CIO may soon include creators alongside other tech employees or contractors within the emerging gig economy. In 2016, leading SME thought leaders, Hank and John Green (the "Vlogbrothers") launched the Internet Creators Guild to focus around increasing peril from "policies, platforms, and the press", as confirmed in our interview with Executive Director Anthony D'Angelo (2018); however, by mid-2019, the organization was shuttered in part from the difficulty with organizing creators globally (Alexander 2019).

SME AND WANGHONG GOVERNANCE COMPARED: WANGHONG

There is no doubt that the state is the most powerful actor in the governance of wanghong. But the state is not unitary and power is unevenly distributed. Power is also enacted both as direct support and indirect facilitation as well as direct censorship, coercion and punishment and indirect "guidance". Platforms have been protected and sponsored through economic initiatives contributing to a more advanced, competitive, and better integrated platform landscape. Simultaneously, the platforms have been enjoined and indeed required to pursue algorithmic and human-curated content moderation aligned with the economic and ideological interests of the state. The surplus of rural Chinese agrarian and manufacturing labor, provided they remain loyal to the Party (large numbers are in fact Party members) and understand cultural protocol, have been transitioned into the Chinese digital economy—from farm and factory workers to working wanghong as well as censors and online monitors of wanghong.

The policy frameworks of cultural industries and the platform economy are designed to manage aggressively what could otherwise be overwhelming Western influence over Chinese tech businesses, advance autarkic control of their own industries, and maintain ideological surveillance of their citizens. Increasingly, the policies are designed to advance China's soft power ambitions transnationally (see Chap. 6 for a discussion of China's going out policies and outcomes in practice). As the Chinese internet has been sponsored by the state, the state has also begun to articulate parallel interest and concerns over its growing social potential and disruptive cultural influence. As set forth by the Cyberspace Administration of China, "Nowadays, the boundary between reality and virtuality is becoming more ambiguous. Cybersecurity is not only related to the security of our country and the society, but more importantly, is related to the personal interests of every netizen" (Cyberspace Administration of China 2017).

Governed to a greater extent than non-Chinese SME by state policy, wanghong platforms and creators thus need to meticulously manage their creativity and business between market needs and state regulation. However, this does not mean that wanghong production in China is shackled as an apparatus to promote only state interests. Political scientists consistently point out that Chinese administration of policy is always full of tensions and negotiations (Lieberthal and Lampton 1992; Xu 2011). As Yu Hong (2017a, p. 4) states in her study of Chinese internet and communication policies, "fragmented class interests, incompatible regional experiments, self-serving bureaucratic interests, and competing developmental visions are pulling the rebalancing in different directions". Although China's political system is typically classified as an authoritarian party-state, its political system is also characterized by resilience and adaptability, which allow for "bottom-up" policy changes and political-economic experiments. Heilmann and Perry (2011, p. 11), for example, note that "China's vast and bureaucratically fragmented political system is animated by policy processes that allow for far greater bottom-up input than would be predicted from its formal structures". Yu Hong underlines this point:

"Competing bureaucratic imperatives and vested state interests in the economy have created and continue to create nonaligned initiatives and diffused commitments", resulting in the non-unitary nature of the state (Hong 2017a, p. 10). It is such diffuse and variable carrying out of broad national policy principles in contestable ways by competing actors that, we argue, creates spaces of agency for various actors we feature in this and subsequent chapters in the Chinese wanghong economy.

Termed "fragmented authoritarianism" by political scientists (Lieberthal and Lampton 1992; Mertha 2009; Yang 2013), the actual process of policy-making and implementing in China involves constant bargaining and competition among government agencies with diverse and often contradictory interests. The wanghong industry has been regulated by multiple governmental bodies, including the Cyberspace Administration of China (CAC), the Ministry of Culture (MoC), the State Administration of Press, Publishing, Radio, Television and Film (SAPPRFT), and the Ministry of Industry and Information Technology. The State Administration for Industry and Commerce and the Ministry of Finance also play a role when policies are related to finance and the market. Fragmented authoritarianism self-evidently poses obstacles, restraints, and dangers, yet it also creates leeway to play "edge-ball"—borderline acceptable online expression, a feature of Chinese popular cultural practice for decades (Keane 1998). As an official from the Ministry of Industry and Information Technology revealed, an effective governance of the livestreaming ecommerce platforms, for instance, requires "coordination of many government departments", yet the reality is "we are still using the old legislative institutions to deal with problems [such as counterfeit products and soft-porn shows]" (Eastmoney 2020).

Given China's uniquely challenging demographics, political administration cannot be fully centralized. According to the Chinese nomenklatura system, the central committee of the Communist Party of China (CCP) holds power in the appointment of senior cadres in leading positions of the party state's bureaucratic apparatus, including the CCP high command, Central Party bureaucracy, State advisory organs, National People's Congress, State Council, state-owned banks, state-owned media, and so forth. (Chan 2004). The nomenklatura system of personnel management reinforces the authority of the Party and central government and is designed to produce an effect of national unity (Chan 2004; Naughton and Yang 2004). Yet, regional governments have significant autonomy in governing at that level. This regionally decentralized authoritarian (RDA) regime—a term coined by Xu (2011)—is distinct from federalism in that Chinese officials are not accountable to their constituents but to higher-ranked leaders. But it is also distinct from the old Maoist command economy. Since Deng Xiaoping embarked on China's marketization reform, GDP growth has become the first reference for official promotions. To stand out in what is fierce regional economic competition, local officials have embraced what Heilmann and Perry (2011) conceptualize as a "guerrilla policy-making style".

Inherited from the CCP's wartime tactics, this "guerrilla approach" characterizes contemporary Chinese policy-making in the sense that the top leadership preserves the power to make decisions on national-wide strategies, while "operationalization and implementation require substantial latitude for local initiative and independence" (Heilmann and Perry 2011, p. 18). As a result, policy making and implementation are always subject to improvisation and adjustment, with pilot efforts and practical experience preferred to abstract theories or models (Heilmann and Perry 2011, p. 18). During the COVID-19 pandemic, for example, the thriving wanghong economy aroused competition among dozens of Chinese cities to promulgate various preferential policies to attract "livestreaming hosts" and MCNs. First-tier cities like Beijing, Shanghai, Hangzhou, and Guangzhou, as well as smaller cities like Yiwu, Qingdao, Quanzhou, Jinan and Heze, have offered support policies such as housing subsidies to top livestreamers. Hangzhou and Yiwu, for example, have offered alluring financial support to top-listed creators in terms of housing, tax, and their children's education. Among these local policies, online traffic and influence is often viewed as the most important criterion in nominating wanghong creators, while downplaying or overlooking the cultural quality, which has been constantly emphasized in national policy.

Chinese governance in practice functions as a network of different, often conflictual, forces emanating from state administrative bodies, local governments, and market entities. As we explore in later chapters, this creates both precarity and opportunity for wanghong platforms and creators. Chinese economic and tech policy, along with its unique social-cultural focus, has allowed wanghong platforms and creators to flourish but also heightened state surveillance. In practice, the wanghong industry features a far more competitive platform landscape than in SME with more advanced integration of technological and economic affordances, while the increasingly greater economic power of the industry does not grant them immunity from the threat of social instability that have contributed to greater cultural policy interventions to advance ideological control of the industry. These conditions are reflected in the following case study of China's livestreaming industry that reflects how commercializing livestreamers have become central focal points in contemporary Chinese governance.

GOVERNANCE OF LIVESTREAMING

The term "livestreaming" refers to broadcast video streaming services provided by web-based platforms and mobile applications that feature synchronous and cross-modal (video, text, and image) interactivity. Live streaming may be the core service of a platform, as with platforms like Twitch or Douyu, or may be an added service on top of other forms of content, like YouTube Live or Kaishuo live. Livestreamers are securing revenue from diverse content genres, or verticals, of onscreen performance that include game play, cooking, painting, karaoke, even what Daniel Recktenwald calls "social eating" (Recktenwald 2017; see also Recktenwald and Du 2016).

Outside China, live streaming platforms have struggled to succeed, apart from the often illicit (and under-researched) porn industry. As with all other forms of technology from early film nickelodeons to home video to online, the porn industry has often led in technological innovation. Referred to as Porn 2.0, live streaming has become "the engine of the porn industry" (Song 2016). The industry has operated under Western, especially United States, liberal values of freedom of speech, although the application of these values to support porn is under increasing review, evidenced by the United Kingdom's Digital Economy Act of 2017, which attempted to severely limit online porn (Tidey 2019).

Outside of *that* application, Twitch remains the one notable exception as a commercial live-streaming site in the West. Launched as justin.tv before YouTube and Twitter in 2005, the site was later purchased by Amazon for USD 1 billion in 2014 (Levy 2014). With recent efforts to expand beyond game play not succeeding (Broussard 2018), the platform remains tailored for game enthusiasts. To date, the platform has received little scrutiny from government. The platform has engaged in layers of self-regulation starting with an iterative array of terms of service to police sexual content and harassment (Alexandra 2018). Twitch creators are encouraged to practice self-regulation and "build a mod team"—a self-selected group of moderators who "ensure that chat is up to the standards of the Broadcaster by removing offensive posts and spam that detracts from conversations" (Twitch n.d.).

Repeated efforts to launch platforms to compete with Twitch have failed (Flynn 2016; Fiegerman 2017). Live streaming, offered as an additional feature on major SME platforms including YouTube and Facebook, has proven a signal failure and has triggered a global backlash against livestreaming technology. Repeated criminal acts and obscene human rights violations have been committed globally across these platforms from live murders, sexual assault, child abuse, torture, and more. The livestream of the New Zealand massacre in 2019 may have proven to be a threshold moment. Western democracies, like Australia, are passing laws to govern live streaming platforms, albeit with limited understanding of how these operate (Oberler 2019). Even platform owners like Mark Zuckerberg have joined the chorus, demanding that governing bodies issue "new rules for the Internet" (Quodling 2019) as others insist the platforms be shut down completely (Grygiel 2019).

All this would suggest "the world is turning against livestreaming" (Newton 2019), but China has a different story both in the growth and governance of livestreaming. As a significant segment within China's larger wanghong industry, which also includes recorded video, image, and text-based platforms, Chinese live streaming has been "booming" (Lavin 2018) for years. At its peak, there were over 200 Chinese livestreaming apps and, while ongoing consolidation has occurred, there remains far more successful live apps in China than the rest of the world (Hallanan 2018). Estimates and predictions of the scale of Chinese live streaming has gone from USD 5 billion in 2016 (Moshinsky 2016) to USD 19 billion in 2022 (iResearch 2018). According to Deloitte, China is the largest live streaming market distinguished by the success of virtual goods, a form of virtual tipping or donations (Deloitte 2018). Integration of livestreaming with China's ecommerce platforms such as Alibaba's Taobao have proven transformative of China's digital, retail, and advertising industries (Wang 2019).

Large numbers of wanghong have crafted sustaining careers in this industry. These creators are also referred to as "zhubo" which translates as host or anchor. China's commercializing gameplay streamers have also prospered on Douyu, a Twitch-like platform. Unlike their Western counterparts, however, they have leveraged their success across an array of competing game platform including Huya, eGame, and PandaTV (although the latter was shuttered in 2018). Their success aligns with the rapid growth of China's videogame publishing and esports industries. These industries are dominated by Tencent Media, which is an investor in all of these game play platforms. This ecology of livestreaming platforms, players, game industries and investors has fueled the launch of successful Western IPOs for Huya in 2019 and Doyu in 2019 (Huang 2019).

In early days, China's "stream queens" (Birtles 2016) engage in more gendered performativity, "singing and slurping soup" (Weller 2017) to appeal to men referred to as "little puppies" (Chen 2018). These conditions have been likened to a "virtual girlfriend" industry (Kaiman and Meyers 2017) helping pretty girls "soothe lonely guys and create fortunes" (Yang 2017). Dating back to 1978, China's one-child policy, designed to inhibit population growth, also contributed to an ever-increasing gender gap, estimated to be near 70 million more men to women by 2020. These conditions have been further exacerbated by rural-urban migration brought about by Chinese economic policy reforms since the late 1970s. The rapid shift from an agrarian to a manufacturing, and then to a service-based economy has led to profound gender- and class-based disparities. Despite restrictions limiting internal migration, rural workers have fled to the cities, despite being forced to live on the outskirts of the city and without local (hokou) recognition. Throughout the country, there are millions of "lonely leftover men" (Sun 2017) with little opportunity for family or romance, even more pronounced in the countryside where there are fewer entertainment options. Even within the cities, socio-economic upheaval has, as a Chinese scholar and live streamer remarked, led to "30 million lonely souls floating above the sky of Beijing" (Cunningham et al. 2019).

More recently, however, livestreaming affordances have been further integrated into major e-commerce platforms like Taobao and Pinduoduo and short video platforms such as Douyin and Kuaishou. Compared to the dedicated livestreaming platforms (for example, Douyu and Huya), the incorporation of livestreaming into these major platforms also signals the mainstreaming, and perhaps normalization, of the livestreaming industry and its culture. As a result, a stricter state regulation of content coincides with the official endorsement of its commercial and employment potential.

The "edge-ball" approach analyzed earlier now tends to be replaced by a "social-benefit" approach. This approach is evidenced by a more stringent content moderation policy that can minimize the potential cultural disruptions, and a more inclusive business network that can benefit the national economic restructuring and mass entrepreneurship and employment. Over the last few years, Chinese state agencies responsible for supervising online activity have shuttered multiple livestreaming platforms along with over 30,000 individual accounts. This crackdown aimed to weed out content that is "vulgar, obscene, violent, superstitious, concerns gambling, or harms the psychological health of underage people" (Lai 2017). In 2018, two leading Chinese short video platforms were "invited for tea" by officials, a euphemism for being threatened with penalties for their "ignorance of the law and disseminating programs that are against social moral values" (Liu 2018). These officials demanded that the platforms give a "comprehensive rectification", prompting them to shut down thousands of user accounts that posted "unhealthy content" and launch channels that promoted "positive and healthy values".

To establish a more inclusive business ecosystem, Chinese livestreaming and e-commerce platforms have been eagerly investing in the so-called "sinking market" (下沉市场 xiachen shichang), a term frequently used by Chinese media and business organizations in the past five years to refer to the small-town and rural markets. The two leading platforms Kuaishou (short video) and Pinduoduo (e-commerce) have invested strategically in social amelioration, targeting the sinking market through rural wanghong creators and cheap consumer products. At the same time, previously urban-based platforms such as Alibaba, Tencent and Jingdong have also lined up to adjust their strategies, addressing rural China. 2018 saw Jingdong, the second largest Chinese e-commerce platform, launching its Super New Star project, in which five new apps (including Fenxiang and Jingxi) were developed to target the Chinese rural market and compete against Pinduoduo (Futunn 2019, n.p.). Alibaba built a new e-commerce platform CunTaobao, still embedded in its original Taobao ecosystem but clearly focused on the rural market. Again, these efforts in expanding leading Chinese ecommerce technology access among rural and marginal populations neatly fit into the state's call for mass entrepreneurship and "poverty-alleviation" through "Internet+". That internet and e-commerce should play an important role in assisting impoverished rural areas to establish online marketing channels for the local products and farmers, to finally advance the model of "internet + poverty alleviation" (The State Council 2018), has been prominent in policy since 2018.

Conclusion

The account of livestreaming given here epitomizes the dynamic management of contradictions in China's governance of the wanghong industry. The mixture of the dual logic of governing the cultural and creative industries for economic and social-cultural benefits as well as social-economic governance through Internet+ and the platform economy has resulted in a far more competitive livestreaming landscape, featuring more sophisticated and integrated commercial features together with increasingly sophisticated, omnipresent censorship and content regulations. Governance beyond state regulation and surveillance in this context not only refers to the governing practices of various platforms and commercial institutions, but also to the everyday labor practice of wanghong production and management. These elements of the wanghong ecosystem are the subjects of the next two chapters. The increasingly stringent policy on content moderation and the competitive market have added to the precariousness as well as increased opportunity for both platform companies and creators' everyday work. The logic of platform capitalism (Srnicek 2017), in conjunction with Chinese state intervention, has both fostered and circumscribed the technological, economic, and social-cultural viability of wanghong industry.

References

Advertising Standards Authority | Committee of Advertising Practice. (2018). New Guidance Launched for Social Influencers. *ASA | CAP*, 28 September. Retrieved August 17, 2020, from https://www.asa.org.uk/news/new-guidance-launched-for-social-influencers.html.

Alexander, J. (2019). YouTubers' First Organizing Attempt, the Internet Creators Guild, is Shutting Down. *The Verge*, 11 July. Retrieved August 17, 2020, from https://www.theverge.com/2019/7/11/20688929/internet-creators-guild-shutting-down-hank-green-youtube-copyright-claims-monetization.

Alexandra, H. (2018). Twitch Gets New Policies for Sexual Content and Harassment. *Kotaku*, 9 February. Retrieved August 17, 2020, from https://www.kotaku.com.au/2018/02/twitch-gets-new-policies-for-sexual-content-and-harassment/.

Birtles, B. (2016). Chinese Social Media 'Stream Queens' Getting Rich by Broadcasting their Lives Online. *Australian Broadcasting Corporation*, 26 July. Retrieved August 17, 2020, from https://www.abc.net.au/news/2016-07-26/chinas-narcissistic-social-media-stars-making-$20k-per-month/7661118.

Broussard, M. (2018). Twitch Plans to 'Aggressively Broaden' Its Content and Expand Beyond Gaming as It Battles YouTube. *MacRumors*, 15 August. Retrieved August 18, 2020, from https://www.macrumors.com/2018/08/15/twitch-expand-beyond-gaming/.

Central Committee of the Communist Party of China. (2016). *The 13th Five-Year Plan for Economic and Social Development of the People's Republic Of China (2016–2020)*. Beijing: Central Compilation and Translation Press.

Chan, H. (2004). Cadre Personnel Management in China: The Nomenklatura System, 1990–1998. *The China Quarterly, 179*(September), 703–734. https://doi.org/10.1017/S0305741004000554.

Chen, L. (2018). China's Risqué Live-Streaming Apps are Now Objectifying Men Too. *Bloomberg*, 10 July. Retrieved March 2, 2019, from https://www.bloomberg.com/news/articles/2018-07-10/china-s-risqu-live-streaming-apps-are-now-objectifying-men-too.

China Information and Communication Research Institute. (2019). White Paper on China's Digital Economy Development and Employment. *CAICT*, 1 July. Retrieved October 8, 2020, from http://www.caict.ac.cn/kxyj/qwfb/bps/201904/P020190417344468720243.pdf.

China Information and Communication Research Institute. (2020). White Paper on China's Digital Economy Development and Employment. *CAICT*, 1 July. Retrieved October 8, 2020, from http://www.caict.ac.cn/kxyj/qwfb/bps/202007/P020200703318256637020.pdf.

China Internet Network Information Centre. (2019). The 44th Survey Report—Statistical Report on Internet Development. *CNNIC*, 1 August. Retrieved September 12, 2020, from https://cnnic.com.cn/IDR/ReportDownloads/201911/P020191112539794960687.pdf.

Couldry, N., & McCarthy, A. (2004). *Mediaspace: Place, Scale and Culture in a Media Age*. London: Routledge.

Cunningham, S., & Craig, D. (2019). *Social Media Entertainment: The New Intersection of Hollywood and Silicon Valley*. New York: New York University Press.

Cunningham, S., Craig, D., & Lv, J. (2019). China's livestreaming industry: platforms, politics, and precarity. *International Journal of Cultural Studies, 22*(6), 719–736. https://doi.org/10.1177/1367877919834942.

Cyberspace Administration of China. (2017). Hold the Key to Internet Security [掌握守护网络安全的密钥]. *Cyberspace Administration of China*, 20 September. Retrieved September 12, 2020, from http://www.cac.gov.cn/2017-09/20/c_1121694996.htm.

D'Angelo, A. (2018). Executive Director, Internet Creators Guild, 1 May, Skype Interview with Stuart Cunningham and David Craig.

Deloitte. (2018). Live Thrives in an Online World. *Deloitte*, 7 December. Retrieved August 18, 2020, from https://www2.deloitte.com/content/dam/Deloitte/global/Images/infographics/technologymediatelecommunications/gx-deloitte-tmt-2018-online-world-report.pdf.

Eastmoney. (2020). How to Regulate Platforms to Improve the Chaotic Livestreaming Wanghong Economy? [网红直播带货乱象不断 平台监管如何完善?]. *Eastmoney*, 5 August. Retrieved September 12, 2020, from http://finance.eastmoney.com/a/202005081477818874.html.

Fiegerman, S. (2017). Twitter Officially Shuts Down Vine. *CNN Business*, 17 January. Retrieved August 18, 2020, from https://money.cnn.com/2017/01/17/technology/vine-shuts-down/index.html.

Flew, T., Ren, X., & Wang, Y. (2019). Creative Industries in China: The Digital Turn. In S. Cunningham & T. Flew (Eds.), *A Research Agenda for Creative Industries* (pp. 164–178). Cheltenham: Edward Elgar Publishing.

Flynn, K. (2016). What Happened to Meerkat? From Hype-Ball to Pivot in Just One Year. *International Business Times*, 9 March. Retrieved August 18, 2020, from https://www.ibtimes.com/what-happened-meerkat-hype-ball-pivot-just-one-year-2333379.

FTC. (2017). FTC Staff Reminds Influencers and Brands to Clearly Disclose Relationship. *FTC.gov*, 19 April. Retrieved November 5, 2020, from https://www.ftc.gov/news-events/press-releases/2017/04/ftc-staff-reminds-influencers-brands-clearly-disclose.

Futunn. (2019). The War Between E-Commerce Giants in 2019: More than the Sinking Market [电商巨头攻防战:别再只关注下沉市场了]. *Futunn*, 31 December. Retrieved September 11, 2020, from https://news.futunn.com/post/4722481.

Galloway, S., & Dunlop, S. (2007). A Critique of Definitions of the Cultural and Creative Industries in Public Policy. *International Journal of Cultural Policy*, *13*(1), 17–31.

Glazer, M. (2018). Social Media Influencers Stump for More Seamless Product Placement. *The Wrap*, 6 February. Retrieved August 18, 2020, from https://www.thewrap.com/were-fresh-meat-social-media-influencers-challenge-ftcs-unequal-ad-tag-requirements/.

Grygiel, J. (2019). Shut Down Facebook Live. *Fast Company*, 22 March. Retrieved August 18, 2020, from https://www.fastcompany.com/90323717/a-modest-proposal-for-facebook-end-live-streaming.

Guthrie, S. (2019). Product Placement Double Standards Affecting Influencer Marketing. *Scott Guthrie*, 29 May. Retrieved August 18, 2020, from https://sabguthrie.info/product-placement-double-standards/.

Hallanan, L. (2018). Top 5 Chinese Live Streaming Platforms You Need to Know in 2018. *Medium*, 12 October. Retrieved August 18, 2020, from https://medium.com/themeetgroup/top-5-chinese-live-streaming-platforms-you-need-to-know-in-2018-d963352124c7.

Heilmann, S., & Perry, E. (Eds.). (2011). *Mao's Invisible Hand: The Political Foundations of Adaptive Governance in China*. Harvard: Harvard University Asia Center.

Hong, Y. (2017a). *Networking China: The Digital Transformation of the Chinese Economy.* Springfield: University of Illinois Press.

Hong, Y. (2017b). Pivot to Internet Plus: Molding China's Digital Economy for Economic Restructuring? *International Journal of Communication, 11,* 1486–1506.

Hong, Y., & Harwit, E. (2020). China's Globalizing Internet: History, Power, and Governance. *Chinese Journal of Communication, 13(1),* 1–7.

Huang, Z. (2019). Douyu Files for US IPO: How China's Answer to Twitch is Really Not Like the US Game-Streaming Service at All. *South China Morning Post,* 23 April. Retrieved August 18, 2020, from https://www.scmp.com/tech/apps-social/article/3007293/douyu-files-us-ipo-how-chinas-answer-twitch-really-not-us-game.

iResearch. (2018). 2018 China's Live Streaming Marketing Market Report. *iResearch Global,* 28 March. Retrieved September 11, 2020, from http://www.iresearchchina.com/content/details8_42342.html.

Jeong, S. (2018). New EU Copyright Filtering Law Threatens the Internet as We Knew It. *The Verge,* 19 June. Retrieved September 11, 2020, from https://www.theverge.com/2018/6/19/17480344/eu-european-union-parliament-copyright-article-13-upload-filter.

Kaiman, J., & Meyers, K. (2017). Chinese Authorities Put the Brakes on a Surge in Live Streaming. *Los Angeles Times,* 24 June. Retrieved July 15, 2020, from https://www.latimes.com/world/asia/la-fg-china-live-streaming-crackdown-20170624-story.html.

Keane, M. (1998). Television and Moral Development in China. *Asian Studies Review, 22*(4), 475–503.

Keane, M. (2007). *Created in China: The Great New Leap Forward.* London: Routledge.

Keane, M. (2009). Creative Industries in China: Four Perspectives on Social Transformation. *International Journal of Cultural Policy, 15*(4), 431–443.

Keane, M. (2010). Keeping Up with the Neighbors: China's Soft Power Ambitions. *Cinema Journal, 49*(3), 130–135.

Keane, M. (2013). *Creative Industries in China: Art, Design and Media.* New Jersey: John Wiley & Sons.

Lai, C. (2017). Chinese Live-Streaming Platform Punished for Broadcasting Fake 'Forbidden City' Video. *Hong Kong Free Press,* 26 May. Retrieved August 19, 2020, from https://www.hongkongfp.com/2017/05/26/chinese-live-streaming-platform-punished-broadcasting-fake-forbidden-city-video/.

Lavin, F. (2018). China's Live Streaming Industry is Booming—Here's How It Works. *Forbes,* 19 June. Retrieved September 11, 2020, from https://www.forbes.com/sites/franklavin/2018/06/19/why-does-china-lead-in-live-streaming/#5ae7e1605dca.

Lee, H.-K. (2016). Politics of the 'Creative Industries' Discourse and Its Variants. *International Journal of Cultural Policy, 22*(3), 438–455.
Levy, K. (2014). Here's Why Amazon Just Paid Nearly $1 Billion for a Site Where You Watch People Play Video Games. *Business Insider*, 25 August. Retrieved October 8, 2020, from https://www.businessinsider.com/heres-why-amazon-paid-almost-1-billion-for-twitch-2014-8?international.
Levy, A. (2019). Apple, Google, Facebook, Amazon Facing Potential Regulatory Scrutiny. *CNBC*, 3 June. Retrieved August 18, 2020, from https://www.cnbc.com/2019/06/03/apple-google-facebook-amazon-facing-potential-regulatory-scrutiny.html.
Liang, F., Das, V., Kostyuk, N., & Hussain, M. (2018). Constructing a Data-Driven Society: China's Social Credit System as a State Surveillance Infrastructure. *Policy & Internet, 10*(4), 415–453.
Lieberthal, K., & Lampton, D. (Eds.). (1992). *Bureaucracy, Politics, and Decision Making in Post-Mao China* (Studies on China) (Vol. 14). Berkeley: University of California Press.
Liu, J. (2018, April 8). Kuaishou and Toutiao got interview! [快手、今日头条、火山小视频被约谈]. People's Daily. Retrieved from http://gongyi.people.com.cn/n1/2018/0408/c151132-29910514.html.
McGuigan, J. (2006). *Modernity and Postmodern Culture* (2nd ed.). London: McGraw-Hill Education.
McIntyre, P., & Srinivasan, A. (2017). Networks, Platforms, and Strategy: Emerging Views and Next Steps. *Strategic Management Journal, 38*, 141–160.
Mertha, A. (2009). 'Fragmented Authoritarianism 2.0': Political Pluralization in the Chinese Policy Process. *The China Quarterly, 200*(December), 995.
Ministry of Culture. (2003). Instructions on Supporting and Promoting the Cultural Industries [文化部关于支持和促进文化产业发展的若干意见]. Retrieved August 12, 2020, from http://www.chinalawedu.com/falvfagui/fg22598/22307.shtml.
Moshinsky, B. (2016). Chinese Millennials Have Created a $5 Billion Industry in their Search for 15 Minutes of Fame. *Business Insider*, 15 September. Retrieved December 29, 2018, from https://www.businessinsider.com/credit-suisse-note-on-chinese-livestreaming-industry-2016-9.
National Development and Reform Commission of China (NDRC) (2016). The Thirteenth Five-Year Plan of China [中华人民共和国国民经济和社会发展第十三个五年规划纲要]. Xinhua News Agency. http://www.gov.cn/xinwen/2016-03/17/content_5054992.htm
Naughton, B., & Yang, D. (2004). *Holding China Together: Diversity and National Integration in the Post-Deng Era*. Cambridge: Cambridge University Press.
Newton, C. (2019). The World is Turning Against Live Streaming. *The Verge*, 04 April. Retrieved August 19, 2020, from https://www.theverge.com/interface/2019/4/4/18294951/australia-live-streaming-law-facebook-twitter-periscope.

Nieborg, D., & Poell, T. (2018). The Platformization of Cultural Production: Theorizing the Contingent Cultural Commodity. *New Media & Society, 20*(11), 4275–4292.

Nye, J. (1990). Soft Power. *Foreign Policy, 80*, 153–171.

O'Connor, J., & Gu, X. (2006). A New Modernity?: The Arrival of 'Creative Industries' in China. *International Journal of Cultural Studies, 9*(3), 271–283.

Oberler, A. (2019). New Livestreaming Legislation Fails to Take into Account How the Internet Actually Works. *The Conversation*, 4 April. Retrieved September 11, 2020, from https://theconversation.com/new-livestreaming-legislation-fails-to-take-into-account-how-the-internet-actually-works-114911.

People's Daily. (2019). The Break-Through of the Platform Economy [平台经济破解"成长烦恼"]. *People's Daily*, 9 October. Retrieved October 9, 2019, from http://www.xinhuanet.com/fortune/2019-10/09/c_1125080668.htm.

Qianzhan. (2020). Analysis of Chinese Livestreaming E-Commerce Market in 2020 [2020年直播电商行业市场规模及发展趋势分析]. *Qianzhan*, 21 May. Retrieved September 11, 2020, from https://www.qianzhan.com/analyst/detail/220/200520-e486bcbc.html.

Quodling, A. (2019) Zuckerberg's 'New Rules' for the Internet Must Move from Words to Actions. *The Conversation*, 2 April. Retrieved August 19, 2020, from https://theconversation.com/zuckerbergs-new-rules-for-the-internet-must-move-from-words-to-actions-114593.

Recktenwald, D. (2017). Toward a Transcription and Analysis of Live Streaming on Twitch. *Journal of Pragmatics, 115*, 68–81.

Recktenwald, D., & Du, Y. (2016). Lagging behind Twitch or on Its Own Path: Pressures and Perks on Domestic Online Live Streaming in China. In *Proceedings of 3rd Annual Chinese DiGRA Conference*, Providence University, Taichung City, Taiwan, 1–2 July 2016.

Rose, N., & Miller, P. (2010). Political Power beyond the State: Problematics of Government. *The British Journal of Sociology, 43*(2), 173–205.

Smith, E. (2018). The Techlash against Amazon, Facebook and Google—And What They Can Do. *The Economist*, 20 January. Retrieved August 18, 2020, from https://www.economist.com/briefing/2018/01/20/the-techlash-against-amazon-facebook-and-google-and-what-they-can-do.

Song, J. (2016). As L.A. Porn Industry Struggles, 'Web Camming' becomes a New Trend. *Los Angeles Times*, 3 August. Retrieved August 19, 2020, from https://www.latimes.com/local/lanow/la-me-ln-porn-camming-20160803-snap-story.html.

Srnicek, N. (2017). *Platform Capitalism*. Oxford: Polity Press.

Stevens, M. (2019). Elizabeth Warren on Breaking Up Big Tech. *The New York Times*, 26 June. Retrieved August 19, 2020, from https://www.nytimes.com/2019/06/26/us/politics/elizabeth-warren-break-up-amazon-facebook.html.

Sun, W. (2017). 'My Parents Say Hurry Up and Find a GIRL': China's Millions of Lonely 'Leftover Men'. *The Guardian*, 28 September. Retrieved August 19, 2020, from https://www.theguardian.com/inequality/2017/sep/28/my-parents-say-hurry-up-and-find-a-girl-chinas-millions-of-lonely-leftover-men.

The State Council. (2005). *Decisions on Allowing Non-Public Capital Entering the Cultural Industries* [国务院关于非公有资本进入文化产业的若干决定]. State Council Bulletin No. 16 of 2005. Retrieved September 11, 2020, from http://www.gov.cn/gongbao/content/2005/content_64188.htm.

The State Council. (2009). Developmental Plan of the Cultural Industries [文化产业振兴规划]. 26 September. Retrieved September 11, 2020, from http://www.gov.cn/jrzg/2009-09/26/content_1427394.htm.

The State Council. (2015a). *Instructions on Promoting 'Internet +'* [国务院关于积极推进'互联网+'行动的指导意见]. State Council Bulletin No. 53 of 2015. Retrieved September 11, 2020, from http://www.gov.cn/zhengce/content/2015-07/04/content _10002.htm.

The State Council. (2015b). *Instructions on Constructing Platforms to Promote Mass Entrepreneurship* [国务院关于加快构建大众 创业万众创新支撑平台的指导意见]. State Council Bulletin No. 53 of 2015. Retrieved September 11, 2020, from http://www.gov.cn/zhengce/content/2015-09/26/content_10183.htm.

The State Council. (2018). *Guidelines on Developing Digital Economies and Expanding Employment* [关于发展数字经济稳定并扩大就业的指导意见]. Development and Reform Employment (2018) No. 1363. Retrieved September 11, 2020, from http://www.gov.cn/xinwen/2018-09/26/content_5325444.htm.

The State Council. (2019). *Guidance on Promoting and Regulating the Platform Economy* [国务院办公厅关于促进平台经济规范健康发展的指导意见]. State Council Bulletin No. 38 of 2019. Retrieved September 11, 2020, from http://www.gov.cn/zhengce/content/2019-08/08/content_5419761.htm.

Tidey, A. (2019). How Will New Law Alter Brits' Access to Porn Sites? | Euronews Answers. *euronews*, 12 March. Retrieved August 19, 2020, from https://www.euronews.com/2019/03/11/porn-websites-to-verify-brits-ages-under-new-law-euronews-answers.

Tong, Q., & Hung, R. (2012). Cultural Policy between the State and the Market: Regulation, Creativity and Contradiction. *International Journal of Cultural Policy, 18*(3), 265–278.

Twitch. (n.d.). Guide to Building a Moderation Team. *Twitch*. Retrieved August 19, 2020, from https://help.twitch.tv/s/article/guide-to-building-a-moderation-team.

Wang, J. (2004). The Global Reach of a New Discourse: How Far Can 'Creative Industries' Travel? *International Journal of Cultural Studies, 7*(1), 9–19.

Wang, Y. (2007). Can Creative Industries Can Replace Cultural Industries? [王永章:创意产业能替代文化产业]? *Techweb*, 16 May. Retrieved September 11, 2020, from http://www.techweb.com.cn/column/2007-05-16/193218.shtml.

Wang, J. (2019). Livestreaming's Transforming E-Commerce in China. *Alizila.com*, 4 April. Retrieved August 19, 2020, from https://www.alizila.com/how-livestreaming-is-transforming-e-commerce-in-china/.

Wang, S., & Xiong, X. (2020). Reports on Agricultural E-commerce in Chinese Impoverished Areas 2020 [中国深度贫困地区农产品电商报告(2020)]. 20 April. Retrieved September 11, 2020, from http://www.farmer.com.cn/2020/04/30/wap_99852276.html.

Weller, C. (2017). Chinese Women are Creating a Billion-Dollar Live Streaming Industry Based on Singing and Slurping Soup. *Business Insider*, 1 May. Retrieved August 19, 2020, from https://www.businessinsider.com/chinese-women-live-streaming-industry-2017-4.

Xi, J. (2015). Xi Jinping on National Cultural Soft Power [习近平谈国家文化软实力]. *Xinhuanet*, 25 June. Retrieved September 11, 2020, from http://www.xinhuanet.com/politics/2015-06/25/c_127949618.htm.

Xu, C. (2011). The Fundamental Institutions of China's Reforms and Development. *Journal of Economic Literature, 49*(4), 1076–1151.

Yang, Z. (2013). 'Fragmented Authoritarianism'—The Facilitator behind the Chinese Reform Miracle: A Case Study in Central China. *China Journal of Social Work, 6*(1), 4–13.

Yang, Y. (2017). In China, Live-Streaming Apps Soothe Lonely Souls and Create Fortunes. *Los Angeles Times*, 5 January. Retrieved August 3, 2017, from http://www.latimes.com/world/asia/la-fg-china-live-streaming-20161128-story.html.

Yang, J. (2020). China becomes the Economic Engine of Internet Celebrities [中国成为网红经济发动机]. *People's Daily*, 14 January. Retrieved September 11, 2020, from http://finance.people.com.cn/n1/2020/0114/c1004-31547337.html.

Zhao, Y. (1998). *Media, Market, and Democracy in China: Between the Party Line and the Bottom Line*. Champaign: University of Illinois Press.

Zhao, E. (2017). The Bumpy Road towards Network Convergence in China: The Case of Over-the-Top Streaming Services. *Global Media and China, 2*(1), 28–42.

CHAPTER 3

Platforms

In the previous chapter, we examined how the wanghong industry has been incubated and protected, if also increasingly surveilled, through state and platform-based policy and governance. In this chapter, we focus on the wanghong platform landscape, which is a subset of China's vast and expanding ICTs, operating centrally in the growth of the country's digital economy and geopolitical ambitions. The larger landscape is populated by massive tech firms, like Huawei, Xiaomi, and Oppo, that span industries from telecommunications to consumer electronics, computer hardware and software to artificial intelligence.

Like the focus on Western platforms like YouTube, Instagram, Facebook, and Twitch which support social media entertainment (SME), in this chapter we focus on that portion of the larger digital and social platform landscape that affords wanghong creators the means to harness platforms for cultural and commercial value. The list here is more expansive, reflective of the breadth and diversity across China's platform ecology. These include first generation video streaming and social media platforms like Youku and Weibo, super-platforms like WeChat integrating nearly every conceivable digitally-delivered service and feature, platforms with niche appeal like AcFun and Bilibili, gameplay livestreaming platforms like Douyu and Huya, former dating apps like Momo and Blued, next-generation social video platforms like Kuaishou and Douyin, and

© The Author(s), under exclusive license to Springer Nature
Switzerland AG 2021
D. Craig et al., *Wanghong as Social Media Entertainment in China*,
Palgrave Studies in Globalization, Culture and Society,
https://doi.org/10.1007/978-3-030-65376-7_3

e-commerce platforms like Taobao now introducing livestreaming features.

We identify platform strategies encountered by the wanghong industry which we name as hyperplatformization and interplatformization, portalization, and the affordances of social presence. These platform strategies advance our understanding of how this industry has become a central driver of China's digital economy while providing the underlying sociotechnological and material conditions for the wanghong industry. As detailed in Chaps. 4 and 5, wanghong platforms nurture and empower dimensions of creator labor and management in many distinct ways from those operating in the SME industry. These conditions have extended wanghong culture deeply into Chinese society, particularly amongst rural and grassroots Chinese netizens. As Chap. 6 explores, the same conditions propelling the wanghong industry forward domestically may also inhibit China's cultural, economic, and political ambitions internationally.

Frameworks

In *Social Media Entertainment*, Stuart Cunningham and David Craig (2019) developed a revisionist account of political economy mapping the SME platform landscape. In contrasting this emerging media ecology from legacy media, we identified a clash of business management cultures between Silicon Valley ("NoCal") strategies of iterative "permanent beta" innovation from Hollywood ("SoCal") strategies of maintaining mass media incumbency at almost any cost. We also exposed the vital distinction between digital and social platforms: closed, professional video streaming, digital platforms like Netflix compared to open access, pro-am video streaming, social media platforms driven by network effects like YouTube.

In our comparative account of these platform landscapes in this chapter, we build off our industrial frameworks of cultural, creative, and social and engage with broader themes of digital and platform capitalism and the platformization of cultural production. Dan Schiller's account of digital capitalism (1999) was an early harbinger of attention to the perilous agglomeration of power and oligopolistic practices of tech conglomerates operating in collusion with state interests. Most of these kinds of large-scale political economic accounts have been Western-centric, focusing on the United States-based, global scaling, tech industries, often referred to as either Silicon Valley or "GAFAM" (Google, Amazon, Facebook, Apple, Microsoft).

Similarly, synoptic accounts of the parallel universe of Chinese platforms are beginning to be developed in media and communication studies. In her field-setting work, Yu Hong (2017) mapped the rise of China's networked economy, framed by digital capitalism, and considered the state's central role in the rise of China's information technology, mobile communication, and online convergence by their media industries. As we noted in Chap. 2, Hong's analysis shows the extent of the alignment of the state and industry unknown in liberal democracies. The tech sector is dominated by the state-protected and incubated "national champion" BATs (Baidu, Alibaba, Tencent) (Jia and Winseck 2018; Xia 2018). As Wilfred Wang and Ramon Lobato (2019) argue, in contrast to "essentially liberal values", such as free speech and free markets, which are the constitutive condition underlying much of Silicon Valley business practice, scholars of China's internet policy and practice do not see communication technologies as being outside the state's political domain. Instead, media and communication technologies have always been conceptualized as part of the state's political apparatus.

As digital and social platforms have increasingly determined how the internet is accessed, political economy scholars have theorized their rising influence. Ann Helmond (2015) first identified "the rise of the platform as the dominant infrastructural and economic model of the social web". In laying out his concept of platform capitalism, Nick Srnicek (2016) extends the definition of platforms well beyond social media to include all webbased infrastructures upon which multiple stakeholders engage in an everexpanding array of business models and services. Srnicek stressed how the network effects of platforms have accelerated not only their access and use, but centrally allow platforms to "gain not only access to more data but also control and governance" (2016, p. 47). Like digital capitalism, the inevitable consequence of platform capitalism, for Srnicek, is the concentration, even tendencies toward monopolization, of political and economic power.

And, as Haiqing Yu (2018) affirms, "China is no exception to platform capitalism" (p. 89). Through the protection and sponsorship of the state, China's tech industry has centrally transformed China's digital economy through the proliferation and development of state-of-the-art platforms, alongside other advances like AI, 5G telecommunications, quantum and cloud computing, and what is denominated as the Internet of Things

(IOT). These studies in political economy provide critical diagnostics of the interplay between platforms and economic systems, but we must be cautious of too neat an application of well-established explanatory Western paradigms that may obscure distinctions in Chinese capitalism as well as platform ontologies, functions, and effects. Prior to the rise of China's digital economy, scholars like Donald Nonini (2008) challenged the framing of China through Western critical models like neoliberalism since China's model of capitalism is differentiated by state-control that shapes and limits how markets operate, determines property rights, and shapes free trade.

We stress that the wanghong platform landscape exhibits *both* greater competition *and* greater collaboration than we see in the SME platform landscape, dominated by the oligopolistic and hegemonic strategies engaged by members of GAFAM (Smyrnaios 2016). These tech behemoths own a handful of SME platforms that dominate the global landscape, whether Google-YouTube, Facebook-Instagram-WhatsApp, or Amazon-Twitch, while Twitter and Snap (Snapchat) remain minor players. In contrast, the BATs compete against, collaborate with, and, in some instances, secure controlling interest of other platform owners, whether Sino Weibo, Bilibili, Bytedance's multiple platforms including Douyin, TikTok, Huoshan, Xigua, and Toutiaou, or Kuaishou. In addition, China's platform economy has witnessed the proliferation of social media affordances across platforms, whether dating apps like Momo and Blued or ecommerce platforms like Taobao or JD.

As we further argue in this chapter, the degree of competitiveness is a consequence of many factors, including the rapid uptake of technology, limited path resistance, diverse financial instruments driving technological investment and differentiation, and, as we saw in Chap. 2, state-based policy incentivization. And collaboration is framed by a shared mission, very much state-aligned, against Silicon Valley hegemony. Some of this competitiveness and yet collaborative spirit is captured by Youku platform executive Bryan Shao (2016) in his interview with us: "They can kill us, and we can kill them. So, we need to stay together so we can both grow faster".

Our other caution is that an application of the platform capitalism framework that stresses uniformity between Western and Chinese models risks under-valuing the technological, social, and economic innovations developed in the Chinese system: technological advances that deliver what we call "social presence", new business models and e-commerce integrations that underpin a broader array of wanghong creators across more diverse markets with greater potential for sustainable careers than in the SME industry.

We also use the concept of platformization. In 2015, Helmond introduced the concept of platformization to account for "the rise of the platform as the dominant infrastructural and economic model of the social web and the consequences of the expansion of social media platforms into other spaces online" (p. 5). David Nieborg and Thomas Poell (2018, p. 4276) define platformization as the process of "the penetration of economic, governmental, and infrastructural extensions of digital platforms into the web and app ecosystems, fundamentally affecting the operations of cultural industries". Platformization, like the concept of the platform society (Scholz 2017; van Dijck et al. 2018), focuses critical concerns for how platform ecosystems are changing societal structure and organization. In China, as Jeroen de Kloet et al. note (2019), platformization is not uniform, rather "follows different trajectories along the vectors of infrastructure, governance, and practice" (p. 254).

We now examine the central trajectories in the wanghong platform landscape, noting their differences with the SME landscape. These trajectories include hyperplatformization advancing the uptake of technologies and nurturing more competitive conditions. Interplatformization refers to collaborative strategies of interoperability across platforms. Portalization refers to an oscillatory process between the social networking, open access, and entrepreneurial affordances of social media platforms and the convergence by legacy media industries on to closed, IP-dominated, internet-driven, video streaming "portals" (the term derives from Amanda Lotz 2017). Finally, we consider how wanghong platforms evidence a more accelerated progression towards the affordances of social presence.

Hyperplatformization and Interplatformization

The twin concepts of *hyperplatformization* and *interplatformization* activate our earlier assertion that the wanghong platform landscape is both more competitive and more collaborative than the SME platform landscape. *Hyperplatformization* refers to the accelerated adoption of ICT and mobile and the underlying material conditions for China's platform economy that, in turn, fuels the growth of the wanghong industry. These conditions are reflected through analysis of the growth of China's rapidly expanding e-commerce industry. Accompanying this strategy is also *interplatformization*, which reveals a more collaborative environment in which platforms engage in greater interoperability than their Western counterparts. As previously mentioned, these strategies are motivated by a competitive focus against Western platform imperialism. Michael Keane and Guanhua Su (2019, p. 4) are quite blunt about this: "China Inc. is directly pitted against Silicon Valley".

From 2009 to 2018, internet use and penetration in China doubled from around 30 percent to 60 percent, while American internet use and penetration has plateaued at 70 percent over the same decade (Fig. 3.1). Internet use operates in tandem with the growth of China's smartphone base. There are now over 800 million internet users in China and 98 percent of them are mobile (Fig. 3.2). Since 2012, China has been the largest smartphone market in the world and, in 2020, smartphone penetration is approaching 60 percent, with nearly 1 billion users (NewZoo n.d.). Affordable access to high speed internet access coupled with such smartphone penetration create the conditions for China's platforms to flourish and, in turn, wanghong creators harnessing them for cultural and commercial value.

China's digital economy in 2019 was claimed to comprise nearly a third of the country's Gross Domestic Product (GDP), according to *The 44ᵗʰ*

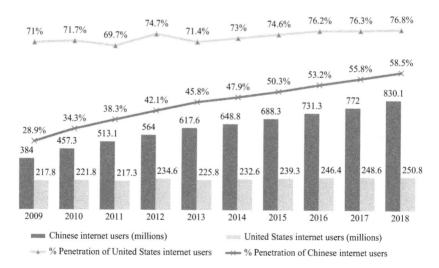

Fig. 3.1 Chinese and United States internet users and penetration 2009–2018

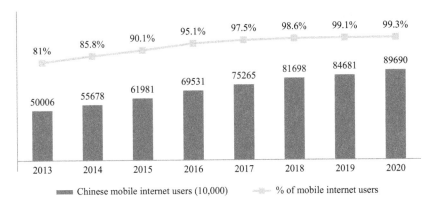

Fig. 3.2 Percent of Chinese internet users who are mobile 2013–2020. (Source: CNNIC 2020)

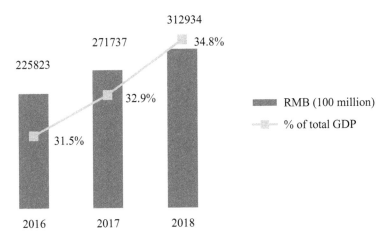

Fig. 3.3 China's digital economy 2016–2018

Survey Report—Statistical Report on Internet Development (CNNIC China Internet Network Information Centre 2019, p. 75). The digital economy's rate of growth is significantly higher than China's overall GDP growth. According to *White Paper on Chinese Digital Economy and Employment 2019*, the rate of growth (Fig. 3.3) was at least 20 percent higher than the growth in national GDP (CAICT 2019, p. 7).

Hyperplatformization has been propelled by China's robust, government-sponsored and -backed venture capital (VC) system, which has fostered a risk-taking, competitive tech landscape underwriting China's digital economy. According to Tim Hardin (2017), a Silicon Valley banker, tech startups are financed by "supportive government guidance funds, cash-rich corporations, high-net individuals, and serial entrepreneurs who are reinvesting their proceeds from China's first wave of successful exits". From 2007 to 2016, China's VC fundraising has grown 10-fold to rival that of the United States, peaking in 2018 before experiencing minor declines in 2019 (Kunthara 2019). According to the China-based Huron Report, as of 2019, China is fostering more tech startups, or "unicorns", than the United States, turning Beijing into the "unicorn capital of the world".

The rise of China's tech sector, platform economy, and wanghong industry can be partly attributed to the influx of global financial capital since the 1990s (Hong 2017; Jia and Winseck 2018; Tang 2020). As Hong (2017, p. 1495) points out, "although the Great Firewall and market restriction shield Chinese Web companies from direct competition from Silicon Valley, Chinese companies tap into the same pool of financial resources as their United States counterparts". The most powerful Chinese internet giants, including the so-called BAT and the new giants such as Bytedance and Kuaishou, all receive a significant proportion of VC investment from the United States, Japan, Singapore, and other countries. This global financial network brings not only money but technology, talent, and international experience to Chinese internet companies, which at the same time are protected from the fierce competition in the global market.

The conditions have persisted into the 2020s despite rising tensions between China and the United States. For example, Silicon Valley-based Sequoia Capital is the largest VC firm in the world and has invested in United States and Chinese technology valued at over USD 1 trillion. Investments include United States tech behemoths, like Google and Facebook, who own platforms, including YouTube and Instagram, vital to the SME industry. Comparably, the firm has invested in Chinese tech conglomerates central to the wanghong industry, most notably tech firms central to the rising competition of their e-commerce platforms, including Alibaba, JD.Com and Pinduoduo. More notably, they have been core investors in ByteDance since 2014, the owner of multiple platforms including Douyin (also referred to as TikTok), Toutiao, Houshan, and Zigua. Bytedance also owns comparable and parallel platforms outside China, including TikTok, which shares similar functions to Douyin and has been the target of a global backlash. TikTok was banned in India in early 2019, and threatened with divestiture by the United States in mid-2020, with Sequoia a potential bidder. Nonetheless, despite these geopolitical headwinds, in late 2019, Sequoia announced USD 2.4 billion for Chinese investors in startup companies, including wanghong platforms. "Setting politics aside…It's a sign that when valuations are concerned …investors can overlook the potential political pitfalls of dealing with China" (Clark and Shieber 2019). Despite the rapidly increasing stress of platform nationalism (a concept further discussed in Chap. 6), United States venture capitalism has been consistently and increasingly attracted to the China tech scene.

In addition to VC investment, both domestic and foreign, Chinese companies have launched IPOs in the United States, securing capital through listing on the NASDAQ, although this practice has slowed in the wake of tougher United States restrictions and relaxed Chinese regulations (Hu 2019). Instead, China has launched the STAR Market, a "tech marketplace", comparable to the NASDAQ but with fewer restrictions and barriers to entry. After receiving a given number of rounds of VC investment, China's tech firms can launch an IPO in this tech market where it may be possible to secure public funding, while operating under far less onerous conditions that demanded by NASDAQ. In comparison, companies listed on the STAR market trade at three times higher value relative to their earnings than on NASDAQ, if also creating untenable conditions that some Western analysts describe as "a bubble ready to burst" (Reuters 2020).

In light of these conditions, the STAR market has fueled an "IPO frenzy…funneling tens of billions into emerging technologies" (Yue 2020). But the consequence is Chinese platforms listed in this market are made vulnerable to control by even larger Chinese firms, most notably the BATs. These firms merely need to acquire controlling market shares rather than more expensive mergers or acquisition, producing greater synergies around their larger tech ambitions within and beyond China. For example, Tencent has secured controlling shares in the two leading gameplay livestreaming platforms, Douyu and Huya, which align with efforts to dominate the Chinese and global game industry. As we will see through this chapter, other wanghong platforms listed on these markets have also been subject to controlling interest by their competitors, but have been able to continue operation. Contrast this pattern to the SME platform landscape where, for example, Twitter acquired the short-video platform

Vine in beta only to shut it down when they failed to successfully monetize the platform, a move short-sighted in the wake of rising Chinese-owned competition like TikTok.

The heart of China's digital economy is their digital and social media platform ecosystem, upon which multiple stakeholders, users, operators, municipalities, and nearly every market and industry have grown dependent, including the wanghong industry. While this system has been dominated by their national champions, known as the BAT (Baidu, Alibaba, and Tencent), it has allowed for emerging major players, like Bytedance and Kuaishou, to potentially threaten their primacy. These Chinese internet giants have engaged in synergistic platform strategies to create an encompassing ecosystem through which Chinese netizens shop, bank, communicate, and play. These firms provide near-frictionless one-stop shops for Chinese netizens' needs at the push of a button and in the palm of their hand. These firms have also created a nested-doll like environment for the growth of next-generation tech firms and platforms, referred to as unicorns. Whether directly or indirectly, the BATs have some form of equity investment in more than half the unicorns (Huxiu 2018).

This networked investment system reflects the centralized role of the BAT champions in the transformation of China's digital economy. Yet, in 2019, this system of outside VCs, STAR Markets, and BAT-investment has also produced more unicorns worth over USD 1 billion than in the United States, and turned Beijing into the "unicorn capital" (He 2019). Beyond the launch of startups, in the wanghong landscape, these underlying conditions foster greater platform competition and nurture more collaboration, if also afford the means for controlling ownership through market-based strategies.

China's hyperplatformization also rests on what economists refer to as "leapfrogging" because of a conspicuous lack of path dependency on older, mature industries and markets. For nearly two decades, China has pursued a "twin-track strategy, which involves merging industrialization and informatization" that embraced ICTs for the purpose of leapfrogging forward into a digital-based economy (Dai 2002). This strategy dates from 2000, when Premier Zhu Rongji launched the Tenth Five-Year Plan, declaring that "Leapfrogging in productivity in development may be achieved by melding informatization and industrialization, the two processes reinforce each other and progress simultaneously" (Dai 2003, p. 8)

Chinese leapfrogging through technological innovation laid the pipeline for the wanghong economy. China's delay in laying copper wire and telephony contributed to the rapid uptake of mobile telephony. In the United States, in the retail sector, massive chain and box stores dominate their sectors whereas in China, these sectors have been far less efficient at servicing the needs of China's rapidly growing middle class (Mozur 2016). These needs are now met through leapfrogging to a more competitive array of e-commerce platforms, just as China's poorly designed credit card system is offset by its online mobile payment system which has resulted in a near-cashless, QR code-driven economy. Tencent's WeChat pay and Alibaba's Alipay account for 90 percent of online transactions and online mobile payments have grown from under USD 1 trillion in 2013 to nearly USD 40 trillion by 2018. According to the NGO, Consultative Group to Assist the Poor (CGAP), China has experienced a "digital payments revolution" (CGAP 2019), particularly through promotion of online payments, mobile phone use, and online access to e-commerce platforms, even in the poorest rural corners of the country.

China's e-commerce system is framed and supported by the state-sponsored drive to move every industry online as quickly as possible through tax initiatives and subsidies. China's e-commerce market is now three times the size of the United States and growing at a rate of 27 percent a year—suggesting that "as China goes, so goes the global e-commerce market" (Lipsman 2019). Unlike the West, dominated by Amazon, China's e-commerce system has fostered a more competitive platform landscape, including Alibaba and JD.com and Pinduoduo. The latter, rival, platform did not exist before 2015 but now has over half-a billion monthly users (Kharpal 2020). As of 2020, JD.com and Pinduoduo not only threaten Alibaba's primacy in the Chinese market but are valued higher than Baidu, one of the original BATs. China's ecommerce platforms are advancing outside their borders, competing directly against United States ecommerce platforms. By 2018, Alibaba's international platform, AliExpress, had already expanded into Russia, Southeast Asia, India, and Latin America (Sun 2018). Of particular note is the success of Taobao which, as *The Economist* (2015) described, "[f]rom shoes to furniture and cosmetics to cars, shoppers in China can find just about anything on Taobao, the country's biggest online marketplace".

Yet, despite vast growth in platform power, the BAT have not monopolized China's tech market in the same way that we now see in the very worrisome dominance of Silicon Valley hegemons Google, Facebook, Amazon, and Apple in their respective markets. Rather, there is greater platform competition that better reflects textbook capitalism. Consider

Sina-owned Weibo, which was launched in 2009 and spun off in an IPO in 2014, after which Alibaba investment comprises a third of the company. Once deemed a serious competitor to Twitter (Zhang and Negro 2013), Weibo has evolved well beyond that comparison. Weibo has become the model of sustainable growth and innovation for Chinese social media. Weibo has surpassed its Western counterpart Twitter in both the integration of more technologically advanced features such as online mobile payments and live streaming, as well as in scale. While limited mostly to Chinese users, domestic and expatriate, Weibo has over half a billion users, as compared to Twitter's 330 million, even though Twitter's reach is global. The company better integrates photo and recorded video, boasts a multi-platform strategy that includes acquisition of livestreaming platform Yizhibo, and the launch of Instagram-like picture-based platform, Oasis or *Lvzhou*. Contrast this with Twitter's inability, after early phase acquisition, to integrate the livestreaming platform Periscope, or monetize the short-video platform, Vine.

Interplatformization—collaboration between rival tech firms and platforms through the interoperability of features, services, and affordances (Lv and Craig 2021)—is another strategy that distinguishes China from the SME landscape. The Silicon Valley model has moved away from the open internet towards a "walled garden" approach, emulating features and services of their rivals, as in the case of Facebook-owned Instagram introducing similar "story" functions like Snapchat and short-video like TikTok. Rather than link to competing e-commerce platforms like Amazon and eBay, Facebook launches its own "marketplaces"—with limited success. Other than Twitch, most SME platforms have struggled to introduce online mobile payment services, whether linked to credit card companies, bank accounts, or bitcoin.

Contrast this with wanghong platforms, particularly the near-frictionless cross-platform integration of ecommerce and online mobile payment services. Tencent-owned platforms like WeChat allow creators to integrate links to rival ecommerce platforms, like Alibaba-owned Taobao and Tmall. This practice would be the equivalent of Instagram and YouTube not only allowing but promoting links to a creator's Amazon page or eBay store. The two largest competing online payment systems, Alibaba-owned Alipay and Tencent-owned WeChat Pay are uniformly available across this platform landscape. In partnership with Alibaba, Sina Corp-owned Weibo launched an in-app online mobile payment systems called WeChat Wallet. (WeChat is owned by TenCent.)

Unlike the app store oligopoly enjoyed by Google and Apple, China has multiple, competing and collaborating, app stores, including stores within platforms like WeChat and Alibaba, referred to "lite apps" and "mini-programs". Even these stores-within-platforms still allow users, including wanghong, to harness features and services from rival platforms. Even though Sina-owned Weibo launched its own e-commerce tool, Xiaodian ("little-shop"), it allows creators to link to ecommerce platforms owned by rival firms. In contrast, Instagram launched an in-app store designed to keep creators and consumers from linking to Amazon (Del Rey 2019).

There are exceptions and complications to this picture. For example, Tencent's innovation and acquisition strategies are monopolistic in intent. Since 2016, Tencent has attempted to corner not only the Chinese social media market but also global media industries. The company has been "taking over global gaming" through either purchase or majority stakeholder investment of game publishers (Custer 2016). Tencent may also replace Baidu as the top investor in iQiyi, which could conceivable merge with Tencent Videos to dominate China's streaming video landscape (Culpan 2020).

With WeChat, or *Weixin*, Tencent has developed a platform ecosystem at a huge scale. As Ge Zhang and Gabrielle de Seta (2018) note, "largely inspired by the app-centric ecology of functions of WeChat, mobile oriented social networking platforms have largely reshaped the local digital media landscape" (pp. 63–64). Breathless business journalism claims that "Facebook wants to be WeChat" (Statt and Liao 2019). Indeed, Facebook and WeChat have been framed in the literature as both platform and infrastructure (Helmond et al. 2019; Plantin and de Seta 2019). To the originally identified properties of platformization that, along with digitalization, include participation, modularity, and programmability, could be added scale, ubiquity, and criticality of use, which refers to the centrality of these platforms to the larger digital economy.

Launched in 2011, WeChat by 2020 has over 1 billion users and combines messenger and social networking services with finance, retail, entertainment, food delivery, and more. Imagine some combination of Uber, Bank of America, eBay, Amazon, Netflix, and Facebook but also add Doordash, Fandango, and Ticketmaster. WeChat has now launched livestreaming features on the platform as well as its own ecommerce platform, decoupling links to Alibaba-owned Taobao and Tmall. These developments signal a shift away from interplatformization and interoperability with rival platforms and towards more of a "walled garden" of self-contained features and services. As we cover in Chap. 6, 2020 has seen the United States Trump administration threaten to ban WeChat, along with Bytedance-owned TikTok, signaling a consolidation of the era of platform nationalism (Mozur and Zhong 2020).

However, Tencent's monopolizing tendencies remain relative outliers and have not inhibited the increased competition and ongoing collaboration across the wanghong platform landscape relative to SME. Rising tech and platform competition throughout China's digital economy contributes to a strategic and disruptive roundelay of platform innovation and oscillation between different value propositions, socio-technological features and affordances, and, in turn, wanghong viability. These patterns may be best reflected in the following account of wanghong platforms converting into streaming video portals—a pattern that, in some instances, abruptly forced wanghong creators and their fan communities to explore alternative platforms.

Portalization

As we have noted, Cunningham and Craig's *Social Media Entertainment* (2019) framed the SME platform landscape in the dynamic tension between two world-spanning but United States-based industrial cultures: tech (Silicon Valley or NoCal) and entertainment (Hollywood or SoCal). YouTube was the prime exhibit in that analysis of the tension between these two cultures, oscillating between the functions of a social media platform and those of an experimental video-on-demand, over-the-top, television-like service.

In this section, we consider how China's tech landscape has comparably oscillated between video streaming, IP-controlled portals that align with the frameworks of cultural industries and social media platforms driven by network effects and online engagement aligned with our framing of social industries. We contrast the evolution of YouTube to Youku, at one point considered the "YouTube of China". While our earlier accounts of hyper-platformization and interplatformization have driven wanghong entrepreneurialism and viability, these oscillations have sometimes proven onerous and sometimes highly problematic for wanghong to manage.

In her treatise on portals (2017), Amanda Lotz showed how internet distributed television services such as Netflix and Amazon Prime Video are different from broadcast and cable television, as well as social media platforms that include video streaming players. Portals, for Lotz, are "crucial intermediary services that collect, curate, and distribute television programming via internet distribution" (Lotz 2017, p. 8). Features of portals typically include professionally-generated content, nonlinearity (on-demand), algorithmic, customer-centric curatorial practices, the prevalence of subscription-based revenue models, and the vertical integration of these operations within traditional media conglomerates—for example, Disney+ and HBO Max. Amongst international SVODs, Netflix stands alone as a pure play streaming video company.

The "streaming wars" (The Verge n.d.) have proceeded, with heightened, now global, competition between deeply capitalized SVOD services, including Netflix, Hulu, Amazon, Disney+, HBO Max, and others. China has its own streaming wars, with increasing competition between Baidu-owned iQiyi, Tencent Video, and Youku, now owned by Alibaba. Their parent companies have since launched parallel portals in Southeast Asia, like Tencent-owned WeTV, in an early bid to compete against United States portals (Lim 2020).

We understand *portalization* as the process by which entertainment IP content is now increasingly curated and delivered by portals. This process includes not only video, but also the streaming audio portals hosting music and podcasts such as Spotify and Pandora. These sites almost exclusively feature professionally generated, licensed, or owned content and are funded through subscription (and sometimes advertising) revenue models. *Portalization* has accelerated during the COVID pandemic that has severely disrupted legacy media distribution and exhibition. As Craig and Cunningham (2021) track, tech-tonic shifts and battles have played out very differently between digital portals and social media platforms, legacy media and tech industries, in the West and China. This is starkly seen in the divergent evolution of YouTube and, at one point, its closest Chinese counterpart, Youku.

Hector Postigo (2016) offers a vivid image of Silicon Valley tech company strategy. It is like "a bettor at a roulette table who is in the happy position of betting on all the numbers, where the payout in aggregate outweighs what appears to be an otherwise wild investment" (p. 15). For nearly two decades, Google's YouTube has cultivated a commercializing environment for native social media creators uploading user-generated content designed for community engagement. Over the same time frame, the platform has repeatedly attempted to compete with the likes of Netflix and Amazon through the distribution (and sometimes commissioning) of professional media. This played out through YouTube's repeated relaunches and renamings of their subscription video platform: from YouTube Music Key, to YouTube Red, to YouTube Premium. They have been mostly unsuccessful. YouTube Premium is now advertising driven, the original content has shifted from expensive scripted fare to reality and lifestyles, and, according to their CEO, operates more like a music streaming platform (Li et al. 2018). YouTube has also struggled to integrate social networking features like their rivals Facebook and Snapchat. Efforts like Orkut, Friend Connect, Buzz, and Google Plus, and their community button, have proved mostly epic fails.

China's platforms and portals have initially been happy to emulate and reverse engineer Western tech models, a strategy called the "flying geese models" of technological development (Keane 2006). Youku was once referred to as "China's YouTube". In 2005, the day after YouTube was launched, the Chinese platform Tudou debuted with an open access platform that allowed users to post and share video content. Youku launched a year later and merged with Tudou in 2012. As Google purchased YouTube a year after its launch, Alibaba purchased Youku, albeit nearly a decade later. In our interview with Youku executive Catherine Zhang (2016), she explained that Youku was also emulating YouTube's user interface, identified similar content verticals, and introduced a comparable user content ID system.

Youku-Tudou also introduced partnership agreements for their native amateur creators, encouraging monetization and professionalization. This helped launch the channels and brands of wanghong supercreators such as Papi Jiang aka Miss Papi. She first emerged on Youku with what Jian Xu and Xinyu Zhao (2019) describe as comedic rants, or *tucao*. This format combines humor, vulgarity, and accents that border on the offensive that endeared large fan communities to Miss Papi, as well as censorship by the state for using foul language (Schoenmakers 2016). Like YouTube Originals, Youku also launched an original channel strategy (*zipindao*) to generate original content fashioned after legacy media fare, such as original web series, produced by both legacy media producers and native Youku wanghong creators. Youku's IP platform strategies helped convert professionalizing amateurs into IP generators, exemplified by the success of Joy Stick's original scripted web series *Surprise (wanwan meixiangdao)* or online talk shows like Baozou Big News (*baozou dashijian*) (Zhao 2016).

But since 2016 the platforms have pursued starkly different trajectories. YouTube continues to foster a creator-centric video ecology alongside channels owned and operated by traditional media companies. Creators like gamer PewDiePie and child unboxer Like Nastya compete with T-Series, run by an Indian music label, and multiple Netflix channels promoting series and topics. Youku has opted for a more dramatic shift, completely abandoning its creator-centric model to compete directly against other video streaming services like Tencent Video and iQiyi. Youku has gone from imitating YouTube to looking like Hulu (Ye 2019).

Youku's wanghong have struggled, ongoing viability limited to those few skilled and trained to convert their content and performative practices into more conventional forms of media IP, like talk shows, web series, and DIY. For the vast remainder of wanghong whose practices are rooted in their commercialization of social engagement with their communities, social platforms becoming portals prove highly disruptive, even disastrous. Papi Jiang has effectively abandoned Youku, first migrating to other platforms like Weibo and WeChat. She has since moved off-screen, launching PapiTube, a multichannel network that represents thousands of wanghong creators, before joining Baidu in 2018 as Chief Content Officer (Li 2019), only posting on her site to announce the birth of her baby. "Whether this marks Papi Jiang's departure from *wanghong* status", Xu and Zhao (2019) remark, "needs further observations" (p. 145).

Chinese social media platform Bilibili has also oscillated between portal and platform strategies. Launched in 2012, Bilibili initially relied on loyal engagement with a cybersubculture of anime and game fans. This culture is known by the acronym ACFUN, although ACFUN is also the name of another competing platform launched by Sina. Bilibili is also distinguished by its unique video platform and player. Niconoco is a Japanese innovation that allows users to comment directly on screen in real time, a process referred to as bullet messaging (*danmaku*). We go into more detail on this affordance in the next section of this chapter.

Like Sina Weibo, Bilibili is not controlled by the BAT although both Alibaba and Tencent are investors. Exemplifying interplatformization, such investment encourages Bilibili to engage in cross-platform interoperability customized to appeal to Bilibili's game and anime fan community. "In a savvy move, Alibaba hooked up food delivery unit Ele.me with Bilibili in December to tap a demographic of anime-watching and game-playing young people reliant on delivered meals" (Liao 2019a). Going public on the NASDAQ in 2018, Bilibili secured investment from Sony America to promote Sony's mobile gaming features. Like Sequoia's prominence in China's VC system, Sony's investment in a Chinese platform signals how foreign tech and media companies can bring capital and investment into the Chinese platform landscape, but not through ownership nor influencing content. For all that, Bilibili has yet to turn a profit. Neither did YouTube during its first decade, relying on its owner, Google's, deep pockets.

After going public, Bilibili was expected to become "the next YouTube" (Liangyu 2020), adding one more flying goose to the flock. The platform entered into original production and licensed IP with traditional media suppliers. The platform live-streamed a New Year's Eve Spring Festival gala that surpassed the ratings of Chinese broadcast TV in part by introducing less traditional performers and more youth-oriented fare, like *World of Warcraft* costumes and *Harry Potter* music. Catering to its game-focused users, the site entered into exclusive deals to live-stream major e-sports tournaments.

Unlike Youku, Bilibili continues to encourage and help monetize their native creators and their channels, referred to a "Up zhu" ("uploaders"). The site maintains the functions of a user-generated platform, allowing for open-access video streaming by creators. The platform launched its "KOL management" division which signs creators to exclusive deals on the platform, includes an MCN talent agency signing creators operating across other platforms, an in-house advertising agency, and production studio (Lawrence 2020). Whereas YouTube demands that creators secure a certain level of followers to enter into a partnership, aspiring Bilibili creators must merely correctly answer a series of questions to enter into their partnership program and secure a portion of advertising revenue. The platform also introduced live-streaming functions, which introduced live-gamers who might appeal to the platform's fanbase.

Nonetheless, platform investment comes with new stakeholders, obligations, and expectations, often at the expense of the older ones. Torn between its twinned portal-platform ambitions, trade stories feature "Bilibili vs Bilibili: The Culture Clash dividing China's YouTube" (Siqi and Davis 2020). Bilibili's attempt to "embrace a wider audience" (Davis 2020) has contributed to a backlash from its ACFUN community. Is this a "subculture sellout" (Liangyu 2020)? As Qin, a veteran user of the platform remarked, "My paradise has been desecrated…Bilibili is no longer that platform where I could watch videos while socializing with others. I now feel like I'm just another user" (Siqi and Davis 2020).

Nevertheless, the platform has doubled down on portalization, launching a "celebrity-driven" creator strategy and entering into deals with the likes of Hollywood star Dwayne Johnson. Bilibili has progressively eroded the culture for their native creators. A number of them have migrated to the AcFun platform. A first-generation platform launched in 2007, AcFun is co-dependent upon its rivals, runs on Sina's video player, and previously secured investment from Youku Toudou. The platform has remained loyal to its niche fan culture. However, in 2018, the platform was purchased by rising tech competitor and Tencent-backed Kuaishou (Li and Jourdan 2018). This aligns with the Tencent's expansive global gaming strategy through ownership of game publishers, investment and control of live gaming platforms Douyu and Huya, and aggregation of wanghong platforms that appeal to game fan communities.

Portalization continues to play out across the wanghong platform landscape. In 2020, Bytedance's long form video platform Watermelon, or Xigua, has aggressively pivoted away from user-generated, open access to compete against the likes of Youku, Tencent Video, and iQiyi. Most notably, this strategy included securing first-run releases of major Chinese feature tentpoles films like *Lost in Russia*, brought about by the collapse of theater distribution due to the coronavirus outbreak. While these portalization tendencies have introduced greater precarity for creators, the next section of the chapter shows that the wanghong landscape has significantly progressed the affordances of social presence, a strategy that has deepened the sustainability and connectivity of wanghong platforms and creators.

Social Presence

Social presence in the wanghong platform landscape is cultivated by technological innovations that allow for social commentary, social streaming, and social video. These affordances, in turn, enhance wanghong platform and creator viability through the near frictionless ability to engage in social tipping and social commerce, the latter two phenomena part of a "social+" business model. These developments have underpinned strong growth in the industry and differentiate wanghong further from SME.

First coined by James Gibson (1977), the concept of affordances more broadly refers to the "actionable possibilities" available to humans within any environment. As Taina Bucher and Anne Helmond (2017) argue, the concept of affordances remains "a key term for understanding and analyzing social media interfaces and the relations between technology and its users" (p. 233). Cunningham and Craig (2019) use the concept of affordances to distinguish social media platforms from other channels of media distribution, whether theatrical, broadcast, cable, or streaming, and the practices of creator labor and management operationalized across them. We identified how communicative affordances (Hutchby 2001) of SME platforms help both users and creators develop "network publics" (boyd 2010). Coupled with commercial affordances, creator entrepreneurialism has the potential to flourish in an environment where "financial and social economies co-exist" (Humphreys 2009, p. 1).

Social presence refers to the perception of being present with a real person. As Joon Lim, Youngchan Hwang, Seyun Kim and Frank Biocca (2015) explain, "the concept of social presence has evolved from interpersonal communication, specifically from Goffman's (1963) notion of the mutual awareness of and attention to each other in a space" (Lim et al. 2015, p. 160). First introduced by John Short, Ederyn Williams and Bruce Christie (1976) in the field of computer science, the term "social presence" captured "the salience of the interactants and their interpersonal relationship during a mediated conversation" (Oh et al. 2018, p. 1). The concept of social presence has featured in more recent discussions—especially from Chinese communication and media scholars (Liu et al. 2020; Lu et al. 2016; S. Wang 2020)—regarding the socio-technological affordances of virtual reality, social media, and livestreaming. As Wang and Lobato (2019) noted, Chinese scholars' focus on social presence signals their awareness of the need to differentiate the ontology of China's platforms from those of the West.

Approximating social presence can foster deeper engagement and intimacy and encourage greater interactivity. For wanghong platforms and creators, these affordances have nurtured new social business models generating greater remuneration and sustainability.

From Social Commentary to Social Streaming

Affordances supporting social presence were introduced relatively early in wanghong history. Around 2008–2009, game and anime-focused platform Bilibili and AcFun were launched, featuring Japanese-designed Niconico video players. These players allowed users to conduct rapid-fire bullet messaging (*danmaku*) in real time across recorded video. Chinese communication scholars have highlighted the socializing affordances that bullet messaging provides users, creators, and their communities. Elaine Zhao (2016) described danmaku as "reinvigorating the meaning of liveness while creating a sense of sharedness amongst audiences" (p. 5454).

Jinying Li (2017) argued that danmaku has changed "video consumption into social communication" (p. 235). Other scholars have pointed to the bullet messaging's "pseudo-synchronicity" (Hamano 2008; Yeqi 2017) and "virtual liveness" (Johnson 2013). Yuhong Yang (2019) argued that danmaku facilitates "the social practice of participatory viewing" (p. 3).

To date, none of the prominent platforms in the SME landscape have ever integrated bullet messaging, including YouTube and Facebook. Chauncey Jung (2018) thinks this may reflect the multilingual nature of these platforms. According to Pew research (van Kessel et al. 2019), 17 percent of YouTube videos posted each week are English-language, although they comprise nearly a third of the views. The ephemeral nature of the social commenting may also pose challenges for platform moderation and state surveillance, although regulations introduced in 2019 have imposed greater censorship (Feng 2019). Nonetheless, at the peak of use, danmaku allowed users to subvert norms and engage in controversial topics. This affordance might explain how danmaku has fostered a subcultural space on Bilibili in which anime and game fans may engage in subcultural and political resistance (Yin and Fung 2017). As Zhen Chen (2018) argues that, despite the platform's intentions for financial gain, Bilibili's features like danmaku allows users to "transform themselves into tactical prosumers… They employ various tactics to resist such control, manipulation and exploitation" (p. 2).

Danmaku was only the beginning. Over the past decade, the uptake of livestreaming technology throughout this landscape has most dramatically advanced the affordances of social presence. (Livestreaming was introduced in greater detail in Chap. 2). Here we offer a brief summary of the evolution and proliferation of Chinese livestreaming in relation to the affordances of social presence. Livestreaming provides the means for social streaming, the ability for users to more deeply engage with their fan community in real time, whether through the streaming screen or a chat room that offers synchronous text-based interactivity.

Social streaming is a vital affordance in the livestreaming vertical of live gaming. Live gaming, also referred to as gameplay, refers to streamers playing video games accompanied by either jokes and/or instruction, while simultaneously interacting with their fan community either on the same screen or in a chat room. With reference to livegaming on SME platforms like YouTube and Twitch, Postigo (2014) described how "the social affordances frame practices such as community participation, systems of subscriber recruitment and exchange and valuation, competition, participatory culture and so forth" (p. 216). For nearly a decade, Twitch has remained the dominant player in the live gaming SME landscape (Bloom 2019) although, in 2020, competition emerged between Twitch competing against Microsoft's Mixer and Facebook and YouTube's gaming platforms. Mixer has since folded, although these platform wars "kicked off a talent war for streamers" (Webster 2020), pointing towards the ongoing influence and entrepreneurial agency of live gaming creators in the SME industry. Outside of live gaming, however, livestreaming has struggled for viability, suffering from a global backlash due to rampant abuse of the platforms hosting criminal activities that the platforms appear incapable of thwarting through content moderation.

In China, livestreaming has tracked a more prolific trajectory. As captured in greater detail in Chap. 2, this trajectory is a consequence of underlying socio-economic conditions coupled with state-driven cultural and creative industries and social policy. Much like the SME livestreaming landscape, the vertical of live gaming has proven a driver of wanghong industry growth and creator viability. Unlike the SME landscape, live gaming comprises only a portion a vastly more diverse array of Chinese livestreaming platforms and verticals advancing more lucrative practices of livestreaming creators, also known as showroom hosts, or *zhubo*.

Launched in the mid-2000s, niche social media platforms dedicated to game culture have accompanied the parallel rise of China's gaming and esports industries, in turn, part of a larger strategy to make China the "global center of the games industry" (Cao 2020). Launched in 2005 at the same time as YouTube and Youku and similar to AcFun, Duowan appealed to gamers and their fans. Five years later, the platform introduced live streaming, was renamed YY Live or Huanjushidai, and pivoted to include a vast array of livestreaming verticals, creators, and affinity communities well beyond gaming. As the vanguard platform leading this innovation, YY Live is known as the "forefather of the country's massive live streaming industry" (Hallanan 2019). Through introduction of virtual tipping, YY Live helped launch the online gift economy, while also integrating its own e-commerce platform Yijan. Virtual tipping and ecommerce integration refer to business models discussed in greater detail in the following section on social+ business models.

In 2018, YY spun off its live gaming platform, Huya, in competition against Douyu, another live gaming platform. China's live gaming sector has proven highly competitive, thus lucrative for live game players, as it has in the SME industry across platforms like Twitch and YouTube Gaming.

In the span of four years, according to iResearch Global (2018), live gaming has grown from USD 2.6 billion in 2016 to USD 23.55 billion in 2020—a growth rate of 900 percent. In 2016, live gaming platform wars were waged between three platforms: Douyu, Huya, and Panda TV. This competition between platforms helped live gamers extract enormous salaries for exclusivity while racking up millions of RMB in virtual goods, or social tipping, as we explain later in this section. After Panda TV folded, Douyu and Huya constituted a duopoly, dominating 60 percent of the live-game market. Both Douyu and Huya have since launched IPOs through the market and Tencent has purchased controlling shares in both platforms, with the anticipation that these will be merged (Sun 2020). On balance, while these strategies may align with the patterns of digital and platform capitalism, we argue that Tencent's platform strategies are more of an outlier, as mapped in this chapter across a vastly more competitive landscape than its SME counterpart.

A decade later, live gaming still dominates livestreaming in SME. In China, however, live gaming represents only 20 percent of the livestreaming industry (Yang 2018). Rather, what has emerged is a more diverse live streaming industry with rapidly scaling streaming platforms (*zhibo*) dominated by native, entrepreneurial, IRL (In Real Life) streamers (*zhubo*). The diversification of livestreaming platforms features deeply gendered and affective creators and performativity. The appeal of and demand for online mediated intimacy afforded by these platforms have contributing to what Kokas referred to as an industry of "virtual girlfriends" (Kaiman and Meyers 2017). Conditions of creator labor and management are elaborated on in Chaps. 4 and 5.

Another core instance of social presence is the introduction of livestreaming across Chinese dating apps in the mid-2010s, which Western platforms introduced only years later. Initially for the purpose of creating real world dating opportunities, as well as sexual hookups, informed by the demand for online and mediated intimacy, livestreaming advanced the affordances of social streaming and presence. Like YY Live, these features allowed the dating apps to introduce social platform business models, like tipping and ecommerce integration, upon which wanghong creators have prospered.

Launched in 2011, Momo was initially compared to the Western-based dating app, Tinder, and pejoratively described as the "one night stand app" (Rosenman 2013) and "a magical tool for getting laid" (Cendrowski 2014). However, in 2015, Momo introduced livestreaming, evolving the platform from "location-based dating to social entertainment" (Lee 2017). By 2018, Momo was one of the largest livestreaming apps in China, Tinder only launched a live video feature in mid-2020 in response to the COVID-19 epidemic (Tilman 2020). While still featuring dating services, Momo promotes livestreaming for other "social activities like chat rooms, karaoke performances, and talent shows", further differentiating the platform from a vast array of United States-owned dating apps like Tinder, Match, and OK Cupid (Sun 2020).

These patterns have been emulated across China's LGBTQ dating apps in contrast to their Western counterparts. Launched in 2012, eleven years after China removed homosexuality from country's list of mental disorders, Blued targeted the LGBTQ community. Three years later, the platform introduced livestreaming and, by 2016, ranked 13th amongst all Chinese livestreaming apps (Shen 2017). By mid-2020, the platform has 49 million registered users, has expanded throughout Southeast Asia, and launched an IPO on NASDAQ (Liao 2020). In contrast, United States-launched gay dating app Grindr has never secured more than 6 million users and struggled to integrate livestreaming features. In need of investment, in 2016, the platform sold majority interest to a Chinese gaming company, Beijing Kunlun Tech. Since then, the United States government has attempted to force the sale of the platform back to Western owners out of concern over data privacy and potential extortion by its Beijing owners (Sanger 2019). As we explore in Chap. 6, this fits a pattern whereby China's newly successful international tech profile is being impacted by the rise of platform nationalism and the growing "splinternet".

Across these platforms and apps, through the affordances of social streaming and presence, creators are securing revenue by deepening virtual intimacy amongst their fan communities, as reflected in recent scholarship. Lik Sam Chan (2019) thought Momo "opened up new possibilities for socializing, relationship-seeking, sexual experimentation, business practices, and so on" (p. 14). Shuaishuai Wang (2019) argued that the rise of wanghong creators operating off the livestreaming features on Blued creates the material conditions for "affective platform economies" and "performative labor".

While livestreaming continues to flourish in the wanghong platform landscape, ongoing competition demands that these platforms advance new strategies, including portalization. While still one of the leading zhibo, YY has integrated a wanghong talent management and IP-incubation strategy. The platform hosts wanghong festivals like the YY festival in

Guangzhou while launching reality shows on the platform designed to identify next-generation wanghong talent. In addition, the platform has secured deals for their native wanghong talent, like the Modern Brothers, a C-pop boy band group, who are encouraged to grow their community across other platforms like Douyin but who return to YY to watch them in concert (Hallanan 2019). Other zhibo have comparably expanded into IP, portal-like practices, emulating some of the SME portalization programming practices like YouTube Premium and Instagram's IGTV. Momo sponsors variety shows like *Plasticity* and *I Love Anime*.

Like YY, Inke is a prominent live streaming platform pursuing a similar talent and IP-management and portal-like strategy. Inke cast their native creators in scripted programs like *Emotional Cuisine 2*, a workplace drama set in a Chinese restaurant whose owner recounts the stories of guest diners. This series has nurtured the careers of aspiring actors and "deconstructed China's star-making factory" inside China's legacy media industries (Ouyangshaoxia 2019). Securing record viewership for Inke, the series has been described as a "live + miniseries" business model as part of the platform's "pan-entertainment" strategy (Wang 2019). The series features short-form video ideal for mobile viewing, distribution well beyond Inke itself, while starring Inke creators whose fans are encouraged to propose future storylines.

Social commentary and social streaming in the wanghong platform landscape afford greater social presence. Social streaming in the form of live gaming has proven profitable in both the SME and wanghong industries. However, as reflected in the diverse evolution of Chinese and Western dating apps, social streaming operates expansively across more Chinese platforms featuring more diverse verticals, while fostering a new wave of creators advantaged by the affordances of greater social presence. While the vast competition amongst streaming platforms contributes to the afore-mentioned patterns of portalization, these features and affordances have also led to forms of social content innovation. We now turn to the rise of "social video" platforms, including Douyin and Kuaishou, as evidence of further affordances of social presence.

The Rise of Social Video

Across industry and academic discourses, the rapid uptake of Chinese platforms, Kuaishou (or Kwai) and Douyin are more hyped and critiqued by their short-video modalities. These discourses, however, more often underdetermine the distinctive socio-technological architecture and engineering that these platforms offer and the user and creator affordances they provide. Varying from 7 seconds to one minute, the hype regarding short video emphasizes the short-lived attention span of digital and mobile youth. The ill-fated consequence of this emphasis has produced expensive flame outs in the Western platform landscape, most notably the collapse of the mobile short-video platform Quibi (Sperling 2020).

In the SME industry, discourses surrounding short video start with the launch of Vine. Vine's appeal and innovation extended well beyond video length to include mobile-first design, a user-interface that feature in-app editing features, looping video that promotes repeat viewing, a channel-less user interface and algorithmic recommendation system that expedited social virality, and a hyper-editing technique that emulated the "Kuleshov effect" (Pavlus 2013). (The latter refers to meaning-making effects generated by the juxtaposition of two diverse images.)

Vine's features and affordances nurtured a new wave of creators and forms of content, such as Zach King's digital illusions. As King (2015) mentioned in our interview, "different platforms give you different rules and boundaries". While still in beta, Twitter purchased Vine and, within two years of launch had 200 million users before it was shuttered. The reasons given for Vine's demise included increased competition from emulating competitor Instagram, the inability to effectively monetize the platform through advertising revenue, as well as poor platform management (Newton 2016). Vine creators had loudly protested the lack of profit participation or revenue partnerships before abandoning the platform for its competition, including Instagram and Snapchat (Chen 2016).

Twitter's failure to accommodate Vine creators signaled that creators had become critical to the growth of next-generation SME platforms. Likewise, in the wanghong industry, where multiple short-video Vine-like competitors launched concurrently with their Western counterparts. Weishi was a Vine-like app that proved an ephemeral example of Tencent's strategy of launching competing platforms that attempt to emulate the features of next-generation platforms. After shutting down the platform, Tencent relaunched Weishi in 2018 to compete with Douyin by offering subsidies to wanghong creators totaling nearly USD 500 million (Zhao 2018). Tencent's competitive management strategy might best be described as "if you can't beat them, buy them", comparable to that of Facebook's acquisition of Instagram and WhatsApp; however, we still advance this agglomerative pattern by Tencent as more Chinese industry outlier than norm.

Driven by competitive pressure, Meitu-owned Meipai integrated the short video modality of Vine and Weishi with the filter functions of Instagram to secure over half-a-billion users. Within a year, however, the platform pivoted rapidly to introduce live streaming and launched and integrated its own ecommerce store called MeituBeauty. The platform has aggressively introduced filtering and AI systems designed for appeal to the beauty wanghong and their communities. These strategies signal platform and market alignment as China's middle class drives growth in domestic lifestyle industries of beauty, fashion, and home décor.

Despite industry discourses hyping overnight success, both Kuaishou and Bytedance-owned Douyin (China's domestic version of TikTok) were launched in the same period as these other short video platforms. However, as Yunwen Wang (2020) shows in her research on Douyin, these social video platforms have been designed to further heighten users' perceptions of "immersion, presence, and entertainment". Their sustainability is testament to their platform management strategies of continuous iteration, innovation, and integration of state-of-the-art social video features and predictive AI recommendation algorithms, as detailed here through comparative platform histories.

Founded in 2012, Bytedance has been acclaimed as the "world's most valuable startup" (Ting 2019). In less than a decade, Bytedance now rivals the BATs in market value, advertising revenue, while eclipsing their global reach. Bytedance owns three short video platforms, Douyin and Huoshan within China and TikTok without. Other platforms include news-focused Headlines, or *Toutiao*, Bytedance has been labelled an "app factory" (Cortese 2020), acquiring, investing in, or launching over 80 platforms across all sectors, signaling that a new "B" has emerged in the pantheon of national champions.

In 2016, Bytedance acquired Beijing-based musical.ly, a Western-facing platform with similar short-video and music integration. The platform was relaunched in 2018 as TikTok and soon became the fastest growing social platform in the world in scale. As we will see in Chap. 6, Bytedance's platform strategy has helped transform the firm into the first global Chinese platform company and affirm the aspirations of founder Zhang Yiming: "From the start, Zhang, a former Microsoft engineer and Chinese serial entrepreneur, had the goal of running a borderless company" (Fannin 2019).

Douyin's platform innovation, much like Vine's was, is not limited to a short-video player but also sophisticated and professionalizing in-app editing, music library integration that fosters content practices like lip-syncing and dancing, and predictive AI recommendation filters. Douyin's advances in social video progress further embed social presence. Recent platform scholarship has begun to focus on social presence. As we have seen, Wang (2020) refers to Douyin's users' perceptions of "immersion, presence, and entertainment". Ethan Bresnick (2019) talks of "virtual play structures" fostering "intensified play" in contrast to conventional video sharing platforms. Zhicong Lu and Xing Lu (2019) argue the platform's appeal lies in its ability for users to develop "virtual intimate relationships" coupled with "positive energy" that aligns with Chinese socio-cultural values of keeping face, or *guanxi*. In fact, Positive Energy or *zhengnengliang*, is the name of the platform's trending video tab. Douyin's features, as Xu Chen, D. Bondy Kaye and Jing Zeng (2020) remind us, also serve the interest of the state "by promoting playful patriotism online" (p. 1).

Lu and Lu (2019) point to how Douyin promote "fashionable lifestyles" along with content designed for "informational and practical purpose". Douyin has rapidly cultivated China's young, cosmopolitan, middle-class netizens, located primarily in Tier 1 and 2 cities. This contrasts with the demographic targeted by platforms like Kuaishou and Bytedance's Huoshan, which targets rural users and creators. This pattern suggests a kind of socio-cultural platform pillarization, segmenting China's platform society by class and location as much as by affinity or interests.

This segmentation contributes to the rise of diverse classes of wanghong creators—and we will look more closely at this in Chaps. 4 and 5. On Douyin, high-end, cosmopolitan creators like Li Jiaqi (Fig. 3.4), a male superwanghong, known as the "lipstick king" can drive 40 million followers to his Taobao store and sell out "15,000 lipsticks in five minutes" (Huang 2020). Alternatively, Xinbao uses Huoshan to amass over 400,000 followers while based in a remote mountainous village in Western China. She demonstrates how to harvest rice and forge iron, before encouraging her followers to visit her ecommerce store to buy her fermented tofu. In their targeting of Tier 4 and 5 cities and villages, both Huoshan and Kuaishou commercially and culturally empowered rural creators and "pushed people from poor villages like Xinbao to the spotlight in a virtual world" (Yuming 2020).

Platform pillarization across diverse segments of Chinese society correlate with how each platform introduces user interfaces, modalities, and

Fig. 3.4 Li Jiaqi promoting a lipstick in livestreaming

platform services that advance social presence. For example, Kuaishou's rural users and creators reflect a slower-paced society with greater emphasis on traditional culture and lifestyles. These strategies and conditions show in different features, including Kuaishou's better integration of livestreaming alongside recorded short-form social video than Douyin. Kuaishou's main discovery page primarily shows videos from a user's own social network as compared to Douyin, which promotes videos based on algorithmically-determined popularity across the entire platform. As a result of these functions and features, Kuaishou users spend up to twice as much time on Kuaishou than Douyin (Iqbal 2010). As confirmed in our interviews with Kuaishou executives (Kuaishou executives 2019), the key objective of Kuaishou's interface has been designed to foster user engagement and stickiness, stated proverbially as "soft fire makes sweet malt".

The consequence of all these features is to make Kuaishou a more "relationship-based" platform than Douyin, which is most notably fostered between the creators and their fan communities. In our interview with Kuaishou executives, they claimed the platform promotes a culture that nurtures brother-like relationships (laotie) between wanghong creators and fans, or as they referred to them, "creator-followers". Similarly, the ability of platforms to foster engagement and closer relationships converts into more revenue for the platform and its creators. All the platforms feature both advertising as well as social business platform models, like social tipping and social commerce, as further discussed in the next section. According to our interview with a senior MCN executive (Kuaishou executives 2019), most of Kuaishou's revenue, and in turn, wanghong revenue, comes from social tipping, which makes the platform more reliable for MCNs and wanghong creators, whereas advertisers revenue proves, in his description, "inconsistent and unreliable". However, these advertising conditions may reflect the socio-economic stability outside of China's fast-growing middle class located within Tier 1 and 2 cities. Douyin secures more revenue through higher advertising rates targeting cosmopolitan, upscale users (Chen 2020).

This platform pillarization may prove mutable as ongoing platform competition and market demand for growth results in constant and rapid platform iteration. As in SME, wanghong platforms are introducing new features and services and, in some instances, pivoting towards an IP-centered portalization model. As Kuaishou strives to secure more revenue from high value advertisers, in recent marketing appeals, the platform is targeting more young, urban, and cosmopolitan users. Like Bilibili, this may result in Kuaishou becoming yet another "subcultural sell-out" (Liangyu 2020). Likewise, in our interviews with Bytedance executives (Bytedance executives 2019), they resisted discussing Huashon, pejoratively dismissing their own platform as "grassroots"; rather, they prefer to tout Douyin, promoting its cosmopolitan users and wanghong creators and, in turn, higher advertising rates and revenue. In 2020, Bytedance renamed Huoshan as Douyin Huoshan and introduced a "ladder plan" designed to "nurture content creators to produce more premium content" (Chen 2020).

For every platform that may appear to abandon the lower tier, rural Chinese netizens, another enters into the fray. As the third social ecommerce platform in China, Pinduoduo's growth story has been called "miraculous", securing RMB 1 trillion (USD 141 billion) in half the time it took Alibaba or JD (Norris 2020). The growth of this platform reflects a commitment to the growth of China's grassroots economy, launching 1 million stores with livestreaming features for Chinese farmers and cooperates to promote agricultural goods. As with all these initiatives, platform innovation is aligned with state interest. "Pinduoduo's latest initiative backs Beijing's efforts to revitalize economic activity after the government started lifting the lockdown on communities and other coronavirus containment measures across the country from last month" (Xue 2020). The ability of these platforms and creators to appeal to multiple segments of Chinese society reflect not only the greater affordances of social presence, but also the integration of social platform business models.

Social+ Business Models

As China's digital and platform economies have evolved, so have policy, industry, and academic discourses around the "+", or plusification of internet technologies. The term Internet Plus or Internet + was first introduced by a Chinese industry consultant in 2012 before it was adopted as a policy strategy in 2015 (Zhang 2017). The adoption of live streaming technologies logically contributed to discourses surround new business models referred to as "live streaming +" (iResearch Global 2018). As mentioned in the last section, a "live + miniseries" model refers to the integration of interactive scripted content with creator talent across social media.

The next iteration of this discourse is *social+*. As first espoused by Chinese tech journalist Zen Soo (2018), the concept of social+ refers to how "different industries such as education, news and E-commerce are anchored by a social pillar that drives user engagement and growth … For companies that have successfully navigated Social+, a model unique to China, victory comes in the form of millions of active users amassed in a relatively short amount of time. Social+ apps are often recognized for their user stickiness, incorporating social elements that incentivize users to come back day after day". As we argue here, the viability of social+ stems from these greater affordances of social presence. The most prolific and lucrative social+ business models are social tipping and social commerce.

Social tipping is also known as online tipping or "da shang", fan tipping, digital tipping, live tipping, gift sending, and virtual goods. The practice involves sending creators money or virtual goods that can be converted into money out of appreciation to grab the streamer's attention

(Chan 2016). Although tipping is not practiced offline, in China, "they tip millions online" (Xiang 2016), which suggests the wanghong industry is introducing new social norms which recognize and reward entrepreneurialism and entertainment values.

This social platform business model has proved lucrative for the growth of wanghong platforms and creators operating across them. As Jilei Zhou et al. (2019) claim, this practice was "invented by Chinese companies...and widely adopted by Chinese live streaming firms" (p. 1) before it was introduced on SME platforms like Twitch. Social tipping took off in China as far back as 2013. When Chinese pop singer Hua Chenyu posted a song on Weibo in 2014, through both download fees and tipping, "he made $17,000 USD in five hours and he wasn't even famous yet" (Frosco 2019). Once Momo introduced a tipping feature alongside integration of livestreaming, within two years, social tipping became a key revenue driver, growing five-fold across Momo, eclipsing both advertising and subscription business models. Inke gamified social tipping, encouraging what has been coined "Player knockout (PK) battles" between live streamers trying to secure the most tips within a given time frame.

According to scholars, the heightened affordances of social presence advanced by these platforms contributes to the desire for social tipping. As Boying Li, Zhengzhi Guan, Fangfang Hou, and Alain Yee-Loong Chong (2018) researched, "we find that contextual factors (that is, interactivity and social presence) are positively associated with consumption intention in live streaming" (n.p.). As poignantly captured in Wu Hao's documentary *People's Republic of Desire* (2018), IRL livestreamers vie for the remunerative affection of their fans through social tips. These business models helped lift rural and uneducated wanghong out of poverty, even if often deriving income from working poor out of gratitude for "helping to ease their loneliness" (Jarowoski 2018). These working conditions are, however, fraught with precarity, demanding long hours that epitomizes affective labor (Hardt 1999) and aspirational labor (Duffy 2017) in these high-stakes platform-driven battles to win the hearts and savings of their fans. One might as easily condemn these platforms, business models, and practices as epitomizing the commodification of the "social" in social industries (Sandvig 2015) as commend them for their advancing social mobility and amelioration within China's hyperplatformized digital economy.

Social commerce is another social+ business model. Shanelle Mullen (2019) defined social commerce as "the ability to make a product purchase from a third-party company within the native social media experience". In China, social commerce and social+ have often been used interchangeably to describe the interplatformization of ecommerce and social media platforms and creator practices. As Haiqing Yu (2019) describes, social+ "combines social networking and entertainment in the context of e-commerce transactions" that have contributed to the popularity of older generation platforms like WeChat and "rising stars like Pinduoduo and Xiaohongshu" (p. 33); the former was discussed in our last section and the latter, also known as Little Red Book, will be further mentioned below.

While Taobao links remain operable across this landscape, the platform also launched Taobao Live in 2016, upon which livestreaming creators, or *zhubo*, like Viya and Li Jiaqi, are flourishing. According to a senior director of e-commerce, "Taobao Live is quickly becoming the model of future retail. Livestreaming is now the primary infrastructure for e-commerce moving forward" (Alibaba Group 2020). Every retailer and sales force exists on this platform: "5000 real estate agents…23 global automakers such as BMW and Audi" (Yi 2020). Competing ecommerce platforms, JD and Pinduoduo, have since integrated their own *zhibo* apps as well.

As with any business model in this landscape, social commerce also introduces risk and precarity for both platforms and creators. Backed by both Alibaba and Tencent, Little Red Book, or Xiaohongshu, is a social commerce site that integrates Instagram-like photo modality and comments promoting beauty and lifestyle wanghong creators along with ecommerce functionality. Founded in 2013, the platform grew rapidly to 200 million users. However, fast growth may have been faux growth, violating the social norms of platform and wanghong engagement. In 2019, the press revealed the platform was populated by fake reviews and reviewers and the platform was suspended from the app stores. In an attempt to reverse the damage, the platform introduced its "brand partner program" and deleted all their creators, numbering over 13,000 (Zheng 2019). Rapid falls from grace can also lead to fast redemption narratives. Little Red Book returned in 2020 seeking half-a-billion in VC investment while also launching livestreaming functions. Even as precarity remains an embedded feature throughout the wanghong industry, these social+ business models driven by the affordances of social presence have advanced the viability of platforms and creators.

Anyone Can Be a Wanghong

The COVID-19 crisis in China may have even further accelerated the growth of the wanghong industry, at least according to Chinese and Western business journalists and websites. "When people were confined to home, the new industry was buoyed to new heights, and many brands turned to wanghong to help boost sales through livestreaming promotions" (Wu 2020). According to business consulting site 1421 (2020), the wanghong industry is one of the few to benefit from the crisis, tripling in revenue from 2019 to 2020, driven by the growth of social video and social streaming sites. Across the ecommerce platform JD.com alone, there were more than 4 million wanghong creators, from rural farmers to mayors, promoting agricultural products and cultural tourism to hundreds of millions (Y. Wang 2020b). In addition to social commerce, the pandemic is also generating new forms of social content. Sponsored by liquor brands, "live clubbing" refers to musician and DJs hosting online dance parties to cope with "the social dis-dance". As one record label executive stated, "it's creating a new entertainment front and a new model of business" (Y. Wang 2020b). In China's near future, it may be conceivable that anyone could become a wanghong accessing—and growing increasingly dependent upon—these platforms to capture commercial, cultural, and social value.

This chapter outlined distinctions between the wanghong and SME platform landscapes. We studied processes of hyperplatformization and interplatformization fostering wanghong entrepreneurialism. We also saw oscillating patterns of platform-portalization that caused brutal outbreaks of creator precarity, evidenced by the collapse of Youku's creator channels. Wanghong platforms, we noted, have advanced the affordances of social presence, evolving from social commentary to social streaming and social video. Accompanying this socio-technological innovation is the rise of social+ business models of social tipping and social commerce. How have these strategies, affordances, and business models shaped wanghong creator culture? In the next chapters, we find out.

References

1421. (2020, June 24). *The Influencer Economy in China*. Retrieved September 15, 2020, from https://www.1421.consulting/2020/06/influencer-economy-in-china/.

Alibaba Group. (2020, March 30). *Taobao Live Accelerating Digitization of China's Retail Sector*. *Alibaba Group*. Retrieved August 20, 2020, from https://www.alibabagroup.com/en/news/article?news=p200330.

Bloom, D. (2019, June 21). Twitch Dominates Gamer Livestreams, But Its Biggest Stars Are The Biggest Winners. *Forbes*. Retrieved September 18, 2020, from https://www.forbes.com/sites/dbloom/2019/07/21/twitch-dominates-gamer-livestreams-but-its-biggest-stars-are-the-biggest-winners/

boyd, d. (2010). Social Network Sites as Networked Publics: Affordances, Dynamics, and Implications. In Z. Papacharissi (Ed.), *Networked Self: Identity, Community, and Culture on Social Network Sites* (pp. 39–58). New York: Routledge.

Bresnick, E. (2019, April 25). Intensified Play: Cinematic Study of TikTok Mobile App. *Medium*. Retrieved September 15, 2020, from https://medium.com/@ethanbresnick/intensified-play-cinematic-study-of-tiktok-mobile-app-b8e848befaa8.

Bucher, T., & Helmond, A. (2017). The Affordances of Social Media Platforms. In J. Burgess, T. Poell, & A. Marwick (Eds.), *The SAGE Handbook of Social Media* (pp. 233–253). SAGE: London and New York.

Bytedance Executives. (2019). Interview with (Anonymous) Bytedance Executive, 9 August, Guangzhou, interview with David Craig.

Cao, C. (2020, February 3) China Has a Big Plan to Become the Global Centre of the Games Industry. *Pocket Gamer*. Retrieved September 16, 2020, from https://www.pocketgamer.biz/asia/comment-and-opinion/72500/china-has-a-big-plan-to-become-the-global-centre-of-the-games-industry/.

Cendrowski, S. (2014, March 11). The Guy Behind China's Tinder. *Fortune*. Retrieved August 20, 2020, from https://fortune.com/2014/11/03/the-guys-behind-chinas-tinder/.

Chan, C. (2016, September 27). 16 Observations on Livestreaming in China. *Andreessen Horowitz*. Retrieved September 18, 2020, from https://a16z.com/2016/09/27/livestreaming-trend-china/.

Chan, L. (2019). Multiple Uses and Anti-Purposefulness on Momo, a Chinese Dating/Social App. *Information, Communication & Society, 22*. https://doi.org/10.1080/1369118X.2019.1586977.

Chen, J. (2020). The Mirage and Politics of Participation in China's Platform Economy. *Javnost-The Public, 27*(2), 154–170.

Chen, X., Kaye, D. B., & Zeng, J. (2020). #*PositiveEnergy* Douyin: Constructing 'Playful Patriotism' in a Chinese Short-Video Application. *Chinese Journal of Communication*. https://doi.org/10.1080/17544750.2020.1761848.

Chen, Y. (2016, May 17). Swinging from Vine: More than Half of Top Vine Influencers Have Left the Platform. *Digiday*. Retrieved August 15, 2020, from https://digiday.com/media/swinging-vine-half-top-influencers-left-platform/.

Chen, Z. (2018). Poetic Prosumption of Animation, Comic, Game and Novel in a Post-Socialist China: A Case of a Popular Video-Sharing Social Media Bilibili as Heterotopia. *Journal of Consumer Culture*. https://doi.org/10.1177/1469540518787574.

China Information and Communication Research Institute. (2019, July 1). White Paper on China's Digital Economy Development and Employment. *CAICT*. Retrieved September 18, 2020, from http://www.caict.ac.cn/kxyj/qwfb/bps/201904/P020190417344468720243.pdf.

Clark, K., & Shieber, J. (2019, December 3). Setting Politics Aside, Sequoia Raises $3.4 billion for US and China Investments. *TechCrunch*. Retrieved September 15, 2020, from https://techcrunch.com/2019/12/03/setting-politics-aside-sequoia-raises-3-4-billion-for-us-and-china-investments.

CNNIC (China Internet Network Information Center). (2019). The 44th China National Statistical Report on Internet Development (第44次中国互联网络发展状况统计报告). Retrieved from http://www.cac.gov.cn/2019zt/44/index.htm

CNNIC (China Internet Network Information Centre). (2020). The 45th China National Statistical Report on Internet Development (第45次中国互联网发展状况统计报告). Retrieved from http://www.cac.gov.cn/2020-04/27/c_1589535470378587.htm

Consultative Group to Assist the Poor (CGAP). (2019). China: A Digital Payments Revolution. CGAP, September 1. Retrieved August 20, 2020, from https://www.cgap.org/research/publication/china-digital-payments-revolution.

Cortese, A. (2020, June 12). ByteDance's Investments Bring a Data-driven Approach to New Sectors. *KrASIA*. Retrieved August 20, 2020, from https://kr-asia.com/bytedances-investments-bring-a-data-driven-approach-to-new-sectors.

Craig, D., & Cunningham, S. (2021). Tech-tonic Shifts: The U.S. and China Models of Online Screen Distribution. In P. Macdonald, T. Havens, & C. B. Donoghue (Eds.), *Media Distribution in the Digital Age*. New York: New York University Press.

Culpan, T. (2020, June 17). Tencent Buying iQiyi Smells a Lot like that Uber Deal. *Bloomberg*. Retrieved September 15, 2020, from https://www.bloomberg.com/opinion/articles/2020-06-17/tencent-buying-iqiyi-smells-a-lot-like-uber-s-china-exit-deal.

Cunningham, S., & Craig, D. (2019). *Social Media Entertainment: The New Intersection of Hollywood and Silicon Valley*. New York: New York University Press.

Custer, C. (2016, June 22). How Tencent is Taking Over Global Gaming. *Tech in Asia*. Retrieved September 16, 2020, from https://www.techinasia.com/tencent-gaming-world.

Dai, X. (2002). Towards a Digital Economy with Chinese Characteristics? *New Media & Society, 4*(2), 141–162.

Dai, X. (2003). ICTs in China's Development Strategy. In C. Hughes & G. Wacker (Eds.), *China and the Internet: Politics of the Digital Leap Forward* (pp. 8–29). London: Routledge.

Davis, R. (2020, May 28). China's Streamer Bilibili Aims to Embrace a Wider Audience Without Alienating its Fans. *Variety*. Retrieved August 20, 2020, from https://variety.com/2020/digital/features/china-streaming-bilibili-1234617963/.

de Kloet, J., Poell, T., Guohua, Z., & Yiu Fai, C. (2019). The Platformization of Chinese Society: Infrastructure, Governance, and Practice. *Chinese Journal of Communication, 12*(3), 249–256.

Del Rey, J. (2019, March 20). Instagram Just Took Advantage of Amazon's Biggest Weakness. *Vox.* Retrieved September 18, 2020, from https://www.vox.com/2019/3/20/18271386/instagram-shopping-discovery-amazon-weakness-checkout.

Duffy, B. (2017). *(Not) Getting Paid to do What You Love: Gender, Social Media, and Aspirational Work.* New Haven, CT: Yale University Press.

Fannin, R. (2019, September 13). The Strategy behind TikTok's Global Rise. *Harvard Business Review.* Retrieved August 20, 2020, from https://hbr.org/2019/09/the-strategy-behind-tiktoks-global-rise.

Feng, J. (2019, February 15). Real-time Censorship for Real-time Comments. *SupChina.* Retrieved September 18, 2020, from https://supchina.com/2019/02/15/real-time-censorship-for-real-time-comments/.

Frosco, M. (2019, May 8). The Rise of Digital Tipping—From Music To Your Own Paycheck. *Ozy.* Retrieved September 18, 2020, from https://www.ozy.com/around-the-world/the-rise-of-digital-tipping-from-music-to-your-own-paycheck/93993/.

Gibson, J. (1977). The Theory of Affordances. In R. Shar & J. Bransford (Eds.), *Perceiving, Acting, and Knowing: Toward an Ecological Psychology* (pp. 67–82). Hillsdale, NJ: Lawrence Erlbaum.

Goffman, E. (1963). Behavior in public places: Notes on the social organization of gatherings. New York: Free Press.

Hallanan, L. (2019, February 12). How YY Used Modern Brothers to Revive its Stagnant Live-Streaming Platform. *Forbes.* Retrieved August 20, 2020, from https://www.forbes.com/sites/laurenhallanan/2019/02/12/how-yy-used-modern-brothers-to-revive-their-stagnant-live-streaming-platform.

Hamano, S. (2008). *Aakitekucha no seitaikei—joho kankyo wa ikani sekkei sarete kita ka (Ecosystems of Architecture: How do Information Environments Come to be Planned?).* Tokyo: NTT Shuppan.

Hardin, T. (2017, October 14). China Now Rivals U.S. in VC Investments. *Venture Beat.* Retrieved September 15, 2020, from https://venturebeat.com/2017/10/14/china-now-rivals-u-s-in-vc-investments/.

Hardt, M. (1999). Affective Labor. *Boundary 2, 26*(2), 89–100.

He, L. (2019, October 23) Chinese Report Counts 206 Unicorns. That's More than America. *CNN Business.* Retrieved September 18, 2020, from https://www.cnn.com/2019/10/23/tech/china-unicorns-united-states/index.html.

Helmond, A. (2015). The Platformization of the Web: Making Web Data Platform Ready. *Social Media+ Society, 1*(2), https://doi.org/10.1177/2056305115603080.

Helmond, A., Nieborg, D., & van der Vlist, F. (2019). Facebook's Evolution: Development of a Platform-as-Infrastructure. *Internet Histories, 3*(2), 123–146.

Hong, Y. (2017). Pivot to Internet Plus: Modeling China's Digital Economy for Economic Restructuring? *International Journal of Communication, 11*, 1486–1506.

Hu, K. (2019, December 20). Fewer Chinese Companies IPO in the US in 2019. *Yahoo! Finance*. Retrieved September 16, 2020, from https://finance.yahoo.com/news/fewer-chinese-companies-ipo-in-the-us-in-2019-115605530.html.

Huang, A. (2020, March 09). Who Is Li Jiaqi, China's Millionaire 'Lipstick King'? *South China Morning Post*. Retrieved August 20, 2020, from https://www.scmp.com/magazines/style/news-trends/article/3074253/who-millionaire-li-jiaqi-chinas-lipstick-king-who.

Humphreys, S. (2009). The Economies within an Online Social Network Market: A Case Study of Ravelry. In *ANZCA 09 Annual Conference: Communication, Creativity, and Global Citizenship*, 8–10 July 2009, QUT Brisbane.

Hutchby, I. (2001). Technologies, Texts, and Affordances. *Sociology, 35*(2), 441–456.

Huxiu. (2018, February 12). More than Half the 124 Unicorns of 2017 are BAT Investments. *Panda Daily*. Retrieved October 7, 2020, from https://pandaily.com/half-124-unicorns-2017-bat-investments/.

Iqbal, M. (2010, September 2). TikTok Revenue and Usage Statistics (2020). *Business of Apps*. Retrieved September 18, 2020, from https://www.businessofapps.com/data/tik-tok-statistics/.

iResearch Global. (2018, March 27). 2018 China's Live Streaming Marketing Market Report. Retrieved September 6, 2020, from http://www.iresearchchina.com/content/details8_42342.html.

Jarowoski, K. (2018, November 29). 'People's Republic of Desire' Review: A Virtual Craze Makes Actual Cash. *The New York Times*. Retrieved September 18, 2020, from https://www.nytimes.com/2018/11/29/movies/peoples-republic-of-desire-review.html.

Jia, L., & Winseck, D. (2018). The Political Economy of Chinese Internet Companies: Financialization, Concentration, and Capitalization. *International Communication Gazette, 80*(1), 30–59.

Johnson, D. (2013). Polyphonic/Pseudo-Synchronic: Animated Writing in the Comment Feed of Nicovideo. *Japanese Studies, 33*(3), 297–313.

Jung, C. (2018, March 19). Will Bullet Comments be Popular in America? *KrAsia*. Retrieved September 18, 2020, from https://kr-asia.com/will-bullet-comments-be-popular-in-america.

Kaiman, J., & Meyers, J. (2017, June 24). Chinese Authorities Put the Brakes on a Surge in Live Streaming. *Los Angeles Times*. Retrieved July 15, 2020, from https://www.latimes.com/world/asia/la-fg-china-live-streaming-crackdown-20170624-story.html.

Keane, M. (2006). Created in China: The New Catch Up Strategy. In *Proceedings International Communication Association, Development and Intercultural Communication Panel*, Dresden June 20.

Keane, M., & Su, G. (2019). When push comes to nudge: a Chinese digital civilisation in-the-making. *Media International Australia, 173*(1), 3–16. https://doi.org/10.1177/1329878X19876362

Kharpal, A. (2020, April 21). Everything You Need to Know about Pinduoduo, the Fast-growing Rival to Alibaba and JD in China. *CNBC*. Retrieved August 20, 2020, from https://www.cnbc.com/2020/04/22/what-is-pinduoduo-chinese-ecommerce-rival-to-alibaba.html.

King, Z. (2015). *Creator, Zach King, 15 July*. United States: Interview with David Craig.

Kuaishou Executives. (2019). Interview with (Anonymous) Kuaishou Executives, 19 May, Beijing, interview with David Craig and Jian Lin.

Kunthara, S. (2019, December 5). VC dollars for China Take a Dip in 2019. *Crunchbase News*. Retrieved September 16, 2020, from https://news.crunchbase.com/news/vc-dollars-for-china-take-a-dip-in-2019/.

Lawrence, H. (2020, January 2). What You Need To Know About Influencer Marketing In China. *Matchmade*. Retrieved September 16, 2020, from https://matchmade.tv/blog/what-you-need-to-know-about-influencer-marketing-in-china/.

Lee, E. (2017, March 10). Chinese Dating App Momo Sees Record Revenue Growth Thanks to Live Streaming. *TechCrunch*. Retrieved August 20, 2020, from https://techcrunch.com/2017/03/09/momo-live-streaming/.

Li, A. (2019). Papi Jiang and Microcelebrity in China: A Multilevel Analysis. *International Journal of Communication, 13*(2019), 3016–3034.

Li, B., Guan, Z. Hou, F., & Chong, A. (2018). What Drives People to Purchase Virtual Gifts in Live Streaming? The Mediating Role of Flow. In *Proceedings of the Twenty-Second Pacific Asia Conference on Information Systems*, 26–30 June, Yokohama, Japan.

Li, J. (2017). The Interface Affect of a Contact Zone: Danmaku on Video-Streaming Platforms. *Asiascape: Digital Asia, 4*(3), 233–256.

Li, P., & Jourdan, A. (2018, May 10). Tencent Backed Kuaishou Buys Rival AcFun in Chinese Online Video Battle. *Reuters*. Retrieved September 16, 2020, from https://www.reuters.com/article/us-kuaishou-m-a/tencent-backed-kuaishou-buys-rival-acfun-in-chinese-online-video-battle-idUSKCN1J10O2.

Liangyu, H. (2020, June 17). Subculture Sellouts: Kuaishou and Bilibili Embrace Normcore. *Sixth Tone*. Retrieved August 20, 2020, from https://www.sixthtone.com/news/1005823/subculture-sellouts-kuaishou-and-bilibili-embrace-normcore.

Liao, R. (2019a, February 14). Alibaba Takes an 8% Stake in Tencent-Backed Anime Streaming Site Bilibili. *Techcrunch*. Retrieved September 16, 2020, from https://techcrunch.com/2019/02/14/alibaba-invests-8-in-bilibili/.

Liao, R. (2019b, June 17). China's Gay Dating App Blued Eyes Nasdaq IPO to Expand Overseas. *Techcrunch*. Retrieved September 16, 2020, from https://techcrunch.com/2020/06/17/blued-ipo/.

Lim, J., Hwang, Y., Kim, S., & Biocca, F. (2015). How Social Media Engagement Leads to Sports Channel Loyalty: Mediating Roles of Social Presence and Channel Commitment. *Computers in Human Behaviour., 46*, 158–167.

Lim, S. (2020, July 14). Why China's Entertainment Giants are Turning Their Focus to South East Asia. *The Drum*. Retrieved September 16, 2020, from https://www.thedrum.com/news/2020/07/14/why-china-s-entertainment-giants-are-turning-their-focus-south-east-asia.

Lipsman, A. (2019, June 27). Global Ecommerce 2019: Ecommerce Continues Strong Gains Amid Global Economic Uncertainty. *eMarketer*. Retrieved August 20, 2020, from https://www.emarketer.com/content/global-ecommerce-2019.

Liu, Z., Yang, J., & Ling, L. (2020). Exploring the Influence of Live Streaming in Mobile Commerce on Adoption Intention From a Social Presence Perspective. *International Journal of Mobile Human Computer Interaction, 12*(2), 53–71.

Lotz, A. (2017). *Portals: A Treatise on Internet-Distributed Television*. Michigan: Michigan Publishing, University of Michigan Library.

Lu, B., Fan, W., & Zhou, M. (2016). Social Presence, Trust, and Social Commerce Purchase Intention: An Empirical Research. *Computers in Human Behavior, 56*, 225–237.

Lu, X., & Lu, Z. (2019). Fifteen Seconds of Fame: A Qualitative Study of Douyin, A Short Video Sharing Mobile Application in China. In *International Conference on Human-Computer Interaction* (pp. 233–244). Cham: Springer.

Lv, J., & Craig, D. (2021). Firewalls and Walled Gardens: The Interplatformization of China's Wanghong Industry. In G. Yang & W. Wang (Eds.), *Engaging Social Media in China: Platforms, Publics, and Production* (pp. 51–74). East Lansing, MI: Michigan State University Press.

Mozur, P. (2016, August 03). China, Not Silicon Valley, is Cutting Edge in Mobile Tech. *The New York Times*. Retrieved August 20, 2020, from https://www.nytimes.com/2016/08/03/technology/china-mobile-tech-innovation-silicon-valley.html.

Mozur, P., & Zhong, R. (2020, September 4). Targeting WeChat, Trump Takes Aim at China's Bridge to the World. *The New York Times*. Retrieved September 16, 2020, from https://www.nytimes.com/2020/08/07/business/trump-china-wechat-tiktok.html.

Mullen, S. (2019, September 09). Social Commerce: What it Is, What it Isn't, and Why You Should Care. *CXL*. Retrieved July 13, 2020, from https://cxl.com/blog/social-commerce/.

Newton, C. (2016, October 28). Why Vine Died. *The Verge*. Retrieved August 20, 2020, from https://www.theverge.com/2016/10/28/13456208/why-vine-died-twitter-shutdown.

NewZoo. (n.d.). Top Countries by Smartphone Users. Retrieved September 16, 2020, from https://newzoo.com/insights/rankings/top-countries-by-smartphone-penetration-and-users/.

Nieborg, D., & Poell, T. (2018). The Platformization of Cultural Production: Theorizing the Contingent Cultural Commodity. *New Media & Society, 20*(11), 4275–4292.

Nonini, D. (2008). Is China Becoming Neoliberal? *Critique of Anthropology, 28*(2), 145–176.

Norris, M. (2020, May 12). Pinduoduo Growth Story Needs a New Chapter. *TechNode*. Retrieved September 18, 2020, from https://technode.com/2020/05/12/pinduoduo-growth-story-needs-a-new-chapter/.

Oh, C., Bailenson, J., & Welch, G. (2018). A Systematic Review of Social Presence: Definition, Antecedents, and Implications. *Frontiers in Robotics and AI, 5*, 114.

Ouyangshaoxia. (2019, January 30). Yingke is Getting Better: Building a Big Stage for the Little Ones. *Artificial Intelligence Technology Information*. Retrieved January 30, 2019, from https://technology-info.net/index.php/2019/01/30/yingke-is-getting-better-building-a-big-stage-for-the-little-ones/.

Pavlus, J. (2013, January 25). Vine's Great Mobile Design is All About Its Engineering. *MIT Technology Review*. Retrieved August 20, 2020, from https://www.technologyreview.com/2013/01/25/180315/vines-great-mobile-design-is-all-about-its-engineering.

Plantin, J., & de Seta, G. (2019). WeChat as Infrastructure: The Techno-Nationalist Shaping of Chinese Digital Platforms. *Chinese Journal of Communication, 12*(3), 257–273.

Postigo, H. (2014). The Socio-Technical Architecture of Digital Labor: Converting play into YouTube money. *New Media & Society, 18*(2), 332–349.

Postigo, H. (2016). The Socio-Technical Architecture of Digital Labor: Converting Play into YouTube Money. *New Media & Society, 18*(2), 332–349.

Reuters. (2020, July 23). China's STAR Market Doubles Nasdaq's Gains This Year, New Benchmark Shows. *Reuters*. Retrieved September 18, 2020, from https://www.reuters.com/article/china-markets-star/chinas-star-market-doubles-nasdaqs-gains-this-year-new-benchmark-shows.

Rosenman, O. (2013, November 13). China's Sexual Revolution: 'one-night stand' App Momo Boasts 80 Million Users. *South China Morning Post.* Retrieved August 20, 2020, from https://www.scmp.com/news/china-insider/article/1355124/chinese-instant-messaging-app-momo-boasts-80-million-users.

Sandvig, C. (2015). The Social Industry. *Social Media + Society, 1*(1). https://doi.org/10.1177/2056305115582047.

Sanger, D. (2019, March 28). Grindr Is Owned by a Chinese Firm, and the U.S. Is Trying to Force It to Sell. *The New York Times.* Retrieved September 18, 2020, from https://www.nytimes.com/2019/03/28/us/politics/grindr-china-national-security.html.

Schiller, D. (1999). Digital Capitalism: Networking the Global Market System. *Education for Information, 17*(3), 268–270.

Schoenmakers, K. (2016, April 18). Internet Star Papi Jiang Censored for Foul Language. *Sixth Tone.* Retrieved September 16, 2020, from http://www.sixthtone.com/news/751/internet-star-papi-jiang-censored-for-foul-language.

Scholz, T. (2017). *Uberworked and Underpaid: How Workers are Disrupting the Digital Economy.* Hoboken, NJ: John Wiley & Sons.

Shao, B. (2016). Vice President Corporate Strategies and PGC Operation, Youku, 31 May, Interview with David Craig, China.

Shen, T. (2017, October 27). Top 5 Chinese LGBT Apps in 2017. *TechNode.* Retrieved September 18, 2020, from https://technode.com/2017/10/27/top-5-chinese-lgbt-apps-in-2017/.

Short, J., Williams, E., & Christie, B. (1976). *The Social Psychology of Telecommunications.* Hoboken, NJ: John Wiley & Sons.

Siqi, L., & Davis, K. (2020, August 7). Bilibili vs. Bilibili: The Culture Clash Dividing China's YouTube. *Sixth Tone.* Retrieved September 16, 2020, from http://www.sixthtone.com/news/1006027/bilibili-vs.-bilibili-the-culture-clash-dividing-chinas-youtube.

Smyrnaios, N. (2016). The GAFAM Effect: Strategies and Logics of the Internet Oligopoly. *Communications & Languages, 188*(2), 61–83.

Soo, Z. (2018, May 12). The Next Big Thing for China's 600 Million Social Media Users is 'Social+'. *South China Morning Post.* Retrieved August 20, 2020, from https://www.scmp.com/tech/enterprises/article/2145750/chinas-internet-companies-adopting-new-social-business-model.

Sperling, N. (2020, May 11). Jeffrey Katzenberg Blames Pandemic for Quibi's Rough Start. *The New York Times.* Retrieved August 20, 2020, from https://www.nytimes.com/2020/05/11/business/media/jeffrey-katzenberg-quibi-coronavirus.html.

Srnicek, N. (2016). *Platform Capitalism.* Hoboken, NJ: John Wiley & Sons.

Statt, N., & Liao, S. (2019, March 08). Facebook Wants to be WeChat. *The Verge*. Retrieved August 20, 2020, from https://www.theverge.com/2019/3/8/18256226/facebook-wechat-messaging-zuckerberg-strategy.

Sun, L. (2018, September 1). Alibaba Is Expanding Its E-Commerce Platform Into These 4 Markets. *Fool.com*. Retrieved September 16, 2020, from https://www.fool.com/investing/2018/09/01/alibaba-is-expanding-its-e-commerce-platform-into.aspx.

Sun, L. (2020, April 09). Tencent Gains Control of Huya: What Does This Mean for JOYY? *The Motley Fool*. Retrieved August 20, 2020, from https://www.fool.com/investing/2020/04/09/tencent-gains-control-of-huya-what-does-this-mean.aspx.

Tang, M. (2020). From "bringing-in" to "going-out": Transnationalizing China's Internet Capital Through State Policies. *Chinese Journal of Communication, 13*(1), 27–46.

The Economist. (2015, June 04). The Everything Creditor. *The Economist*. Retrieved August 20, 2020, from https://www.economist.com/china/2015/06/04/the-everything-creditor.

The Verge. (n.d.). Streaming Wars. Retrieved September 16, 2020, from https://www.theverge.com/streaming-wars.

Tilman, M. (2020, May 6). Tinder Is Rushing a Live Video Feature So You Can Virtually Date in the Pandemic. *Pocket-lint*. Retrieved September 18, 2020, from https://www.pocket-lint.com/apps/news/tinder/152086-tinder-is-rushing-a-live-video-feature-so-you-can-virtually-date-in-the-pandemic.

Ting, D. (2019, October 30). Everything You Need to Know About ByteDance, the Company Behind TikTok. *Digiday*. Retrieved August 20, 2020, from https://digiday.com/media/everything-you-need-to-know-about-bytedance-the-company-behind-tiktok/.

van Dijck, J., Poell, T., & de Waal, M. (2018). *The Platform Society: Public Values in a Connective World*. Oxford: Oxford University Press.

van Kessel, P., Toor, S., & Smith, A. (2019, July 25). A Week in the Life of Popular YouTube Channels. *Per Research Centre*. Retrieved September 16, 2020, from https://www.pewresearch.org/internet/wp-content/uploads/sites/9/2019/07/DL_2019.07.25_YouTube-Channels_FINAL.pdf.

Wang, S. (2020). Chinese Affective Platform Economies: Dating, Live Streaming, and Performative Labor on Blued. *Media, Culture & Society, 42*(4), 502–520.

Wang, W., & Lobato, R. (2019). Chinese Video Streaming Services in the Context of Global Platform Studies. *Chinese Journal of Communication, 12*(3), 356–371.

Wang, X. (2019, January 15). Over Ten Million People Chase Dramas, Yingke Starts the First Shot of "Live + Miniseries". *WeChat Official Accounts Platform*. Retrieved August 20, 2020, from https://mp.weixin.qq.com/s/-4LSmJP3QfQS7IWyg4gcRA.

Wang, Y. (2020, May 13). In-depth Report: Amid COVID-19, e-Commerce Livestreaming Becomes Phenomenon. *JD Corporate Blog*. Retrieved August 20, 2020, from https://jdcorporateblog.com/in-depth-report-amid-covid-19-e-commerce-livestreaming-becomes-phenomenon/.
Webster, A. (2020, June 23). Mixer Was a Failure, but it Kicked Off a Talent War for Streamers. *The Verge*. Retrieved September 16, 2020, from https://www.theverge.com/2020/6/23/21299479/mixer-closure-streaming-talent-war-ninja-shroud-twitch.
Wu, H. (2020, June 22). Binjiang Steps Forward to Support Livestreaming. *Shine*. Retrieved September 16, 2020, from https://www.shine.cn/biz/event/2006220662/.
Xia, B. (2018). Capital Accumulation and Work in China's Internet Content Industry: Struggling in the Bubble. *The Economic and Labour Relations Review*, 29(4), 501–520.
Xiang, T. (2016, March 7). China Doesn't Tip In Restaurants, But They Tip Millions Online. *TechNode*. Retrieved September 18, 2020, from https://technode.com/2016/03/07/digital-tipping-economy-china/.
Xu, J., & Zhao, X. (2019). Changing Platformativity of China's Female Wanghong: From Anni Baobei to Zhang Dayi. In S. Cai (Ed.), *Female Celebrities in Contemporary Chinese Society* (pp. 127–158). Singapore: Palgrave Macmillan.
Xue, Y. (2020, April 23). Pinduoduo Doubles Down on Rural China, with Five-year, US$7.1bil e-Commerce Campaign. *The Star*. Retrieved September 16, 2020, from https://www.thestar.com.my/tech/tech-news/2020/04/23/pinduoduo-doubles-down-on-rural-china-with-five-year-us71bil-e-commerce-campaign.
Yang, P. (2018, September 9). A Primer on China's Live Streaming Market. *Hackernoon*. Retrieved December 28, 2018, from https://hackernoon.com/a-primer-on-chinas-live-streaming-market-352409ad2c0b.
Yang, Y. (2019). The *Danmaku* Interface on Bilibili and the Recontextualised Translation Practice: A semiotic technology perspective. *Social Semiotics*, 30(2), 254–273.
Ye, J. (2019, July 19). How Douyu Won the Live-streaming War to Become China's Twitch. *South China Morning Post*. Retrieved August 20, 2020, from https://www.scmp.com/abacus/who-what/what/article/3028270/how-douyu-won-live-streaming-war-become-chinas-twitch.
Yeqi, Z. (2017). Intertextuality, Cybersubculture, and the Creation of an Alternative Public Space: 'Danmaku' and Film Viewing on the Bilibili.com Website, a Case Study. *NECSUS. European Journal of Media Studies*, 6(2), 37–54.
Yi, D. (2020, February 20). Alibaba-owned Livestreaming Platform Taobao Live Sees Rapid Growth Amid Outbreak. *Caixin Global*. Retrieved August 20,

2020, from https://www.caixinglobal.com/2020-02-20/alibaba-owned-livestreaming-platform-taobao-live-sees-rapid-growth-amid-outbreak-101518181.html.
Yin, Y., & Fung, A. (2017). Youth Online Cultural Participation and Bilibili: An Alternative Form of Democracy in China? In R. Luppicini & R. Baarda (Eds.), *Digital Media Integration for Participatory Democracy* (pp. 130–154). IGI Global: Hershey.
Yu, H. (2018). Game On: The Rise of the eSports Middle Kingdom. *Media Industries Journal*, 5(1). https://doi.org/10.3998/mij.15031809.0005.106.
Yu, H. (2019, June 27). China's 'social+' Approach to Soft Power. *East Asia Forum*. Retrieved October 08, 2020, from https://www.eastasiaforum.org/2019/06/27/chinas-social-approach-to-soft-power/.
Yue, X. (2020, July 16). IPO Frenzy Grips China's Nasdaq-Style STAR Market. *The Wall Street Journal*. Retrieved September 16, 2020, from https://www.wsj.com/articles/ipo-frenzy-grips-chinas-nasdaq-style-star-market-11594893290.
Yuming, Q. (2020, April 23). The Story of a Rural Vlogger. *China Today*. Retrieved September 16, 2020, from http://www.chinatoday.com.cn/ctenglish/2018/sl/202004/t20200423_800201917.html.
Zhang, C. (2016). Interview 31 May with David Craig, Beijing, China.
Zhang, G., & de Seta, G. (2018). Being 'Red' on the Internet. In C. Abidin & M. Brown (Eds.), *Microcelebrity Around the Globe* (pp. 57–67). Bingley: Emerald Publishing Limited.
Zhang, H. (2017). Dean of School of Journalism and Communication, Beijing Normal University, Livestreamer, 15 June, with Junyi Lv, China.
Zhang, Z., & Negro, G. (2013). Weibo in China: Understanding its Development through Communication Analysis and Cultural Studies. *Communication, Politics & Culture*, 46(2), 199–216.
Zhao, E. (2016). Online Entertainmentl Professionalization of Amateur Production in Online Screen Entertainment in China: Hopes, Frustrations and Uncertainties. *International Journal of Communication*, 10(2016), 5444–5462.
Zhao, X. (2018, April 11). Tencent Bets on its Revived Weishi App to Take on TikTok in Short-video Streaming. *KrASIA*. Retrieved August 20, 2020, from https://kr-asia.com/tencent-bets-on-its-revived-weishi-app-to-take-on-toutiaos-tik-tok-in-short-video-streaming.
Zheng, R. (2019, November 10). Kim Kardashian Meets Chinese Top Livestreamer Viya. *Jing Daily*. Retrieved August 20, 2020, from https://jingdaily.com/livesteam-goldmine-kim-kardashian-meets-chinese-top-livestreamer-viya/.
Zhou, J., Zhou, J., Ding, Y. and Wang, H. (2019), "The magic of danmaku: a social interaction perspective of gift sending on live streaming platforms", *Electronic Commerce Research and Applications*, Vol. 34 No. 2019, p. 100815.

CHAPTER 4

Creators

In this chapter, we consider conditions and varieties of *wanghong* labor. Wanghong labor demands efficient management of dynamic networked relationships between multiple stakeholders, including platforms, advertisers, management firms, fan communities, and the state. Like creator conditions in social media entertainment, conditions of wanghong labor and entrepreneurialism are both markedly precarious while also significantly enriching. We map the diversity of Chinese creators through a taxonomy of cultural, creative, and social wanghong. The always-present governance by the state exposes platforms and creators to risk while placing onerous responsibility for content moderation, self-regulation, and censorship on intermediaries and individual wanghong. Socio-technical innovation underpinning social presence in the platform ecology means wanghong are exposed to heightened psychological demands as well as enhanced commercial opportunity. Much of the organization of wanghong labor is accomplished by Chinese multi-channel networks (MCNs)—a term generalized to mean any intermediary management firm facilitating the growth of platforms and creators, advertisers, and manufacturers. While in the SME industry, MCNs have experienced a steep fall from grace, China's MCNs number in the thousands, advancing the careers of millions of Chinese creators, while vulnerable to permanent disruption in governance and platform change.

© The Author(s), under exclusive license to Springer Nature
Switzerland AG 2021
D. Craig et al., *Wanghong as Social Media Entertainment in China*,
Palgrave Studies in Globalization, Culture and Society,
https://doi.org/10.1007/978-3-030-65376-7_4

Framing Wanghong Labor

Examining working conditions in the cultural and creative industries, critical scholars have mapped the conditions of creative labor that may have grown more precarious in the digital age. Cultural work proves neither as fulfilling nor autonomous as often touted by policy or industry boosters (Deuze 2009; Hesmondhalgh and Baker 2011; Curtin and Sanson 2016). Creative workers' aspiration for self-realization in practice is often compromised by the lack of labor protection and market competition (Hesmondhalgh and Baker 2011; McRobbie 2016). Gender, intersecting with race and ethnicity, age, (dis)ability and sexuality, can often lead to occupational segregation and unequal access to creative work and its reward system (Banks 2007). The rise of the platform society (van Dijck et al. 2018) and the analytical frameworks of platform capitalism (Srnicek 2017) and platformization (Helmond 2015; Nieborg and Poell 2018) have magnified concerns about the role of these technologies in causing greater labor precarity and exploitation. Critical scholars have offered accounts for how platform users are converted into "prosumers", operating effectively as exploited creative labor (Ritzer and Jurgenson 2010; Fuchs 2010). Niels van Doorn (2017) notes that in the platform economy, contracted labor has been replaced by "platform labor", which adopts "a more austere and zero-liability peer-to-peer model that leverages software to optimize labor flexibility, scalability, tractability, and its fragmentation" (2017, p. 901). As a consequence, workers are more readily regarded as subcontractors, instead of employees, of the platform companies, thereby exempting them from benefits or labor protection. Focusing less on value generation by creators operating entrepreneurially across digital and social media platforms, scholars further these critical concerns around inequality and risk that maintain and perpetuate preexisting social divisions. While they may operate entrepreneurially and independently within a flexible work regime (Gill 2007; Gregg 2013), creators are also operating under the adverse conditions of aspirational labor (Duffy 2016) and visibility labor (Abidin 2016). "While a select few may realize their professional goals—namely to get paid doing what they love—this labour ideology obscures problematic constructions of gender and intersectionalities with class" (Duffy 2016 p. 3).

Many of these concerns about this form of labor are very real, but creators' aspirations are not illusory, nor are they symptoms of false consciousness. Their entrepreneurial work also connects to their pursuit of a "better self" (Rose 1990): advancing in income, being more creative, better known, or fashionable. Wanghong strive to navigate work opportunity and pursue social mobility in a highly stratified and fiercely competitive society that places enormous weight and prestige on formal education and has historically and ideologically discounted entertaining self-display as rampant individualism.

Critical concerns about creator labor need to be framed against concrete comparisons of actually existing, alternative regimes of cultural worker rights and freedoms. Stuart Cunningham and David Craig (2019) have set out the points of difference between SME creator labor and cultural producers and media professionals operating in established media industries. SME creators were seen to advance from amateurism and hobbyism to more sophisticated and platform-determined professionalization and entrepreneurialism. Creators skills were more often self-taught rather than through specialized training, collapsing any division of creative labor between producing and production, and emerging from well-outside of the protocols and places of incumbent media industries, whether Hollywood, Bollywood or Chollywood.

Creator labor was most distinguished from cultural producers in the established media industries by platform dynamics. David Nieborg and Thomas Poell (2018) describe how platforms operate across "multi-sided markets" that foster more diverse opportunities and agency for individual creators. These conditions may prove as collaborative and symbiotic, as they are iterative and precarious. More specifically, sustainability demands that creators engage in a suite of risk management strategies to navigate the constant iteration of platforms, whether ever-changing algorithms, user-interfaces, features, services, or business models. In media, value is often generated through the control of either entertainment IP (intellectual property) or media distribution. In contrast, creators are more likely to secure cultural and commercial value through platform practices that engage, aggregate, and motivate their fan communities. These practices align with the conditions of relational labor (Baym 2015, p. 16), in which the social networking features of platforms afford, indeed demand, that cultural producers, whether creators, artists, or musicians, must engage in "regular, ongoing communication with audiences over time to build social relationships" in order to further their careers. In the case of creators, these online relationships are commodified across a portfolio of business models and practices, as further detailed in this chapter. In the wanghong industry, distinguished by the deeper strength of social affordances on platforms, wanghong are arguably even more subject to the demands of relational labor in order to successfully navigate and monetize their careers through social platform business models, like social tipping and social commerce.

We argue in this chapter that, like creators operating in the SME industry, the careers of wanghong are both acutely precarious but substantially enriching at the same time. In our taxonomy of wanghong labor across cultural, creative, and social, we map the evolution of creator labor. Like the progression of SME creators, this evolution has proven rapid and dynamic, which vast changes in platform and content practices, entrepreneurialism, and community engagement. These differences in this evolution align with rapid uptake of new platform features and affordances in the wanghong industry. As mapped in Chap. 3, these include the affordances of social presence that advance the social media business models, like social tipping and social commerce.

One means of tracing this evolution of creator labor is through the changes of names for social media entrepreneurs. In SME, these names have progressed from content creators to influencers or, as more readily adopted by most platforms as of 2020, just "creators". We witness similar parallels in the evolution of wanghong nomenclature. For example, early cultural producers operating across social media were referred to as KOLs (Key Opinion Leaders), but this term came to be used for native amateur and professionalizing creators emerging off these platforms. Early terms like zhubo referred to livestreaming showroom hosts. As stressed in Chap. 1 and also by Zhao (2021), the term *wanghong* is polysemic. It may refer to social media creators or the entire industry. The term also includes culturally-specific pejorative connotations to describe those female livestreamers who operate as "virtual girlfriends", exploiting the affective needs of lonely Chinese men.

Along with the taxonomy, we identify differentiating conditions of precarious wanghong labor. These conditions are notably advanced by ongoing and iterative state intervention (Chow 2019; Lin 2019). As we have seen, the party-state's dual agenda for restructuring the economy and social/cultural governance expects creative workers to "be creative" for the market and the state. Likewise, for wanghong, all practices of platform labor and entrepreneurialism are deemed cultural and creative, and therefore subject to government surveillance, control, and potential censor (Lin 2019). These top-down, highly contingent, conditions of wanghong control place even more onerous demands on wanghong for self-censorship and self-governance. Through greater reliance upon the affordances of social presence and relational labor, wanghong are vulnerable under conditions of affective labor and online harassment, exacting a psychological and emotional toll on their personal lives. As further described below, as platforms have advanced the affordances of social presence, so too the risks of boundary-less exposure of all aspects of online life, particularly through always-on livestreaming.

On the other hand, wanghong entrepreneurialism has been advanced through platform innovation and, most notably, social platform business models like social tipping and social commerce. The success and viability of these business models have fostered more viable and sustainable economic conditions for wanghong than that of SME creators. While SME operates globally (outside China) and multi-culturally, we find wanghong culture is most distinguished by divisions of class and geography. Cosmopolitan wanghong in top tier cities have often proven even more successful than their SME counterparts, but more significant has been the social uplift and financial opportunity for rural, lower social class, grassroots wanghong to become what Jian Lin and Jeroen de Kloet (2019) call "unlikely creative workers".

Cultural, Creative, and Social: A Taxonomy of Wanghong Labor

After graduating from Chinese Communication University in 2017, one of our interviewees Xian Jing with his three friends started a WeChat public account called "Business Review on Culture and Entertainment" (文娱商业观察), a subscription service that provides business commentaries on Chinese creative industries. By September 2020, this account had gained approximately 200,000 subscriptions and achieving an estimated value of RMB 286,000 on the market.[1] However, Xian Jing does not have any educational or occupational experience in business finance. He studied arts at college. His only related experience came from an internship in a new media company. Compared to the offline working conditions in Chinese creative sectors, content production on social media platforms looks to have lowered the entry threshold for creative workers and has

---

[1] The statistics are provided by NewRank, a leading Chinese data analytic platform targeting wanghong industries and social media platforms. https://services.newrank.cn/trade/#/appraiseIndex.

provided workarounds to alleviate problems such as bureaucracy and inequality of class and gender, all of which are prevalent in Chinese media industries like film, television, music, and publishing (Lin 2019).

Min is a Chinese woman in her forties. After working for 16 years as a writer for a state-run magazine, she resigned in 2017 and started writing for digital platforms. According to her, her account has over 60,000 subscribers and brings RMB 50,000 in revenue per month from advertising that sits alongside her content. The flexible work is both highly profitable and allows her to stay at home and raise her two children. People from rural areas untouched by Chinese economic advance also see an opportunity to become creative entrepreneurs, indicated by the abundant cases of video-makers on Kuaishou, a platform, as we saw in Chap. 3, with a majority of its users from rural China and urban lower social classes. According to the statistics provided by He Yang, who runs an intermediary agency YouMeiYou for selling and buying WeChat Public Account channels, 80 percent of these channels are operated by people born after 1985, 40 percent of them born between 1990 and 1995, with the majority women.

These examples tell a story of wanghong distributed across geography, class, and gender in ways that address inequality of opportunity. Going further in this chapter, we propose a taxonomy of three types of creators based on their sphere of creativity and social background (see Fig. 4.1). There are *cultural* wanghong—the most successful referred to as "Big V" or KOLs; *creative* wanghong—professionalizing amateur creators native to social media platforms generating content built around lifestyles and affinities; and *social* wanghong. The latter have emerged most notably on social streaming and social video platforms and have cultivated followers and revenue less by their content practices than through mediated social interaction.

Cultural wanghong are typically media professionals and experts, for example, authors or actors, who use wanghong platforms to extend their celebrity status or advance their expertise. A number of these creators were previously employed by legacy media organizations in television, news media and film. Before creating *Luogic Talkshow*, Luo Zhenyu, for example, was a well-known television producer at China Central Television (CCTV) (He 2019). The rise of the internet and social media entertainment motivated Luo to resign from CCTV in 2012 and found his own company and content channel on Youku and WeChat. In this show, Luo shares his reading experiences in history, economics, and management with the audience in a practical and comprehensible manner. By 2014,

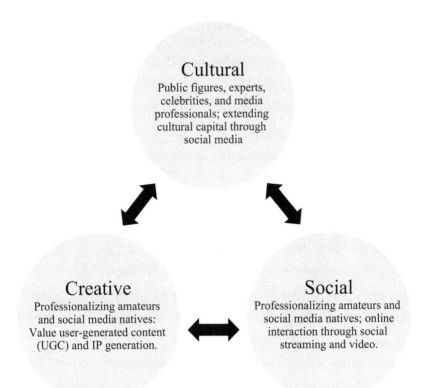

Fig. 4.1 Wanghong labor

Luogic Talkshow had become the most influential online program in China. Facilitated by the fame and popularity he managed to achieve in these two years, Luo started integrating his knowledge business (advertising and subscription fee) with ecommerce and community outreach. In 2015, he launched his own set of apps named Dedao, which translates to "get" but is referred to by Chinese users in English as iGet (得到)—a reference to Apple's use of "i" nomenclature. Dedao is a so-called "knowledge sharing platform", which invites university lecturers, business consultants and writers to offer online courses, podcasts, and e-books. Users need to pay monthly subscription fees for most of the online content including Luo's own *Luogic Talkshow*. Luo himself transformed from a wanghong creator to a wanghong investor and entrepreneur. By May

2020, Dedao has accumulated over 38 million users with an estimated valuation of RMB 30 billion (Yang 2020; iponews 2020).

Cultural wanghong usually already have expertise in their respective fields before going online. And before launching their wanghong enterprises, they had built influence and social networks. The online content they create extends their cultural capital and appears more serious and elitist than that created by native and amateur creators. The cultural creators who have built large followings and launched successful brands are often regarded as Big V[2] (大V), or Key Opinion Leaders (KOLs). Their content production has the look and feel of professionally generated content and has less of a classless entry threshold due to its requirement for higher production values and creator expertise.

Creative wanghong are professionalizing amateurs native to platformized culture. Across diverse verticals of content (see Chap. 5), creative wanghong range from urban-based, university-educated young hipsters through to rural peasants and migrant workers. We see Chinese and international multilingual creators vlogging about their cosmopolitan tastes and lifestyles, but we also see rural fishermen and farmers recording their skills derived from generations of practice. Across a breadth of platforms, from first-generation Weibo and WeChat to next generation Bilibili and Douyin, creative wanghong have built careers creating tutorials about fashion, make-up, or game play, but also their attitudes and values about relationships, marriage, career, and so on.

Compared to the Big V wanghong, creative wanghong are amateurs operating with limited budgets and self-taught media skills (photography, audio-visual editing, and make-up). This amateurish style is categorized as "User-Generated Content" (UGC), although UGC has become associated with both monetized and non-monetized content in the earlier development of this industry. We will later discuss similar developments around the adoption of the terms MCN, an acronym for "multichannel networks" that has since been adopted within the wanghong industry to describe any intermediary firm operating between platforms and creators. As we will see in Chap. 5, their "grassrootedness" lends to creative wanghong an aesthetics of "performative authenticity", which resonates with the everyday life of their followers. Wang Rui, for example, lives in a small village in Anhui, a hinterland province west of Shanghai. His future was rather

---

[2] "V" stands for "verified", referring to those who have their identity and profession verified by the social media platforms.

uncertain, chances were high he would become one of the migrant workers in the bustling eastern seaboard Tier 1 cities, most likely Shanghai. But already at a young age he developed a strong interest in computer games, and with the emergence of platforms like Douyin, he slowly started a career as an online game commentator. Based in his countryside village, he posts short videos and writes commentaries on games, a job that earns him enough money to sustain himself.

A Feng and Lao Si both live in a fishing village in southern China. They started their channels on Bilibili in 2018, producing and posting how-to-catch-fish videos almost every day. By 2020, their seemingly unsophisticated personality and exotic fishing life have garnered millions of subscribers on Bilibili, Xigua, and YouTube and their fishing videos can easily obtain 200,000 views in a few days after uploading to the platforms. The online traffic generates decent financial returns. Since Bilibili has a special reward system that pays RMB 3 (or USD 0.50) per 1000 views, without even doing advertising or ecommerce, A Feng and Lao Si can easily earn RMB 900, roughly USD 140, per video.

Along with the growth of popularity and revenue, however, such amateur production is also gradually professionalized and creative wanghong have the potential to develop sizable brands comparable to, if not surpassing, the size and value of cultural wanghong. Before her career took off, Zhang Dayi was an unknown model working for fashion magazines and occasionally posting selfies on Weibo. After accumulating a small number of followers, she started sharing her fashion tips and some rough-cut videos. In 2014, MCN company Ruhnn approached her and helped establish a professional team in charge of Taobao ecommerce and personal branding around her content. The professionalized operation led to explosive growth of Zhang Dayi's business. With over 12 million followers on Weibo (by September 2020) and a prosperous ecommerce business together with advertising, she is not only the most influential Chinese beauty blogger, but also one of the most successful wanghong entrepreneurs in China.

As mentioned in Chap. 3, Papi Jiang or Miss Papi is one of the most successful, and even prototypical, creative wanghong in the industry. Prior to her wanghong career, she was an unsuccessful actress and aspiring media professional. From 2015, she started posting videos first on Maipai and then on Weibo. Her short-form video content featuring fast-paced rants, which Jian Xu and Xinyu Zhao (2019) refer to as *tucao*, lightly satirized Chinese culture. As her channel and follower numbers expanded, in

2016 she secured nearly USD 2 million in investment from Luogic Show. That same year, she signed with Mountain Top, a talent management firm, and launched her own MCN, PapiTube, which manages a newer generation of creative wanghong.

Whether it is text, images, audio, or video, for most creative and cultural wanghong, content still plays a central role in the success of their careers. In contrast, *social* wanghong are distinctive in their ability to harness the affordances of social presence across wanghong platforms, nurturing mediated relationships through extraordinarily dynamic communicative competence—online interactivity and fan-community building—rather than through content creation. The creativity involved in their production process is less about fashioning a text and more about fostering social relationships. What attracts users to subscribe to their channels is not the acquisition of cultural capital or the enjoyment of particular genres, but the intimacy and reciprocity generated by the production of social presence.

Social wanghong have emerged most notably on livestreaming platforms, which refers to broadcast video streaming services provided by web-based platforms and mobile applications that feature synchronous and cross-modal (video, text, and image) interactivity. Across these platforms, users ("livestreamers" or *zhubo*, which translates as showroom hosts) have generated content genres ("verticals") of onscreen performance that include gameplay, cooking, painting, karaoke, and mukbang, or "social eating" (Recktenwald 2017). Livestreamers convert their onscreen practice and interactivity with their followers into revenue streams, generated through features and affordances both on and off platforms.

Also mentioned in Chap. 2, once the most successful vertical of social wanghong featured attractive female livestreamers, often wearing heavy makeup and sexy outfits, talk, sing, and dance online for their male fans. Offended by the deeply gendered and performative nature of these social creators, the Chinese press has condemned the creators for their "vulgar and sexual content" (Wang 2016) and for "going low" (Yang 2016). As Aynne Kokas remarked, China's livestreaming industry has become "an entire industry of virtual girlfriends" (Kaiman and Meyers 2017).

In press accounts, the term "wanghong" has been used pejoratively for these female livestreamers engaging in deeply-gendered performativity, exploiting and profiting from the desire and needs of lonely men. Beyond these normalized critiques, as previously noted in Chap. 2, the success of these social wanghong are testament to underlying socio-economic policy and material conditions. China's one-child policy—now modified to some extent—has contributed to a vast gender imbalance estimated to be near 70 million more men-to-women by 2020 that has produced millions of "lonely leftover men" (Sun 2017). China's shift from a rural agrarian and manufacturing base to a more consumer-oriented, service-based economy has contributed to mass migration from rural to urban centers (Johnson 2013) and the rise of a "feminized service sector" (Grossman 2012).

The consequence of these conditions has left millions of Chinese men partnerless with little opportunities for family formation and romance. Rural Chinese men rely on smart phones for basic communication but these also provide entertainment and interactivity previously limited, inaccessible, or unaffordable. Their phones provide access to hundreds of applications, which now include any number of livestreaming applications and, in turn, helped cultivate their "virtual girlfriends". As Beijing Normal University scholar and livestreamer, Hongzhong Zhang, claimed

> Chinese people are lonely due to the fast pace of urbanization. A large number of people are going into big cities where they feel lonely. 30 million lonely souls are floating above the sky of Beijing. Alternatively, these conditions apply in the countryside because rural Chinese have fewer entertainment options. (Zhang 2017)

As for these female livestreamers, normative social critiques can simultaneously occupy diverse positions. Female streamers have been empowered by the underlying socio-cultural, material, and technological conditions of the industry. For some, particularly those less educated and from more traditional cultures, lower classes, and remote areas, female zhubo may be afforded greater entrepreneurial agency and the means for social mobility. To be eligible, they need a good-looking face and body, some basic creative skills such as singing and dancing and most importantly special communicative skills (for example, seductive posture and talking) that can cultivate intimacy with their audience. As social wanghong, these female livestreamers thus distinguish from cultural and creative wanghong creators in the sense that the communicative skills and the cultivated social relationship transcend content (singing or dancing) to become the primary goal and talent of livestreaming wanghong. This highly-gendered industry has a lower entry threshold for its relatively small production cost, yet the industrial inclusiveness also induces fierce platform competition and, as we will show in the next section, cause formidable precarity facing these social wanghong performers, especially given a significant number of these livestreamers are signed and controlled by MCNs and guilds. Alternatively, as social wanghong has become even more central to the rise of the digital economy, these wanghong garner greater cultural respect for their entrepreneurialism. As Chinese news headlines remark, "after years of derision, China's Internet celebrities finally win mainstream success" (Wang 2019).

This distinction between creative, cultural, and social wanghong, however, is by no means comprehensive or always clear-cut (see Fig. 4.1). All wanghong, even the Big V, engage in visible (Abidin 2016), affective (Duffy 2017), and relational (Baym 2018) labor, exploiting the affordances of social presence on platforms to aggregate and engage their community for value. Likewise, creative wanghong, like Papi Jiang and Zhang Dayi can transform into cultural wanghong (the Big V), extending their careers offline, whether in legacy media or launching lifestyle brands. Finally, many social wanghong creators share a similar background with creative wanghong in terms of their class, education, and previous profession. As they evolve their wanghong careers, they expand their repertoire of creativity, innovation, and entrepreneurialism.

Our taxonomy is meant to help make sense of the extraordinary variety of wanghong practice. In effect, we better view these three categories as *tendencies* embodied in the process of wanghong labor and production as determined by platformativity. Coined by Thomas Lamarre (2017), platformativity refers to how the progression of affordances of platforms for creators advance new forms of creativity, innovation, and business models. In their historical account of wanghong, Ge Zhang and Gabriele de Seta (2018) detailed "how shifting intra-actions between infrastructures, platforms, and modes of performativity have shaped the construction of internet celebrity in China" (p. 61). Xu and Zhao (2019) also described how the professionalization of female wanghong has evolved these labor practices "from a stigmatized non-mainstream (feizhuliu) culture online to a new type of digital economy and a trendy profession" (pp. 149–50). Aligned with these accounts, in our taxonomy of wanghong, we understand these categorical distinctions as dynamic, constantly shifting in the wake of repeated disruptions and expansions throughout this industry.

WANGHONG CONDITIONS

While offering work opportunities and identity enhancement, the wanghong economy is also permeated with uncertainty and precarity. Increasingly stringent internet censorship in China and the rapidly evolving social media industry demand a continuous self-governance that incorporates self-censorship, continuous learning, and emotional management.

As we saw in Chap. 2, while Chinese policy makers have regarded the wanghong economy as an integral part of national economic advance, the state also keeps a vigilant eye on the content and culture it produces. To investigate and stop practices that may "harm social morality" (Horwitz 2017) and threaten political "harmony", Chinese authorities since 2016 have accelerated its regulation and censorship of productions on various social media platforms. In mid-2016, the State Administration of Press, Publication, Radio, Film and Television (SARFFT) banned female livestreamers from "erotic banana-eating" (Phillips 2016). In one instance, a livestreamer was detained for five days after she was presumed to have streamed from the Empress Dowager's bedroom in the Imperial Palace. However, it proved to be a set in a studio.

Platforms increasingly are as subject to direct censorship as wanghong and the effects on company practice are now manifest, often as much where moral surveillance is accomplished through machine learning. All the platforms we interviewed have divisions dedicated to supervision and censorship. Once content creators are discovered to have erotic or sexually explicit behaviors, their account is shut down. Platforms have developed diverse strategies that combine human and automated curation. According to He Jinkai, a marketing manager at Yi Live, of the 2000 employees at their firm, half of them (1000) are involved in online supervision (He 2017). Kuaishou also established a team of over 5000 employees responsible for manual censorship (Yu and Wenting 2018).

For individual creators, this stringent censorship regime forces them to meticulously self-censor themselves, balancing the demands of the state, platforms, brands, and fans. Sisdon is a queer beauty/fashion blogger based in Dongguan, Guangdong. After his cross-dressing video went viral on Iqiyi in 2015, he opened Weibo and WeChat accounts featuring crossdressing images and beauty and fashion tips. As he described in our interview (Sisdon 2018), he is a "small, local wanghong" whose fans are mostly local in Southern China. Even so, he has managed to develop multiple revenue sources including influencer marketing with beauty and fashion brands, social commerce, and social tipping through live streaming. His queer content has encountered ongoing problems:

> Weibo suspended my account last year. You cannot be too obvious as an LGBTQ. They didn't gave me a reason but I guess I cannot be so obvious anymore…I cannot post things that I want to pose anymore…if I become bigger, I might be considered dangerous…Now I'm afraid to be suspended again…I actually have a really famous video on TikTok (Douyin) of me dancing. But it got deleted again. (Sisdon 2018)

As Sisdon's comments suggest, the more successful the wanghong, the more potentially vulnerable their career, particularly those who may be perceived as violating cultural norms, if not explicit state policy. Tianyou was the most successful zhubo in 2017 (Sohu 2019). His livestreaming shows on Kuaishou attracted over 35 million followers and earned him more than USD 2 million a year from social tipping and influencer marketing. He even released his own songs and aired programs on Chinese state-owned television. However, in early 2018, Tian You was accused by the state-run China Central Television (CCTV) of talking about pornography and drugs while livestreaming. Shortly after, Tian You was banned across all Chinese platforms and in established media and his career appears over (eastmoney 2020).

Aside from career uncertainty resulting in censorship, the affective labor of wanghong creators exhaustively blurs the boundaries between life and work, personal and public. Like those for SME creators, these conditions place extraordinary demands on wanghong management of self-representation and fan engagement. As Elaine Zhao (2021, n.p.) avers, "wanghong operate in a liminal space where the line between public personae and private selves is shaky". High interactivity and connectivity online expose creators to both praise, celebration and "public shaming, humiliation and harassment".

These conditions were confirmed in our interview with Anna (2019). She was initially hired as an employee for Bigo, a livestreaming platform. Then the firm asked her to become a livestreamer on the platform. The blurring of her professional and personal life contributed to an untenably toxic environment marked by cyberbullying and sexual harassment that forced her to leave her job and abandon her livestreaming career:

I have one follower who knew my Instagram. He started stalking me and my friends. He started to ask why I'm not streaming and why I stopped replying to his messages. He started to send me messages like, "I know what you did, I know who you were, you are not allowed to be with other men, I've been supporting you, you cannot go out with other man". Then he started texting my boyfriend, "who are you, why are you always with her, you're not allowed to be with her because she is mine". He started sending me things anonymously, like flowers, and when I refused to accept them, he got really angry. I tried to report it to the company even though I was no longer there. They responded with "don't worry about it, you're just popular, they'll go away, there's nothing much we can do anyway, just ignore it." I tried to ignore it. I ended up with blocking him on all my social media, and I told him to stop bothering me. Now I am no longer livestreaming.

The affective demands of relational labor while navigating the commercial dynamics of social presence prove challenging, even exhausting, contributing to feelings of loneliness and social insecurity. In our interview with Bobby Kiki (2017), the pseudonym for a livestreamer operating on multiple platforms including Huoshan (Volcano), she remarked:

Livestreaming is a job but it is different from nine-to-five jobs. We sit for 6 hours and talk and dance. We have to imagine what our top followers like. We need to know their favorite songs, the colors they hate, and the clothes they like. We need to be aware every time they enter the room. If we treat them seriously, they will send me the gifts. Gradually, we will develop more of a connection…Sometimes, when fans have conflicts with me and when I am alone, I feel lonely. Streamers actually do not have many people to keep them company…We do not have a private life. We post pictures to fans everyday with posts like: "I am eating breakfast at 8:00, going to the gym at 9:00, doing my nails at 10:00, taking a nap at noon… but nobody realized that I am doing these things all alone. This is hard for me. We have fans who want to take care of us, but we rarely have time to meet friends in real life and offline. Gradually, I feel I am not living in reality. (Kiki 2017)

Despite these challenges and the potential emotional and psychological toll, these creators are still motivated by the promise of a "better self"—a successful career, including financial success, social mobility, and personal transformation. We have seen how this calculation requires balancing the often onerous and often contradictory demands of followers, advertisers, platforms, and the state. Having said that, the financial and career upside for wanghong—as we discuss now—can be much more than the disappointing letdown that critical scholars have often argued. Lucrative business models like social tipping and social commerce, coupled with the stabilizing effects of wanghong MCNs, contribute as a general rule to greater financial reward and sustainability than experienced by wanghong's SME counterparts.

Wanghong Monetization

SME creator entrepreneurialism and monetization involves developing a portfolio of revenue streams to mitigate risk and increase sustainability. Varying by platform, content verticals, and the nature and size of their fan communities, creators can secure revenue through advertising, subscription revenue, and, in the case of livestreaming, virtual goods. Across platforms, successful creators have entered into high-touch brand deals for influencer marketing and launched subscription and crowd-funding pages on platforms like Patreon and Kickstarter. Only a small percentage of creators have secured fees through deals with mainstream media in film and television, although some have secured book publishing and music recording deals. Pre-COVID, creators may also have commanded lucrative performance fees, whether through touring or live appearances at venues like clubs, malls, or cafes, or appearances at fashion shows, whether on the red carpet or modelling down. Some SME creators are able to secure licensing and merchandising fees for their self-branded consumer products.

Despite this array of options, commercial affordances for SME creators lag behind that of their wanghong counterparts. We go into these differences now, but one which stands out as fundamental is the difference between wanghong's accepted place in China's digital economy as delivering on goals of Internet+ and mass innovation and the more contingent place of SME creators as nominal stakeholders within their industry. Many United States platforms have lagged in empowering creators, as witnessed in the collapse of the short-video Vine platform. In 2018, YouTube began demonetizing creators in the disastrous "Adpocalypse" (see Cunningham and Craig 2019, pp. 111–13). Despite creators being the engine of Instagram's explosive growth of the platform, that platform's creator studio, designed to assist creators with growing their channels and generating more revenue, only launched in 2020.

The one consistent exception in the West is, ironically, Bytedance-owned TikTok which, like its Chinese-counterpart, Douyin, considers creators as vital stakeholders in its growth. The platform allows creators to secure revenue from virtual goods and provides an influencer marketing service coined the "creator marketplace". Unlike Douyin, the platform also established a multi-billion-dollar fund to support creators in the United States and Europe (Weiss 2020), which is strong evidence that Bytedance understands the dramatic difference in sustainability that SME creators face relative to their wanghong counterparts.

Influencer marketing remains a core business model for most cultural and creative wanghong. The Big Vs entered directly into deals with brands, while smaller wanghong connect with advertisers through third-party MCN agencies. Like YouTube, some wanghong platforms such as Bilibili, Toutiao and Xigua offer creator partnership programs and advertising marketplaces, in which creators are compensated by receiving a share of advertising revenue based on their online traffic. Overviewing these fundamental components of the wanghong industry, Lin and de Kloet (2019) observe that "the long-term financial success of digital platforms is thus not simply based on the exploitation of platform labor, but is contingent upon commercial collaboration between platform companies, content producers and other complementors" (p. 6).

Hyperplatformization, portalization, and interplatformization, discussed in Chap. 3, each create revenue opportunities for wanghong. In turn, these inform the viability and sustainability of wanghong careers. Interplatformization, for example, affords the means for wanghong to engage in near frictionless cross-platform use of multiple platform features and services. Through enhanced social presence, wanghong can generate forms of revenue little developed in the West through business models like social tipping and social commerce, as illustrated in the following.

Whether called virtual or social gifting, live or social tipping, or *da shang*, this business model has become a significant income source for both livestreamers and livestreaming platforms. Xiaoxing Zhang, Yu Xiang, and Lei Hao (2019) are clear in their analysis that the infrastructure of livestreaming platforms "is purposely designed to maximize content monetization through virtual gifting" (p. 13). Most of these platforms have their own virtual currency (for example, Kuaibi on Kuaishou, Huyabi on Huya), through which users exchange their real money and buy and send virtual gifts to livestreamers. Whereas livestreaming in the SME industry remains mostly limited to social live gaming, wanghong livestreamers secure tips though a far more diverse array of live socializing practices, including singing, dancing, hosting talk shows, fishing, and mukbang. Originating in Korean, mukbang refers to a kind of fetishized performance in which strangers watch creators eat massive amounts of food on recorded video platforms like YouTube. This content has since migrated to livestreaming platforms like Twitch and spread across Asia, if not, worldwide. In China, this phenomenon aligned with the larger progression of the affordances of social presence and has grown with so much popularity that it has experienced a backlash in the press. In the wake of the COVID-19 crisis, ongoing trade wars with the United States, and rising fears of food insecurity, in their "Clean Plate campaign", the government has condemned this practice as amoral and "food waste", shaming these creators to explore alternative content (Tidy 2020). This pattern of creators engaging in popular content practices that push the boundaries of taste, both literally and figuratively, and socio-cultural norms of Chinese society reflects strategies of "edge ball", as discussed below.

Social tipping has proven lucrative for both platforms and wanghong. As Chap. 3 notes, first generation live streaming platforms like Momo and Inke not only rely on social tipping, but have gamified the process through "PK, or Player Knock-out Battles". Similarly, game-focused platforms Huya and Douyu secure between 86 to 95 percent of their revenue through their share of social tips paid to live gamers (Liao 2019). Platform dependency on the social tips generated by live gamers has led to a race to secure exclusive access to these gamers, in exchange for both salaries and higher cuts from social tipping, particularly those who belong to esports teams and compete in tournaments. Outside of live gaming, other platforms and verticals allow for social tipping and streamers operate across as many platforms and rooms as they can navigate to secure the largest number of followers and gifts. For example, Wang Qian, a Kuaishou creator we interviewed in 2018, performs magic tricks in his livestreaming shows and has over 1 million followers. He claimed in our interview with him that his average monthly income can reach USD 9000—mostly derived from social tips from his followers.

Social commerce also generates high returns for wanghong and platforms. Using social commerce—the near frictionless integration of e-commerce links coupled with online mobile payment services across their social media platforms and channels—wanghong can directly sell products to their fan communities and audience. In earlier developments, wanghong platforms created user interfaces and the ability to post links that would drive traffic over to ecommerce platforms. Since 2018, next generation platforms like Kuaishou, Douyin, and Xigua have launched e-commerce services, called mini shops. These shops remain cross-platformed and inter-operable with and in collaboration with those platforms run by rival tech firms, whether Taobao, JD, or Pinduoduo—a strategy we describe as interplatformization.

In addition to ongoing collaboration between tech companies and platforms, the uptake of social commerce in China has contributed to platform co-dependency between e-commerce platforms and wanghong creators. As scholar Anett Dippner (2018) notes, these are "intrinsically inseparable...many wanghongs either started their careers as Taobao models and expanded their online shops successively on social media platforms by advertising their products as their own-tested best choice (and thus blurring the line between authentic self-representation and business) or they gained their fan reputation with beauty product recommendations and styling tutorials over years. This makes wanghong the perfect advertising medium for the fashion and cosmetics industry" (p. 11).

Even Dippner underestimated the breadth and scale of this phenomenon, as wanghong e-commerce now extends well beyond the lifestyles industry, driving sales and services throughout the digital economy. Whether "made in" or "created by" China, everything can and is likely already being sold by wanghong through social commerce practices. Consider superwanghong Viya who, in addition to selling beauty and lifestyle products, has used her social commerce platforms to sell houses and even rocket systems (Jain 2019). Viya's main platform is Alibaba-owned Taobao, as previously described, an ecommerce platform prominently featured in the interplatformization strategies within the wanghong platform landscape and these social commerce business models.

We have seen in this section that, as wanghong platforms introduce new socio-technological and commercial features, wanghong have continued to flourish, if remain precariously interdependent upon the platforms for their careers. Whether creative, cultural, or social, these wanghong must perpetually engage in dynamic and iterative changes in creator management, multiplatform maintenance, content production, and entrepreneurialism. Within this new media ecology, a growing wave of intermediary firms called MCNs and media professionals have emerged to assist in these developments, as discussed in the next section.

Wanghong Management and Chinese MCNs

Wanghong management is increasingly the domain of MCNs, a term that generally covers any intermediary firm operating between platforms and creators, established media and advertisers. These firms offer a suite of content production and management services that advances the interests of platforms and professionalizes wanghong entrepreneurialism. As outlined in this part of the chapter, this intermediary layer of the wanghong industry has emerged at a scale and with viability significantly greater than their SME counterparts. Nonetheless, MCNs are still subject to precariously disruptive conditions.

In the SME industry, "the MCN is synonymous with failure", admits the blog lead by one of China's leading MCNs, Parklu (Rapp 2019). Most of these firms first emerged in the late 2000s, fostered by YouTube's creator-focused advertising partnerships and the redesign of the platform's user interface to allow creators to operate multiple channels. Companies like Fullscreen, Maker Studios, Machinima, Awesomeness TV, and The Style Network entered into management service agreements with tens, even hundreds, of thousands of creators. Most firms offered services that claimed to help creators monetize their channels on and across multiple platforms, grow their fan or subscriber base, create more professional content that will be distributed through more channels including legacy media, secure influencer deals with advertisers, and provide the tools and strategies that fostered sustainable career development.

Most of these promises proved as hollow as their services proved redundant. Platforms elbowed them out of the way with automated and low-touch management services, like YouTube's Creator Academy. In her account of the "deconstruction of MCNs", Digiday journalist Kerry Flynn (2019, n.p.) describes how, "as YouTube matures, middlemen lose ground". Inflicting further damage, traditional Hollywood talent agencies and management began to siphon off the top-tier creator talent from MCNs, leveraging their larger portfolio of services to broker deals for creators throughout the arts and legacy media industries. Within a few years, most MCNs had either collapsed or pivoted to offer a new array of services and value propositions, leaving creators in their wake. Some MCNs secured investment from or were bought outright by media conglomerates; for example, the lucrative deal between Maker Studios and Disney. As soon as the deals were signed, the owners of the firms cashed out, fully aware of the ephemeral value their firms represented. As experts like Kendra Chamberlain (2017) opined, the Maker Studios deal signaled "the final chapter of the MCN era".

On the other hand, in the wanghong industry, MCNs have flourished over the past decade. Depending on the source, there were between 2000–3000 MCNs in 2018 (Han 2020), and as many as 28,000 MCNs in

2020 together valued at over USD 3.4 billion (Jiang 2020). Unlike their counterparts in SME that scaled while over-promising services, Chinese MCNs may typically manage only a handful of wanghong clients and deliver a more high-tough experience. These firms do not need scale to succeed as these creators have more lucrative business models afforded to them than their Western counterpart, especially social tipping and social commerce. Most operate in close cooperation with platforms, delivering high-touch management services critical to the growth of both platforms and creators, brands and advertisers. In their 2016 Annual report for the United States Security Exchange Commission, the Chinese platform Weibo openly declared:

> The role of multi-channel networks, MCNs, as talent agencies for content creators, are becoming increasingly important. We have built a large network of MCNs in different domains, such as e-commerce and video, and rely on these platform partners to incubate and grow content creators and help them share more and better content on Weibo. If we are unable to expand our network of MCNs and content creators and entice them to share more content, our content offerings may not be as robust and competitive and our user base and user engagement may be adversely and materially affected. (Weibo 2016, p. 11)

Chinese MCNs provide an array of services to platforms and wanghong, as well as, more broadly, across multiple markets and industries in China's diversifying digital economy. The firm Ruhan (or Ruhnn) is a prime example. As Dippner (2018) notes, "companies such as TopHot and Ruhan call themselves 'hotbeds' that make future Internet stars fit for fame, but they also hire established top talents and assume responsibility for content creation, marketing and all kind of business aspects such as market development, negotiations with business partners and business management" (p. 18). MCNs are referred to as "wanghong incubators" in Xiaofei Han's (2020) account of how MCNs like Ruhan have expanded their service beyond beauty and lifestyle management to place themselves closer to the center of the larger value chains of ecommerce and retail in the wanghong economy: "Wanghong incubators have, therefore, become a critical intermediary which progressively fills—and institutionalizes—the space between different types of dominant platforms such as Weibo and Taobao. … such value chains have clung into, and now are becoming increasingly central to, the business strategies of both Weibo and Alibaba" (p. 7).

Chinese MCNs are as subject to conditions of precarious management as those for platforms and wanghong themselves. Ruhan serves again as an exemplar. Launched in 2001 as an e-commerce firm called Leilin, Ruhan became a top fashion brand in partnership with the Alibaba-owned ecommerce platform Taobao and Tmall. In 2014, the firm partnered with Zhang Dayi, who was, at that time, a relatively unknown beauty and lifestyle wanghong. Within two years, Dayi could sell clothing worth USD 3 million in two hours on Taobao and was making more money than Fan Bingbing, China's largest movie star (Xu and Zhao 2019). Even though Dayi remains the top wanghong, Ruhan continued to sign and launch the careers of multiple wanghong and, in 2016, launched an IPO on the Nasdaq valued at USD 125 million (Liao 2019). However, in 2020, Dayi and Ruhan suffered a remarkable fall of grace, when Dayi was accused of having an affair with Jiang Fan, the President of Tmall, by Jiang's wife. Referred to as a "melon" in the press, the scandal cost Jiang's job and Ruhan has reportedly lost USD 1 billion in value and may be delisted from the Nasdaq (DayDayNews 2020). These accusations of infidelity, coupled with unfair business dealing, have also compromised Dayi's fan loyalty leading to Dayi's descent "from being highly sought after to being forgotten" (jqknews.com 2020). This story reminds us how the wanghong industry places great value on the performance of authenticity which, in the instance of MCN management, includes transparent business practices. The performance of authenticity—which we know from Sarah Banet-Weiser's (2012) important account of brand culture—represents both commercial and cultural capital in creator-driven industries. We take this analysis further in Chap. 5.

One type of MCN in the wanghong industry that differs radically from those in the SME industry are MCNs managing livestreaming wanghong, or zhubo. These MCNs are referred as "gonghui" (guild 公会), a word that is a synonym for union (工会gonghui) in Chinese. As Zhicong Lu (2020) described, guilds have been vital to offering support, promoting, and managing zhubo. The rapid growth of these MCNs were a consequence of livestreaming features and platforms introduced throughout the industry that fostered lucrative social platform business models for social wanghong. In contrast to MCNs in the West, Chinese gonghui have succeeded in securing extensive employment contracts with their creators, securing exclusivity if also creating the conditions for exploitation, including exhaustive demands for streaming around the clock and more heightened forms of affective performance bordering on censorable fare.

While social wanghong featured skills for engaging their online communities through live interaction, these MCNs proved vital to their business development and career management. In the earlier period of development, these guilds developed a reputation for exploiting streamers, often engaging in less transparent, even borderline criminal, business practices. As depicted in the documentary, *People's Republic of Desire* (Wu 2018), guilds would often demand exclusivity from streamers while commanding a large percentage of their revenue secured primarily through social tipping. The streamers are forced to compete in winner-take-all PK battles with other streamers, funded by unknown benefactors who may either be the guild owners or the platforms. Driven by the demands placed by these guilds, zhubo sometimes engaged in outlandish sexual behavior bordering on pornographic to their highest bidders, or tuhao, to pay more. In some instances, this behavior can lead to prostitution. In a press interview, a livestreamer admitted "there are hidden rules in this world. Tuhao will ask to meet in person, or something else" (Yang 2018).

As the industry has become more formalized, and these social wanghong, platforms, and guilds have become more critical to the growth of China's digital economy, the state has introduced more oversight. As discussed in our governance chapter but briefly described here, these regulations sought not only to contain bad and exploitative practices, but exert social control. In 2017, SARFFT, an earlier iteration of China's complex policy bureaus responsible with oversight of their internet, introduced regulations for livestreaming platforms, creators, and firms that "harm national security, damage social stability, disturb societal order, violate the rights of others or broadcast obscene or erotic activities" (Kaiman and Meyers 2017). Shortly after, nearly 400 livestreaming platforms and guilds were either closed or fined for sponsoring "violence, pornography, gambling, superstition, and other values harmful to public morality" (Yang 2018, p. 1).

This pattern of formalization from illicit behavior followed by government control is also not unusual throughout the growth of Chinese cultural industries. As Michael Keane (1998) identified, borderline acceptable behavior, or "edge ball", has long been a feature of Chinese cultural practices for decades. With regards to livestreaming, Cunningham, Craig, and Junyi Lv (2019) observed that "these violations of Chinese norms that make livestreamers subject to an ever-increasing level of state regulatory restraint, signal the return of ideology designed to mold online expression and behavior" (p. 719). As alternatively reported in popular media, "for

China's livestreaming craze, the party is over it seems—now that the Communist Party has arrived" (Horwitz 2017).

The supervening conditions of hyperplatformization, limned in Chap. 3, see MCNs forced to regularly pivot to new business strategies reactively, rather than through strategic innovation. In our interview with the co-founder of Star-Station TV, a leading MCN agency in China, co-owner Heng Cai (2019) describes practices of risk management that border on desperation. "We keep experimenting…. We call this 'horse riding'—the channel that rides the fastest garners our support. As a management company, we cannot be an artist. We must be product managers".

Earlier in this chapter, we classified wanghong as cultural, creative, and social, and pointed to evidence of movement between these types of wanghong practice. MCNs may be similarly understood. The CEO of Xinpianchang, or New Studios Media, gave us a sense of the dramatic shifts in that company's identity in a series of interviews. First launched in 2012, Xinpianchang was a first-generation MCN that started by financing and producing short films at the height of their appeal in China. But, "as many distribution platforms, like iQiyi, Youku, Tudou, 56 emerged at that time, and it is very hard for an individual to put their content on those platforms, we become a bridge between the content creators and the platforms" (Yin 2016). Their focus then shifted from streaming video portals toward social media platforms—"social media is our battlefield—we gather fans on social media first, then use the fan base to do other things". As for managing wanghong, they described how a process of identifying KOLs (key opinion leaders) on Weibo, but then converting them into "PGC", a term he used to describe professional web series producers.

By 2019, Xipianchang's value propositions had expanded. While still financing, producing, and distributing web series, the firm launched a web portal for production talent operating across legacy and social media industries, while it was also signing and managing wanghong talent. "In the wanghong area, personality matters … most of our clients sell products on Tmall. So, we select personalities like make-up, beauty, lifestyle." In 2020, Yin told us, "the MCNs have changed a lot here again, not because of the crisis [COVID] but because of the rise of new platforms like TikTok (Douyin) and Bilibli. They have become the leader and renew the roles". Xinpianchang is now dedicated to managing social wanghong across these platforms, while also running their own Douyin channels hosted by Xinpianchang employees.

As the wanghong economy grows, so stakeholder scrutiny heightens. In 2019, another MCN, Hive Media, was accused of inflating data and revenue when a high-profile ad campaign for a client went bust. The firm was kicked off the Weibo platform and charged with crimes by the Prosecutor's General Office, which is the highest criminal court of the land (Jiang 2020). Prosecutions like these throw further light on "China's perennial struggle with data faking" (Lee 2019)—although fake data remains a concern across the global social media landscape.

* * *

For Chinese MCNs, dealing with precarity and risk while calibrating entrepreneurial opportunity is a condition of survival. The labor conditions for wanghong are distributed unevenly by their background, their cultural and social capital, type of content and part of the country they work in. Governance, whether by the state and platforms or through self-censorship, is borne by wanghong because of the lucrative opportunities afforded them. As the next chapter will show, contingencies of this kind in this industry have also produced a kaleidoscope of commercialized brand culture, where authenticity intermingles with performativity, self-censorship conflates with parody, and the state's oversight is sustained and tested simultaneously.

REFERENCES

Abidin, C. (2016). Visibility Labour: Engaging with Influencers' Fashion Brands and #OOTD Advertorial Campaigns on Instagram. *Media International Australia*, *161*(1), 86–100.

Banet-Weiser, S. (2012). *Authentic™: The Politics of Ambivalence in a Brand Culture* (Vol. 30). NYU Press.

Banks, J. (2007). Opening the Production Pipeline: Unruly Creators. In J. Jenson & S. de Castell (Eds.), *Worlds in Play: International Perspectives on Digital Games Research* (pp. 143–150). New York: Peter Lang.

Baym, N. (2015). Connect with Your Audience! The Relational Labor of Connection. *The Communication Review*, *18*(1), 14–22.

Baym, N. (2018). *Playing to the Crowd: Musicians, Audiences, and the Intimate Work of Connection*. New York: New York University Press.

Cai, H. (2019). Partner, COO, Star Station TV. 17 May, with David Craig, Beijing, China.

Chamberlain, K. (2017, May 11). Maker Studios Hints at End to the MCN Era. *ReThink*. Retrieved September 17, 2020, from https://rethinkresearch.biz/articles/maker-studios-hints-end-mcn-era/.

Chow, Y. (2019). *Caring in Times of Precarity: A Study of Single Women Doing Creative Work in Shanghai*. Cham: Palgrave Macmillan.

Cunningham, S., & Craig, D. (2019). *Social Media Entertainment: The New Intersection of Hollywood and Silicon Valley*. New York: New York University Press.

Cunningham, S., Craig, D., & Lv, J. (2019). China's Livestreaming Industry: Platforms, Politics, and Precarity. *International Journal of Cultural Studies*, 22(6), 719–736.

Curtin, M., & Sanson, K. (Eds.). (2016). *Precarious Creativity. Global Media, Local Labor*. Oakland, CA: University of California Press.

DayDayNews. (2020, April 20). Zhang Dayi Responded for the First Time: I Have Never Seen the President Alone, I Have a Boyfriend. *DayDayNews*. Retrieved September 18, 2020, from https://daydaynews.cc/en/technology/516426.html.

Deuze, M. (2009). Media Industries, Work and Life. *European Journal of Communication*, 24(4), 467–480.

Dippner, A. (2018). Social Media Celebrities and Neoliberal Body Politics in China. *KFG Working Paper Series, 2018*. Retrieved September 17, 2020, from https://www.polsoz.fu-berlin.de/en/v/transformeurope/publications/working_paper/wp/wp91/WP_91_Dippner_WEB_und_Druck.pdf.

Duffy, B. (2016). The Romance of Work: Gender and Aspirational Labour in the Digital Culture Industries. *International Journal of Cultural Studies*, 19(4), 441–457.

Duffy, B. (2017). *(Not) Getting Paid to Do What You Love: Gender, Social Media, and Aspirational Work*. New Haven, CT: Yale University Press.

Eastmoney. (2020, August 10). Zhubo Blacklist Since 2018 [48名主播被列入黑名单]. *Eastmoney*. Retrieved September 17, 2020, from http://finance.eastmoney.com/a/202008101587708730.html.

Flynn, K. (2019, April 8). The Deconstruction of the MCN: As YouTube Matures, Middlemen Lose Ground. *Digiday*. Retrieved September 17, 2020, from https://digiday.com/marketing/deconstruction-mcn-youtube-matures-middlemen-lose-ground/.

Fuchs, C. (2010). Labor in Informational Capitalism and on the Internet. *The Information Society*, 26(3), 179–196.

Gill, R. (2007). *Gender and the Media*. Cambridge: Polity.

Gregg, M. (2013). *Work's Intimacy*. Cambridge: Polity Press.

Grossman, B. (2012). The Feminised Service Sector: From Micro to Macro Analysis. *Work Organisation, Labour and Globalisation*, 6(1), 63–79.

Han, X. (2020). Historicising Wanghong Economy: Connecting Platforms Through Wanghong and Wanghong Incubators. *Celebrity Studies.* https://doi.org/10.1080/19392397.2020.1737196.

He, J. (2017). Director of Commercial Department, Yi Live, 9 June, with Junyi Lv, China.

He, J. (2019, May 13). The Underestimated Luo Zhenyu. *36Kr.* Retrieved September 17, 2020, from https://www.36kr.com/p/1724561801217.

Helmond, A. (2015). The Platformization of the Web: Making Web Data Platform Ready. *Social Media + Society*, 1–11.

Hesmondhalgh, D., & Baker, S. (2011). Toward a Political Economy of Labor in the Media Industries. In J. Wasko, G. Murdock, & H. Sousa (Eds.), *The Handbook of Political Economy of Communications* (pp. 381–400). Oxford: Blackwell.

Horwitz, J. (2017, February 11). China's Crackdown on the Country's Livestreaming Craze Is Getting More Intense. *Quartz.* Retrieved August 24, 2020, from https://qz.com/1013018/chinas-crackdown-on-the-countrys-livestreaming-craze-is-getting-more-intense/.

Iponews. (2020, August 17). Estimated Valuation of 30 Billion! Dedao to Be Listed [保守估值300亿]. *Sina Finance.* Retrieved September 17, 2020, from https://finance.sina.com.cn/stock/kechuangban/qydt/2020-08-17/doc-iivhvpwy1413268.shtml.

Jain, M. (2019, November 8). Kim Kardashian West Joins China's Livestreaming Ecommerce Craze Ahead of Singles' Day. *Radii.* Retrieved September 17, 2020, from https://radiichina.com/kim-kardashian-west-livestream/.

Jiang, Y. (2020, June 2). How COVID-19 Reshaped This Part of China's Influencer Economy. *Jing Daily.* Retrieved September 17, 2020, from https://jingdaily.com/how-covid-19-reshaped-this-part-of-chinas-influencer-economy/.

Johnson, D. (2013). Polyphonic/Pseudo-Synchronic: Animated Writing in the Comment Feed of Nicovideo. *Japanese Studies, 33*(3), 297–313.

jqknews.com (2020 18 Apr) From being highly sought after to being forgotten, Zhang Dayi, the first generation of Internet celebrities who fell into scandal, became popular again. *Jqknews.com.* Retrieved from https://www.jqknews.com/news/441532-From_being_highly_sought_after_to_being_forgotten_Zhang_Dayi_the_first_generation_of_Internet_celebrities_who_fell_into_scandal_became_popular_again.html

Kaiman, J., & Meyers, J. (2017, June 24). Chinese Authorities Put the Brakes on a Surge in Live Streaming. *Los Angeles Times.* Retrieved July 15, 2020, from https://www.latimes.com/world/asia/la-fg-china-live-streaming-crackdown-20170624-story.html.

Keane, M. (1998). Television and Moral Development in China. *Asian Studies Review, 22*(4), 475–503.

Kiki, B. (2017). Livestreamer, YouKu-Laifeng and Houshan, 13 June with Junyi Lv, China.
Lamarre, T. (2017). Platformativity: Media Studies, Area Studies. *Asiascape: Digital Asia*, 4(3), 285–305.
Lee, E. (2019, October 22). Fake Data Scandal Rocks Chinese Ads Giant. *Technode*. Retrieved September 17, 2020, from https://technode.com/2019/10/22/fake-data-scandal-rocks-chinese-ads-giant/.
Liao, R. (2019, April 22). Douyu, China's Twitc Backed by Tencent, Fiels for a $500M U.S. IPO. *Techcrunch*. Retrieved September 17, 2020, from https://techcrunch.com/2019/04/22/douyu-us-ipo/.
Lin, J. (2019). *Schizoid Creators: Creative Work and Subjectivity in the Chinese Cultural Economies* (Doctoral dissertation, Universiteit van Amsterdam).
Lin, J., & de Kloet, J. (2019). Platformization of the Unlikely Creative Class: Kuaishou and Chinese Digital Cultural Production. *Social Media + Society*, 5(4). https://doi.org/10.1177/2056305119883430.
Lu, Z (2020). Live streaming in China for sharing knowledge and promoting intangible cultural heritage. *Interactions*. XXVII: Jan-Feb 2020; 58
McRobbie, A. (2016). *Be Creative: Making a Living in the New Culture Industries*. Malden, MA: Polity Press.
Nieborg, D., & Poell, T. (2018). The Platformization of Cultural Production: Theorizing the Contingent Cultural Commodity. *New Media & Society, 20*(11), 4275–4292.
Phillips, T. (2016, May 9). Gone Bananas: China Bans 'Erotic' Eating of the Fruit on Live Streams. *The Guardian*. Retrieved August 19, 2020, from https://www.theguardian.com/world/2016/may/09/gone-bananas-china-bans-erotic-eating-live-streams.
Rapp, J. (2019, March 29). How Do Multi-Channel Networks (MCNs) Work in China? *Parklu*. Retrieved September 17, 2020, from https://www.parklu.com/multi-channel-networks-mcns-china/.
Recktenwald, D. (2017). Toward a Transcription and Analysis of Live Streaming on Twitch. *Journal of Pragmatics, 115*, 68–81.
Ritzer, G., & Jurgenson, N. (2010). Production, Consumption, Prosumption: The Nature of Capitalism in the Age of the Ddigital 'Prosumer'. *Journal of Consumer Culture, 10*(1), 13–36.
Rose, N. (1990). *Governing the Soul: The Shaping of the Private Self*. London: Routledge.
Sisdon. (2018). Wanghong Creator, 8 August with David Craig, Shenzhen, China.
Sohu. (2019, August 6). How Popular Was Tian You in 2017? [MC天佑最火时候有多火?]. *Sohu*. Retrieved September 17, 2020, from https://www.sohu.com/a/319220518_100076530.
Srnicek, N. (2017). *Platform Capitalism*. Oxford: Polity Press.

Sun, W. (2017, September 28). 'My Parents Say Hurry Up and Find a Girl': China's Millions of Lonely 'Leftover Men'. *The Guardian*. Retrieved August 19, 2020, from https://www.theguardian.com/inequality/2017/sep/28/my-parents-say-hurry-up-and-find-a-girl-chinas-millions-of-lonely-leftover-men.

Tidy, J. (2020, August 20). Mukbang: Why Is China Clamping Down on Eating Influencers? *BBC News*. Retrieved September 18, 2020, from https://www.bbc.com/news/technology-53840167.

van Dijck, J., Poell, T., & de Waal, M. (2018). *The Platform Society: Public Values in a Connective World*. Oxford: Oxford University Press.

van Doorn, N. (2017). Platform Labor: On the Gendered and Racialized Exploitation of Low-Income Service Work in the 'On-Demand' Economy. *Information, Communication & Society, 20*(6), 898–914.

Wang, J. (2016). Toushi zhongguo wangluo zhibo dangqian de wenti yu fazhan qushi (See Through the Current Problem and Future Development of Chinese Online Livestreaming). *Journal of News Research, 7*(13), 321.

Wang, S. (2019, December 30). After Years of Derision, China's Internet Celebrities Finally Win Mainstream Success. *Pandaily*. Retrieved September 17, 2020, from https://pandaily.com/after-years-of-derision-chinas-internet-celebrities-finally-win-mainstream-success/.

Weiss, G. (2020, July 23). TikTok Establishes $200 Million Fund to Get Its Creators Paid. *Tubefilter*. Retrieved September 18, 2020, from https://www.tubefilter.com/2020/07/23/tiktok-establishes-200-million-creator-fund/.

Weibo. (2016). United States Securities and Exchange Commission Washington, D.C. 20549 FORM 20-F. Retrieved September 18, 2020, from http://ir.weibo.com/static-files/bb5320ad-2466-4f4d-9e75-97ad3e9e0063.

Wu, H. (2018, February 25). People's Public of Desire. *PBS.org*. Retrieved September 17, 2020, from https://www.pbs.org/independentlens/films/peoples-republic-of-desire/.

Xu, J., & Zhao, X. (2019). Changing Platformativity of China's Female Wanghong: From Anni Baobei to Zhang Dayi. In S. Cai (Ed.), *Female Celebrities in Contemporary Chinese Society* (pp. 127–158). Singapore: Palgrave Macmillan.

Yang, S. (2016). Wangluo zhibo luanxiang beihou de sikao—yi Douyu weili (A Thought on the Mess of Online Livestreaming – Using Douyu as a Case). Retrieved August 24, 2020, from http://www.wenku1.com/news/FD0D92C8E710E891.html.

Yang, P. (2018, July 21). A Primer on China's Live Streaming Market. *Hackermoon*. Retrieved September 18, 2020, from https://hackernoon.com/a-primer-on-chinas-live-streaming-market-352409ad2c0b.

Yang, Y. (2020). Four Years Later, Dedao Has Accumulated 387 Million Users. [得到四周年,用户数已达3870万]. *ChinaVenture*. Retrieved from http://www.chinaventure.com.cn/news/110-20200527-355093.html.

Yin, Xinglian (Ethan). (2016). Interview with CEO Ethan Song, 2 June with David Craig, Beijing, China.

Yin, Xinglian (Ethan). (2020). (WeChat Exchange with David Craig on July 26, 2020).

Yu, Z., & Wenting, X. (2018, April 16). China's Huge Pool of Web Moderators Required to Have an Eagle Eye for Dangerous Content. *Global Times.* Retrieved September 17, 2020, from https://www.globaltimes.cn/content/1098173.shtml.

Zhang, H. (2017). Dean of School of Journalism and Communication, Beijing Normal University, Livestreamer, 15 June, with Junyi Lv, China.

Zhang, G., & de Seta, G. (2018). Being 'Red' on the Internet. In C. Abidin & M. Brown (Eds.), *Microcelebrity Around the Globe* (pp. 57–67). Bingley: Emerald Publishing Limited.

Zhang, X., Xiang, Y., & Hao, L. (2019). Virtual Gifting on China's Live Streaming Platforms: Hijacking the Online Gift Economy. *Chinese Journal of Communication.* https://doi.org/10.1080/17544750.2019.1583260.

Zhao, E. (2021). Wanghong: Liminal Chinese Creative Labor. In S. Cunningham & D. Craig (Eds.), *Creator Culture: An Introduction to Global Social Media Entertainment.* New York: New York University Press.

CHAPTER 5

Culture

INTRODUCTION

When online traffic becomes monetizable, it also becomes someone's faith. Catching attention is the "bible" of many "wanghong". 10,000 likes can drive some of them to go against science and common sense; With 100,000, they may ignore social justice and moral ethics; When it goes to 1 million, they will dare to challenge our social order and law.
CCTV (2019)

Many people call me wanghong, but what makes me different is that I have something real. I never attempt histrionics but do things step by step. I'm taking this seriously. People like me because I'm simple and direct, with nothing garish. This's also how I view myself. I'm just an ordinary person—a cook. On the right platform, at the right time and by the right expertise, I became a so-called "wanghong", yet I still prefer people addressing me as a cook. This title wanghong actually doesn't matter.
Wang Gang (2018)

The complexities of wanghong we have explored so far, involving governance, the industry, platforms, and labor, cannot be fully understood without an account of its culture, its textuality, and the intersubjective relations developed in its vigorous cyberspaces. Its immense popularity, coupled with the rich diversity, has given rise to as much discursive controversy as economic and social vibrancy. Anyone might be a wanghong, as we suggested at the end of Chap. 3, yet as the epigraphs to this chapter testify, it has also been stigmatized to the extent that almost no one will faithfully identify with this notorious job description.

This surrounding stigma testifies to the cultural dilemma of wanghong in today's China. On the one hand, wanghong have often been criticized by the public media and elites for being irresponsible and hedonistic, with regard to the materialistic values that are practiced by these grassroots individuals who obtain popularity and financial success in such a short time, without sufficient, or professional, training. The success of amateurs offends the deeply Confucian value placed on education, but it should not be forgotten that many of the stars of Western tech and entertainment were often dropouts. Ostensibly, wanghong signify a commercial culture that is deeply depoliticized and non-revolutionary, far distanced from those rebellious youth of the May Fourth movement as well as those Red Guard youth active during the Cultural Revolution in the 1970s. It is individualism and consumerism that defines the values and lifestyles performed by these online influencers and their fans.

On the other hand, suggested by the remark on the official Chinese TV channel CCTV in the epigraph, in the eyes of the authorities the vibrant mass participation and inclusiveness of wanghong also pose a potential threat to the social, political, and cultural order fashioned by China's one-party system. The focus on domestic consumption and the digital economy, as we saw in Chap. 2, is the cutting edge of national restructuring and employment, yet the diversity and creative spirit shown in wanghong culture also may unleash disruptive expression that may undermine the legitimacy of a "harmonious" national culture.

Skepticism from the elites and the state has never managed fully to inhibit the online vibrancy of wanghong culture, yet it does point to, and genuinely reflect, the paradoxical nature of its reception. Fundamentally, if consumerism and commodified entertainment culture embedded in wanghong practice is degrading and apolitical, why is it also dangerous and disruptive to such an extent that the party-state becomes so wary and censorially intervenes so often? To address this question and to unravel the cultural dilemma of wanghong, we need to take the poetics and politics of wanghong seriously. We first need to locate it in the trajectory of cultural history in contemporary China.

WANGHONG IN CULTURAL HISTORY AND NOW

The birth of wanghong can, arguably, be recognized as the continuation of the transforming "revolutionary" youth culture of previous decades. Consumerism and individualism did not originate when China went online, but was ultimately the cultural result of China's marketization reform program and its one child policy since the 1980s. From the indie rock music in late 1980s to Wang Shuo's "hooligan" novels and to Han Han's online blogs, a cynical yet euphoric, rebellious and anti-hegemonic posture intermingles with consumerism and individualism facilitated by the burgeoning market economy (Rofel 2007; de Kloet 2010; Clark 2012; Strafella and Berg 2015; de Kloet and Fung 2017).

There is a bright line to be drawn from these phenomena to *A Bloody Case Caused by a Steamed Bun* (Hu 2006), a viral video widely circulated online in 2006 which marked the inception of Chinese online participatory culture. Saturated with parody, mimicry and remix, the video spoofs Chinese "official" culture in the form of Chen Kaige's film *The Promise* (2005) in its bricolage of CCTV news program, entertainment shows and popular music. At first sight, the aesthetics of *A Steamed Bun* are amateurish: the rough visual quality and the non-professional editing of footage, thus echoing the often-claimed authenticity of user-generated content, or "grassroots creation", as referred to by the video's creator Hu Ge himself (Xiong 2018).

This grassroots aesthetic pinpoints the inauthenticity of Chinese blockbuster cinema, represented by Chen Kaige's film. Besides this, in Hu Ge's mimicry of the CCTV program *Report on Chinese Rule of Law*, we can also trace a more muted implication of inauthenticity in the supposed solemnity of the state media, teased and dissolved into the amusing and entertaining effects of the video. The playful use of visual and vocal language is subversive in the sense coined by Haiqing Yu: it is a form of "light-hearted resistance", which does not "challenge the mainstream culture (be it political or business), but rather deconstructs it through playful (mis)use (and often juxtaposition) of the available resources" (Yu 2007, p. 429).

Fast forward more than a decade and this light-hearted resistance continues to be detected in Chinese cyberspace. For example, a special genre of visual culture that has become widely popular on the platform Bilibili is named guichu (鬼畜) videos, which literally means Ghost Beast. Similar to mashups widely popular on western platforms, guichu refers to those online videos remixing a variety of existing audio-visual clips to create highly amusing content (see Chap. 4 and Fung and Yin 2019). Moreover, as we will show in this chapter, with increasing capitalization and state territorialization of the Chinese internet, social media spaces have witnessed a massive expansion in wanghong expressive genres or, "verticals". In the western context, as we have seen, the three verticals native-to-SME culture are categorized as vlogging, gameplay and Do-It-Yourself (how-to videos) (Cunningham and Craig 2019). Chinese wanghong culture, however, includes a greater diversity in formats and content verticals, from old-fashioned text-image-based online writing (mostly circulated on Weibo, WeChat and Douban) to more visualized short videos (mostly notably on Douyin, Kuaishou, Xigua and Bilibili) and live-streaming (Douyu, Huya and Kuaishou).

Across these different platforms, we identify three categories of wanghong content: cultural, creative, and social (see Figs. 5.1 and 5.2). *Cultural*

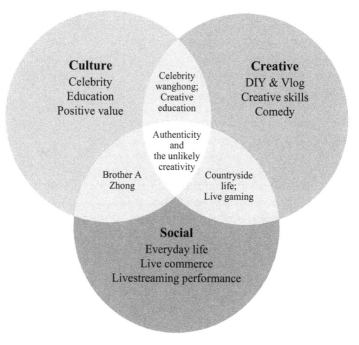

Fig. 5.1 Taxonomy of Wanghong content

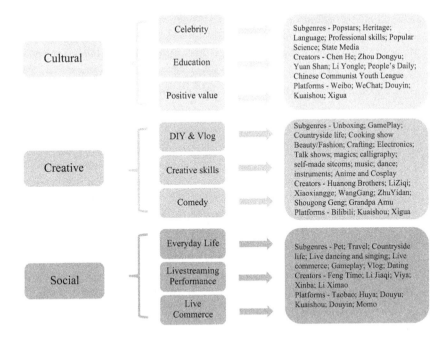

Fig. 5.2 The main genres of content

wanghong content refers to those performers, genres, and formats highly related to the established media industries and mainstream heritage culture, including genres of celebrity (pop stars active on wanghong platforms), education (various contents promoting popular science, knowledge, language, and professional skills), and positive values (channels run by Chinese state-media and official institutions promoting the so-called positive values (正能量 zheng nengliang)). *Creative* wanghong content, in comparison, includes more diverse and vernacular creative genres on the platforms, including DIY and vlogging (such as unboxing, cooking, beauty and fashion), creative skills (magic, cosplay, gameplay, crafting, rural living, and singing) and comedy (fictional short sitcoms, talk shows, and food commentaries) (Fig. 5.2). The creators of the content fall in the creative wanghong category as identified in Chap. 4 (see Fig. 4.1). Finally, *social* wanghong content is characterized by the social nature of online content and their emphasis on the social skills (instead of cultural and creative expertise). Among them, most notably are the various shows documenting creators' pets, travel and food tasting, livestreaming shows featuring beautiful girls' and boys' performance and interaction with their online followers, and more recently live commerce (as shown in the following, Li Jiaqi's livestreaming channel resembles the traditional television shopping shows, but offers a seemingly more objective comparison and evaluation of products, as well as a more convenient shopping experience).

As we also stated in Chap. 4, the boundary between these categories are not always well-defined. There are both commonalities and overlaps that bridge cultural, creative, and social content. Primarily, behind such an immense and diverse pool of content is the deepening of commodification of the platform economy (van Dijck et al. 2018) that also manages to offer widespread opportunity to all manner of individuals in a "participatory" and "convergence" culture (Jenkins 2006; see also Jenkins et al. 2013). Wanghong culture constitutes an extension and intensification of the cultural industries and the commercial popular culture, in which cultural production and commodification have been expanded to incorporate the vernacular creativities (Burgess 2006) of massive numbers of individuals from almost all social classes. Typifying Sarah Banet-Weiser's (2012) account of brand culture, commercial interests are no longer seen as separate from cultural meaning but are inherent in the motivation and practice of symbolic creation.

The anti-hegemonic spirit embedded in the youth culture of previous decades has continued but morphed into a version of Yu's light-hearted resistance which we read through the lens of Esther Peeren's notion of "boredom creativity" (Peeren 2019). The current generation of wanghong creators, such as Huanong Brothers, Wang Gang, Li Ziqi, and Li Jiaqi, exhibit a content aesthetics in which "the product of creativity is not valued aesthetically but solely in terms of whether it draws and engages the attention of the nominally bored" (Peeren 2019, p. 105). What kind of boredom drives millions of online followers to watch cooking, fishing, unboxing, gaming and even sleeping videos made by wanghong creators? Wanghong, similarly bored by their routine and often marginalized lives, turn those lives and routines creatively into entry-level light-hearted resistance. As we show in the following sections, this "boredom culture" does not challenge the social and political order, but teases, refuses and disrupts everyday lives that have been made "boring" in a real-world of hierarchy, constraint, and conservatism.

The two dynamics that energize and underpin wanghong popularity are their claims to authenticity and the "unlikeliness" that such marginalized people could rise to such prominence. The widely shared discourse of authenticity is performed through creators' accents, dress, speech, and tools, leading to user participation and social intimacy between creators and their followers. Claims to authenticity are reinforced by the unlikeliness of such creators—in the sense that those marginal and previously voiceless Chinese individuals have become popular online figures and, as we will see, their tedious everyday experiences are transformed into "grotesque", "useless", "spectacular", "meaningless", but creative and entertaining content. Wanghong culture is characterized, like Chinese youth culture portrayed by de Kloet and Fung (2017, p. 27), by a "paradoxical co-creation" between individuals, the state, and the market. It produces spaces for "experimenting with different cultural repertoires" (2017, p. 16), while not necessarily qualifying as "anti-hegemonic struggles". Instead, this vibrant online culture, evidenced also by de Kloet and Fung's discussion of memes (2017, p. 86), provides "a joyful playground" for Chinese netizens to "express what cannot be expressed" in the established screen culture.

Wanghong as Authentic

In September 2019, a video titled *One Hundred Reasons to Eat Bamboo Rats* went viral on Chinese social media. In this video, creator Liu Suliang stands inside the farm shed and "teases" the bamboo rats he raises. Some have sunstroke, he remarks dryly, some are depressed, some have lost their fight, and some have eaten too much. All these "misbehaviours" lead to the same destiny: they will be cooked into a nice meal, either barbecued, steamed, or braised. Aside from few critiques of being cruel to animals, most online viewers find amusing Liu Suliang's deadpan style of interaction with bamboo rats. Since 2017, Liu Suliang and his partner Hu Yueqing have launched their channel Huanong Brothers (华农兄弟) on Xigua and Bilibili, two of the most popular wanghong video platforms in China. Their videos document their everyday life on their farm, such as feeding and petting the bamboo rats, pigs, and dogs, as well as exploring local fruits and vegetables grown in their village. By 2020, they have managed to obtain over 5 million followers on Bilibili, 3 million on Xigua and 500 thousand on YouTube, becoming one of trendiest wanghong teams in China. Liu Suliang expertly appears shy in front of the camera, and the non-professional production and the rough quality of their videos add to the claimed "authenticity" of their online aesthetics. Everything looks and feels real in the video: Liu Suliang is a real farmer, as well as his animals (Fig. 5.3). It is this authentic documentary of life in the countryside that attracts followers—"it brings us the simple happiness of country life" (Short Video Factory 2018, n.p.).

Huanong's videos represent a widely popular group of wanghong contents we call simply "countryside life" (see Fig. 5.2). Popular creators such as Grandpa Amu (wood crafting), Dianxi Xiaoge (cooking), and A Feng and Lao Si (fishing) are other exponents of this category. These creators often choose short videos and livestreaming as main formats to document their everyday rural life and authenticity is produced through exotic food, local accents, as well as unfashionable clothes and no make-up. These videos are both creative and social (see Fig. 5.2), demonstrating the interplay of vernacular creativity coupled with online sociality.

Fig. 5.3 Liu Suliang and his bamboo rat

Authenticity is not only produced by creators' appearance and demeanor, but also by epitomizing deeply-held, residual symbolic values. Li Ziqi provides a sharp contrast to the aesthetics represented by Huanong Brothers. Li Ziqi's videos are also made in the Chinese countryside yet showcase a much more exquisite, professional aesthetic. If the key feature of Huanong content is raw authenticity, Li's videos invoke traditional Chinese watercolor portraiture of country life. Soybean, peanut, pomelo, cotton, bamboo, corn, rice—familiar everyday ingredients are made into delicate dishes or artefacts through her extraordinary artisanal handiwork framed in the videos' evocative visual language (Fig. 6.2, see Chap. 6). In these typically 10-minute shows, Li rarely speaks but performs her proficient cooking and crafting skills in the scenes that are elaborately set and filmed. These spectacles of the Chinese country life echo Chinese traditional idyll verses like *In people's haunt I build my cot; Of wheel's and hoof's noise I hear not* by the ancient poet Tao Yuanmin (translated by Xu Yuanchong, Ye 2016), whose poems have been read as depicting the utopian dreams of Chinse traditional intellectuals.

The popularity of Li Ziqi, according to her followers, is attributed to her archaic depiction of nature, falling into the imagined tranquility of the pastoral in the eyes of those who live a hectic urban life (Wang 2018). In comparison to the Huanong Brothers, the embellished rurality in Ziqi's videos enacts a different sense of authenticity, which is constructed in the classic dichotomy between the mechanistic urban-and the organic-natural. The performative character of her authenticity thus becomes necessary, given the fact that the real village life can be as much mechanical and arduous as urban life. In any case, the actual production work of either Huanong Brothers or Li Ziqi takes intensive work.

Aside from content depicting countryside life, the authenticity approach is widely adopted by almost all forms of wanghong contents across the three categories (Fig. 5.2) mapped earlier. On Douyin, for example, the well-known Chinese film actress Zhou Dongyu posted short videos of her funny moment with an elephant in the zoo, her imitation of Papi Jiang (a popular wanghong comedian), or the simple food she cooked at home. In stark contrast to characters that she played in her films, Zhou's Douyin content goes "off-screen" to depict her home life in all its simple banality. She even uses her phone camera and the built-in editing tools offered by the platform.

Zhu Yidan's Boring Life traverses the border between fiction and nonfiction, documentary and scripted, and cultural, professionally-generated

Fig. 5.4 One episode of *Zhu Yidan's boring life*

wanghong content and amateur, creative, content. Like series television, *Boring Life* is a scripted, comedic web series inspired by real-world accounts of boss Zhu Yidan and his employees. Yet, as shown in Fig. 5.4, Yidan cast amateur actors in all the roles and the series is shot in real-world offices, restaurants, and streets with little cinematic or artificial production design. Coupled with simple directing and minimal editing, this production has found a loyal fan following through its appeals to authenticity in the storytelling and production values.

The question of wanghong authenticity occupies a space in a long tradition of Chinese popular culture. Directors active in the independent documentary movement in the 1990s, for example, also trumpeted their work as creating a sense of "xianchang" (现场 on-the-spot) through their work of filming on location. This practice was chosen by these indie directors as a resistance to their predecessors in the Maoist era when films and documentaries had to serve the propaganda and educational rules and thus were mostly made in studios with pre-planned scripts or archival footages (Zhang 2006; Robinson 2013). Documentaries characterized by xianchang are recognized as independent and alternative to the mainstream Chinese cinema because they attempt, Luke Robinson observes, "a certain spontaneous quality understood as inherent to such filmmaking, for since what happened on the physical space of 'the scene' was beyond the control of the filmmaker, xianchang as a practice was considered to be intrinsically open-ended and indeterminate" (2013, p. 5). The aesthetics of *xianchang* thus emphasize the authenticity of their filming and challenges the dominant cinematic ideology. But compared to Chinese independent documentaries, wanghong content in contemporary China is by and large apolitical and is intricately involved in commercial, mainstream society. Its amateurish spirit echoes populism instead of the elitism as practiced by the 1990s indie directors. Their authenticity is invoked and relies on the online interaction and participation to create emotional, intimate, and inter-personal relevance with online communities. It is more entertaining than documentary or educative.

The authenticity adopted by Chinese wanghong creators also has its own specificities compared to the SME creators in the West. If certain content is regarded authentic, it also denounces, either implicitly or explicitly, something inauthentic, the identification of which is both social-historical and personal. But this political aspect can only be apprehended by unravelling the hidden cultural and political contexts in which these authenticities are performed and received. To do so, we need to delve into the specific aesthetics of wanghong culture (interactive content) and situate it in the landscape of contemporary Chinese cultural politics, which together weaves these narratives of authenticity. At the same time, as Stuart Cunningham and David Craig argue, the authenticity of SME always lies in the online practice of community building as the basis for any possibility for commercial branding (2019, p. 156). It is sociality and branding that distinguishes the culture of social media entertainment from established forms of professional cultural production such as television and film. As we have reiterated throughout this book, the wanghong economy has developed a similar, more salient, social dimension, enabled by both state governance and particular affordances of wanghong platforms. Branding and social functions have become indispensable for wanghong content and creator practice. This intersection of sociality and branding further complicates the politics of wanghong culture, given the state's both protective and restrictive role in governing the wanghong economy as we analyzed in Chap. 2.

To explicate the specificities of wanghong culture, especially the ambivalence of its politics, the following two sections will introduce the concept of "unlikely creativity" (content) and "sociality culture" (participation) as two distinctive features charactering Chinese wanghong authenticity and its cultural politics.

Wanghong as Unlikely Creators

Shougong Geng (Handcraft Geng) is a popular wanghong channel on Bilibili and Kuaishou that posts videos of handcraft inventions made by Geng Shuai, a local farmer from Baoding, Hebei province. Named bizarrely as "head knocker", "Gatling gun", "robotic washing machine" and "handstand hairwasher" (Fig. 5.5), these inventions are all ingeniously designed and crafted yet are mostly "useless" in everyday life. For instance, "handstand hairwasher" allows Geng Shuai to wash his hair when doing a handstand; "smile assistant" is a device that can "assist" those who do not like to smile; "robotic washing machine" is made of a waste gas cylinder that can automatically wash clothes with its electric mechanical arms. These sophisticated yet quirky instruments have made Geng Shuai very popular online. By late 2020, he had 4.3 million followers on Bilibili, 4.5 million on Kuaishou and over 2 million on Weibo. His fans make fun of him as "the useless Thomas Edison", "the most miserable wanghong" (all of his inventions seem torturous to use) and "jeans lover". In the videos, Geng Shuai introduces the design and "uses" of his devices, often in a self-deprecatory tone, with his "provincial" Hebei accent. Together with his iconic jean overalls, thick and long hair and big round eyes, these videos generate a particular sense of absurd humor, which according to Geng imitate Hongkong *Mo lei tau* comedy, represented by Stephen Chow's films (Zhu 2019).

Geng's inventions were inspired by his early, itinerant working-class life. Prior to his wanghong career, his average income was around RMB 900 per month and saw him moving to five different cities taking all kinds of jobs including as a plumber, a construction worker, and a phone seller. His dream through all that was to open a fireworks factory. Geng mocks himself for being part of "the mobile builder of Chinese cities": either

Fig. 5.5 Shougong Geng and his robotic washing machine

working on remote construction sites or on his way to the next job. Later, learning from his father, Geng became a skilled welder, working for the local railway. In 2016, tired of his mundane working life, Geng built a studio to build his machinery-inspired artwork. After he launched channels on Kuaishou and Bilibili, fascination with his "useless" inventions secured millions of viewers.

The story, and aesthetics, of Geng Shuai's online creations illustrate wanghong's "unlikely creativity". As we saw in Chap. 4, participatory social media platforms such as Douyin, Kuaishou and livestreaming apps have enabled an "unlikely creative class" that expands Chinese popular cultural production among more marginalized groups of population: working class, less-educated, living in rural China or on the peripheries of urban society (Lin and de Kloet 2019). Wanghong culture in that sense does not necessarily map to well-established critical categories such as youth culture, urban culture, or subculture. Chinese popular culture of the 1990s and early 2000s—that is, before its platformization—was mostly produced in or from cities, "especially large conurbations on the eastern seaboard were the nodes through which international and other new influences presented themselves to young Chinese" (Clark 2012, p. 7). Wanghong culture has expanded beyond such spatial segregation and the urban imagery of popular culture. It resonates with what Henry Jenkins terms convergence culture, "where old and new media collide, where grassroots and corporate media intersect, where the power of the media producer and the power of the media consumer interact in unpredictable ways" (2006, p. 2).

As well as working class, grassroots and marginal individuals like farmers, migrant workers, teachers, students, women, and older Chinese forming an unlikely creative class, convergent wanghong culture also influences mainstream entertainment culture, in a process of the "wanghongization" of celebrity (a popular subgenre in cultural wanghong content, see Fig. 5.2). In another trend in the platformization of culture, established, professional celebrities such as film actors and pop stars are now opening channels on social media platforms and creating tailored, wanghong-style content. Besides the case of Zhou Dongyu cited earlier, Chen He, a popular actor known for his casting in the trendy television series *iPartment*, has attracted over 60 million followers on Douyin, where his posts adopt the wanghong vernacular of light-hearted, everyday amateurism. When film and television production was heavily disrupted by the novel coronavirus outbreak in early 2020, television networks (for example, Hunan TV) and online portals such as Tencent Video, Youku and Iqiyi have aligned to create "wanghong-style" reality shows by inviting celebrities to document their performance at home or in their private studios (Cai 2020). *Eat Well*, for example, a show that runs on Youku, invites celebrities such as Zhao Benshan, Pan Changjiang, Lin Yongjian and Ma Weiwei to livestream their cooking and dining experiences with their family members at home. In these new reality shows, we observe an increasingly fluid boundary between wanghong and celebrities.

The formation of an unlikely creative class brings with it the formation of an unlikely aesthetics. Offering a significant break with the solemn, predictable content on broadcast media, the creative repertoire of wanghong absorbs everyday experiences from hugely disparate individual backgrounds. Like Geng Shuai's inventions, those that might be viewed as "bizarre", "useless" and "nonsensical" in the mainstream culture are celebrated by their followers as authentic, funny, and creative. Such upending of notions of what counts as culture can be seen across most of the wanghong content categories (see Fig. 5.1). In his unboxing videos, we see Xiao Xiangge (vlogging and unboxing) using a traditional corn-popper to cook crawfish, nibbling a RMB 3,000 king crab, and getting stuck by a light bulb lollipop (Fig. 5.6). A Feng and Lao Si (countryside life) display the fishes, crabs, and shrimps they have caught from the choppy sea in their short videos and vlogging shows. In his daily livestreaming on Taobao, Li Jiaqi (DIY culture and live commerce) brags about his selected lipsticks and cosmetic products from L'Oréal, SK-II, Armani, and such. On Douyin, we find a divergent mixture of trendy dances, music and comical performances, while on Kuaishou we learn magic tricks, cooking and crafting. Even high school teachers like Li Yongle (knowledge sharing) can catch attention from his 9 million fans through his popular science lectures such as *Do aliens really exist? Why is fart so smelly? Can we create a time machine?*

The state also "participates" fulsomely in wanghong culture. There are numerous "official" channels widely circulated on social media platforms. And they appear to be popular. According to data analytics company NewRank (https://www.newrank.cn/), People's Daily and CCTV, the

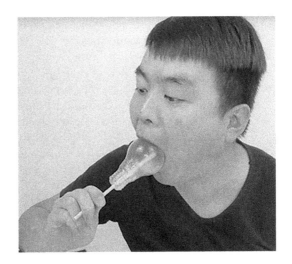

Fig. 5.6 Xiao Xiangge eating a light bulb lollipop

two most important state propaganda outlets, are the most subscribed channels across all short video platforms including Kuaishou, Douyin and Bilibili. On Douyin, for example, People's Daily has attracted over 100 million followers (by September 2020). Videos posted here include not only video clips from the news reports published on its own website, but also native content designed and produced for the short video platform. In a video paying tribute to an old veteran who fought during the Korean War in 1950, a younger solder was filmed saluting the "old hero"; the military medals were shown to the camera and some upbeat pop song was used as background music with a subtitle stating "Salute to veterans; Respect to heroes!" (People's Daily 2020)

This range of style and content and the embeddedness of official, positive value content within it underscore the "unlikeliness" of wanghong culture as a component of China's peculiar cultural system. The above-analyzed creativities are unlikely not because that they are impossible to organize or make, but simply because of the unlikeliness of their presence in Chinese popular culture. From television to commercial cinema, the production of Chinese screen culture for decades has been dominated by state-owned television networks and film studios. The national discourse of "double responsibilities" (Lin 2019)—generating revenue alongside conforming politically—makes the autonomy of creative labor highly contingent and places responsibilities on creative workers to "be creative for the state". The participatory nature of the online cultural economy, in contrast to the established media industries, has unleashed vast creative impulses from below. Though by no means de-territorialized—outside the Chinese cultural system—and thus not immune to censorship and calls to conform to official culture, the wanghong economy operates as a platform for vernacular creativity (Edensor et al. 2009, p. 10)—the "neither extraordinary nor spectacular" but "mundane, intensely social practices"—to thrive, shifting the dynamics of Chinese popular cultural production from the professional and the state to the vernacular and the individual.

This wanghong creativity distinguishes from professional and legacy forms of creativity in the sense that it is arises from the vernacular, grassroots, and banal everyday life. It can be seen as a form of "boredom creativity"—the participation of creators and their followers in the wanghong culture functions as both resistance to and reproduction of the very state of boredom. Following Esther Peeren (2019), to find something boring is to devalue and critique it as "inadequate and unfulfilling" and in contemporary Chinese capitalism boredom has become both a stigmatized shameful experience and a productive force. The incorporation of this often idle and even redundant labor force into wanghong creator labor, as Chaps. 3 and 4 noted, echoes the expectations of the state's agenda for "Mass Entrepreneurship and Innovation" (The State Council 2015). While for creators, wanghong creativity and subjectivity also become desirable alternatives to the work and title as cook, farmer, high school teacher or college graduate waiting to be hired by companies. The banality of the everyday has been converted into the productive footage of their online creativity, signifying a moment when boredom, creativity and career converge.

Demonstrated by Geng Shuai's case, his "grotesque" inventions only become meaningful and "creative" when they are shown in his videos and catch the attention of his millions of bored followers. Together with his accent, dresses and gestures, the nonsensical devices invented all transfer into comical authenticity contributing to "unlikely" but productive wanghong creativity. The subjectivity of wanghong thus constitutes a mixed process of becoming, transcending the simple identity of either their "authentic", everyday job or the professionalized creative worker. Through accessible digital platforms, these online visual contents create a cordial resonance with their viewers' similarly mundane and boring life and fills their empty time that is both unavoidable and intolerable. Wanghong culture light-heartedly reframes mundane everyday life and legacy screen culture, both of which can be experienced as "boring" within the Chinese hierarchical social, cultural, and economic order. Its scale, diversity and sheer energy makes the guardians of this order nervous, as suggested by the CCTV remark with which we started the chapter. Without however posing a direct challenge to that social and cultural order, it absorbs them into its own production.

Sociality as Culture

Wanghong's authenticity, appeal and energy lie not only in its creators' socio-economic profiles and content aesthetics, but also in the relationship between creators and spectators. Powered by affordances that, as we saw in Chap. 3, create the conditions for social presence, wanghong constantly reinforce its viewers as followers, fans, and community participants. "Come on Laotie! Double click, 666 and subscribe to my channel!" Laotie is a popular slang originated from North-East China, meaning "brother" or "old friend". The action of double clicking on a video equals a "like" and "666" in Mandarin is homophonic to liu (溜), referring to "cool" or "awesome". This mode of intimate address is not only overtly spoken by creators in their online shows, but is encoded into the entire process of content production. Wanghong's mode of address is designed to produce a consistent personality, whether outspoken, righteous, fun, gentle, humorous, which contributes to sustained intimacy between creators and their followers. In his videos posted on Bilibili, A Feng is not only a local skilled fisherman, he also helps his disadvantaged neighbors, shares fishing skills with his friends, treats his fans with nice seafood meals and volunteers to deliver food for people in quarantine during the coronavirus outbreak. He is humble and not greedy. Occasionally, fans are invited for a fishing boat tour with him, which always ends with a seafood feast. As a result, A Feng becomes a friendly and virtuous figure, beloved by his fans and also his fellow villagers.

For celebrity wanghong, their personalities are often depicted as cool, fashionable, trustworthy, or even patriotic. In August 2019, for example, famous Chinese actors and actresses such as Zhang Yixing, Liu Yifei (playing Mulan in Disney's 2020 film *Mulan*), Yang Mi, Huang Xiaoming and Lu Han posted on their Weibo accounts with lines such as "I stand with Hong Kong police", "I love Hong Kong and I love China" or "Hong Kong is part of China". The great online popularity and the social nature of wanghong culture seem to have forced these celebrities to publicly perform their "patriotism" to echo the surging online nationalism. A consistent performance of personality proves to be even more crucial for social wanghong production. As mentioned in Chap. 4, livestreaming shows are characterized by the live interaction between streamers and fans and social skills often outweigh other creative skills in obtaining online success. Buqiuren, a well-known PUBG livestreaming gamer on Huya, often claims he is more of an entertaining zhubo (livestreamer) than a professional game player. His good-looking appearance, gentle and polite communication style has won him over 11 million subscribers on Huya and 510 thousand subscriptions to his YouTube English Channel.

This community-oriented, relational, and relatable nature of wanghong creation is driven by the inherent business model of the wanghong economy. As a central platform mechanism, commercial social media transforms "online and offline objects, activities, emotions, and ideas" into tradable data through the process of datafication: "the massive amount of user data collected and processed by online platforms provide insight into users' interests, preferences, and needs at particular moments in time" (van Dijck et al. 2018, p. 37). The datatification allows platforms to generate substantial revenue through advertising while also empowering creators to become entrepreneurs and monetize the online traffic of their content (subscriptions, likes, shares, comments, and so forth). As we saw in Chap. 3, many platforms, including YouTube, Bilibili and Kuaishou, have adopted "traffic-based incentive models" to facilitate a highly interactive creator culture. Besides platform incentives, creators also collaborate with multichannel networks (MCN) and creator agencies to further exploit online traffics to seek for more sustainable monetization such as e-commerce and advertising. This "micro-platformization", according to Jonathan Hutchinson (2019, p. 11), ensures "the advertisers receive the most appropriate influencer for their products or services". Similar to the process of platformization that "makes data platform ready", "micro-platformization makes influencers brand ready" (Hutchinson 2019). Sophia, a wanghong MCN manager based in Shenzhen, confirms this during our interview that their job is to "pair up" their creators with the right platform:

> We differentiate the platforms for different wanghong needs. Live streaming platforms like Yizhibo, Lang Live, and Douyu are where you make money based on the gifts that the viewers give you. Short video platforms such as Weishi, Douyin, Kuaishou are where you get paid like on YouTube based on views and followers and engagement combined with commercials being added. Weibo and the Little Red Book is where money comes from brand-making posts for soft marketing and also building a bond with followers and turning that into actual value. (Sophia 2020)

Fans, community, and interaction thus become crucial for transforming creator culture into a sustainable wanghong business. If the unlikely creativities investigated in the previous section construct authenticity at the aesthetic level, wanghong authenticity is further reinforced by the community-building and interactivity inherent in the process of wanghong production, in which branding culture both characterizes and circumscribes such discourses of authenticity. To do so, wanghong creators often choose to develop a special *"renshe"* (人设character)—to perform a certain personality—that can fit into the imagined audience and community that creators want to address. Through quite performative creative practice such as language, accent, dress, gesture and even props used, wanghong content adopt highly interactive formality that will affect and provoke intimacy among viewers, who will later become their followers, fans and even consumers of their promoted brands. In terms of social wanghong content, income is secured through virtual gifting or online ecommerce. Here, the "coin of the realm", so to speak, is personal charisma. The more outgoing, charming, and trustworthy, the more followers.

For creative wanghong, success relies more on some form of skill or talent, whether performing a funny character or generating innovative creative projects. Among thousands of food bloggers on Bilibili, for example, we can identify a wide range of creator personalities. Most notably, Xiao Xiangge mocks himself as "Guizhou Eddie Peng[1]". Ge combines the affective and the corporeal, including silly facial expressions and chubby body shape, with comedic skill, using an array of accents and clever one-liner while experimenting with kitchen appliances. Combined, Ge has secured over 2.7 million followers on Bilibili and 615K subscribers on YouTube. In contrast, Da Xiangge features a more curated food channel with higher production values, if still securing a high following comparable to Ge. Set in a newsroom-like studio, his food shows are beautifully edited, the food selected is mostly expensive and his narration is delivered in a somber tone. As a result, Da Xiangge is regarded as a serious, knowledgeable, and professional food vlogger.

For most of this online content, a frequent discourse that often emerges out of their diverse stylizations is "real-life" and "jiediqi" (接地气 down to earth); these personalities should be relevant, but not identical, to the everyday life of digital users. Becky Li (Li Beika, DIY culture and beauty blogging), a popular Chinese on-line writer, posts articles on fashion and luxury wear on Chinese platforms WeChat and Weibo, using the name "*Li Beika's fantasy world*". After four years of operation, her account has become one of most popular wanghong channels in the vertical of fashion. In August 2020, her WeChat account had about 3 million visits per month on average and over million active followers on WeChat and over 6 million Weibo followers in total. Afforded by the large fan group and data traffic, Becky became a favorite of both domestic and international fashion and luxury brands and advertisers. Unlike popular stars and celebrities, Becky used to be a political and entertainment journalist at Southern Metropolis Daily, a Chinese newspaper based in Guangzhou.

---

[1] Eddie Peng is a Canadian Chinese film actor who has been famous for his handsome appearance.

The success should be attributed to her mastery of "renshe" through her individualized writing style. As one of her followers shares, "it is her style of writing that is the most attractive. She always affectionately teaches us what you should buy, in a tone like a caring little sister. This tone really attracts fans, with high loyalty" (Guiqulaixi 2018).

The same approach has also been employed by Viya and Li Jiaqi in their livestreaming shows (DIY culture and beauty blogging, livestreamer). Belonging to the category of DIY culture (Fig. 5.1), their promotion of various products and brands follows the "authenticity approach" through their outspoken and ostensibly objective review of products, yet all of this is realized through their extraordinary social skills and appealing personalities. "Oh my god! The matte look of this lipstick does not feel dry at all!" "It doesn't look old-fashioned on yellow skins, absolutely not!" "There is a feeling of first love, thanks to its moist texture: exquisite and smooth, even with a slight honey peach smell. A must buy for elegant ladies!" "What so special is its velvet violet colour—the lekvar purple. Wear it and you'll be a lady!" "The very high-class strawberry colour makes it perfect for big occasions! It gives you an absolute disposition as a confident hostess!" "Yellow skin? White skin? No bother. This is for you!" These are the words uttered by Li Jiaqi in his livestreaming shows to promote lipstick on Taobao and Douyin. As many commentators point out, Li's success is largely by virtue of his special way of communication with the online audience. The exaggerative, assertive, and authoritative tone demonstrates his knowledge of cosmetic products and brands, while his male identity and his impeccably crafted appearance (skin care, hairstyle, dress, and so forth) gives him further credibility with his mostly female followers. Interpellated in his narratives as "elegant lady", "princess", "first love" and "hostess", followers of Li Jiaqi are mobilized into an imagined community that, bonded by Li's provocative while "reliable" online branding shows, actively participates and contributes to his wanghong business.

Moreover, behind all these commercial branding elements we can also identify an intriguing politics of gender and sexuality played by Li Jiaqi and his interaction with fans. His try-out and promotion of lipsticks and cosmetics have ostensibly reinforced his "feminine" outlook, the presence of which in Chinese online space at least implicitly displays the "queerness" or homosexuality that has long been underrepresented in Chinese popular culture. His forthright embracing and promotion of consumption echoes the individualism and consumerism deep-seated in the Chinese youth culture since the 1980s (de Kloet and Fung 2017). Such individualist, consumerist and even "cosmopolitan" outlook, however, distances from his revolutionary predecessors and thus does not promise a dissent, resistant culture. Li's livestreaming is by no means an undisguised, radical "coming-out" that pose a direct challenge to the existing gender and sexual norms; instead, the way in which he promotes beauty products and addresses hetero ladies reinforces the existing heteronormativity and gender stereotypes. This resembles, though in a different way, what Shuaishuai Wang (2019) discovers in his ethnographic study of gay live streamers on Chinese homosexual dating platform Blued. As Wang notices, virtual gifting as the main monetizing affordance of Blued not only enables a transformation of the online participation of gay users and their affective intimacy into tradable data of the platform economy, but does indeed cultivate a virtual community and fosters online intimacy among Chinese gay individuals, whose gender and sexual identity seems more circumscribed in the offline society.

Conclusion: The Power and Politics of Wanghong

Seeking to understand wanghong culture, we need to avoid viewing this particular form of online culture as a contingent unity held together by authoritarianism, nationalism, and censorship. Unravelling the poetics and light-hearted resistance of wanghong helps us move beyond paranoid and simplistic descriptions of Chinese culture that "not only identifies an ideological enemy to the liberal-democratic West, but also precludes any patient or meaningful engagement with the many dimensions, such as culture, of a living society" (Tang 2015, p. 7). Relatedly, following Xiaobing Tang, we also avoid the "dissidence hypothesis" that views cultural politics in China as political dissidence and "therefore worthy of sympathy and outside support". Hypercommercial branding cultures and the prevalence of censorship online may have seen historically more overt dissident politics diluted into more subtle, ostensibly apolitical forms. From the early video of "the steamed bun" to Geng Shuai, Li Jiaqi and the like demonstrate that "light-hearted resistance" coined by Haiqing Yu (2007) has carried on in Chinese cyberspace during the past decade. It is less of a form of resistance and politics that directly challenges the power of the state and mainstream culture, but more of trivialized practices of discontent with everyday quotidian lives, which can be experienced as "boring" within the Chinese hierarchical social, cultural, and economic order. Wanghong as career and identity offers a massive number of Chinese a window from which they may see and experience alternative futures of work and life, which all appear "unlikely" and "grotesque" in offline society where everyone fits a class, profession, gender, or demographic position.

The power of wanghong culture reaches beyond the realm of popular culture and media production. It sparks the creative impulse of vast numbers from below and fosters potential upward social mobility that seems to allow wanghong to imagine and organize their lives outside of the normalized hierarchical structure of Chinese society. It disrupts the micro-social fabric in which Chinese populations are organized: the established division between urban and rural, rigid social distinctions in terms of profession, class, and education. This disruptive power is amplified by the commercial nature of wanghong production as it aligns with the state's agenda of economic development and employment while being at least of regular concern in terms of political order and social stability. In their study of YouTube, Burgess and Green point out:

> The commercial drive behind and the hype around YouTube may have produced the possibility of participation in online video culture for a much broader range of participants than before. This idea allows us to shift our concern away from the false opposition between market and non-market culture.... YouTube is generating public and civic value as an unintended and often unsupported consequence of the practices of its users. (Burgess and Green 2018, p. 66)

Burgess and Green question whether this "unintentionally produced cultural, civic and social value of YouTube" is "being truly valued and supported by the platform" (Burgess and Green 2018, p. 66). We would ask if the social and economic value of wanghong culture is truly valued most particularly by the state—platforms seem to have a decent grasp of its value. Given the increasing uncertainty of the contemporary world and Chinese society, which is only exacerbated by the pandemic and the geopolitical tensions, we are unable to deliver a clear answer but would affirm the vibrant and schizophrenic state of becoming in the subjective formation of wanghong creators and culture. It is a culture that results from the state-platform-capitalism complex but also may, if not disturb it, then at least distress it, from within and below.

References

Banet-Weiser, S. (2012). *AuthenticTM: The Politics of Ambivalence in a Brand Culture*. New York: NYU Press.

Burgess, J. (2006). Hearing Ordinary Voices: Cultural Studies, Vernacular Creativity and Digital Storytelling. *Continuum, 20*(2), 201–214.

Burgess, J., & Green, J. (2018). *YouTube: Online Video and Participatory Culture*. Cambridge: Polity Press.

Cai, X. (2020, February 20). Reality Shows Present Slice of Indoor Life During Epidemic. *Sixth Tone*. Retrieved August 25, 2020, from http://www.sixthtone.com/news/1005218/reality-shows-present-slice-of-indoor-life-during-epidemic.

CCTV. (2019, October 15). Wanghong Should Not Cross the Baseline of Our Society *["网红"再红也不能触碰社会"红线"]*. 新闻频道_央视网. Retrieved August 25, 2020, from https://news.cctv.com/2019/10/15/ARTIgUdncF0Y95tieXIvCLkt191015.shtml

Clark, P. (2012). *Youth Culture in China: From Red Guards to Netizens*. Cambridge: Cambridge University Press.

Cunningham, S., & Craig, D. (2019). *Social Media Entertainment: The New Intersection of Hollywood and Silicon Valley*. New York: New York University Press.

de Kloet, J. (2010). *China with a Cut: Globalisation, Urban Youth and Popular Music*. Amsterdam: Amsterdam University Press.

de Kloet, J., & Fung, A. (2017). *Chinese Youth Culture*. New York: Polity Press.

Edensor, T., Leslie, D., Millington, S., & Rantisi, N. (2009). Introduction: Rethinking creativity: Critiquing the Creative Class Thesis. In T. Edensor, D. Leslie, S. Millington, & N. Rantisi (Eds.), *Spaces of Vernacular Creativity* (pp. 15–30). London: Routledge.

Fung, A., & Yin, Y. (2019). New Productive Culture: Shanzhai or Second Degree of Creation? In J. de Kloet, Y. Chow, & L. Scheen (Eds.), *Boredom, Shanzhai, and Digitisation in the Time of Creative China* (pp. 149–170). Amsterdam: Amsterdam University Press.

Guiqulaixi. (2018). Why is *Li Beika's Fantasy World* So Popular? [公众号《丽贝卡的异想世界》为什么会这么火?]. *Zhihu*. Retrieved September 30, 2020, from https://www.zhihu.com/question/54917390.

Hu, G. (2006). A Bloody Case Caused by a Steamed Bun [一个馒头引发的血案]. *YouTube*. Retrieved September 30, 2020, from https://www.youtube.com/watch?v=xIU4udZRKEY.

Hutchinson, J. (2019). Micro-Platformization for Digital Activism on Social Media. *Information, Communication & Society*. https://doi.org/10.1080/1369118X.2019.1629612.

Jenkins, H. (2006). *Convergence Culture: Where Old and New Media Collide.* New York: NYU Press.
Jenkins, H., Ford, S., & Green, J. (2013). *Spreadable Media: Creating Value and Meaning in a Networked Culture.* New York: NYU Press.
Lin, J. (2019). Be Creative for the State: Creative Workers in Chinese State-Owned Cultural Enterprises. *International Journal of Cultural Studies, 22*(1), 53–69.
Lin, J., & de Kloet, J. (2019). Platformization of the Unlikely Creative Class: Kuaishou and Chinese Digital Cultural Production. *Social Media+ Society, 5*(4). https://doi.org/10.1177/2056305119883430.
Peeren, E. (2019). You Must (Not) Be Bored!: Boredom and Creativity in Global Capitalism. In J. de Kloet, Y. Chow, & L. Scheen (Eds.), *Boredom, Shanzhai, and Digitisation in the Time of Creative China* (pp. 101–109). Amsterdam: Amsterdam University Press.
People's Daily. (2020). Short Video Clip. *Douyin.* Retrieved September 30, 2020, from https://v.douyin.com/JASd67E/.
Robinson, L. (2013). *Independent Chinese Documentary: From the Studio to the Street.* London: Palgrave Macmillan.
Rofel, L. (2007). *Desiring China: Experiments in Neoliberalism, Sexuality, and Public Culture.* Duke University Press.
Short Video Factory. (2018, September 30). Very Earthy and Very Red! "Hua Nong Brothers" Accepts Advertisements and Recruits Teams. What Is the Secret Behind The Explosion? [很土, 也很红!"华农兄弟"接广告、招团队, 背后的爆火秘籍是?]. Retrieved August 25, 2020, from https://www.sohu.com/a/257196681_100005778,.
Sophia. (2020). 3 July, interview with Jian Lin via WeChat.
Strafella, G., & Berg, D. (2015). The Making of an Online Celebrity: A critical analysis of Han Han's blog. *China Information, 29*(3), 352–376.
Tang, X. (2015). *Visual Culture in Contemporary China.* Cambridge: Cambridge University Press.
The State Council. (2015). Instructions on Constructing Platforms to Promote Mass Entrepreneurship [国务院关于加快构建大众 创业万众创新支撑平台的指导意见]. Retrieved from http://www.gov.cn/zhengce/content/2015-09/26/content_10183.htm
van Dijck, J., Poell, T., & de Waal, M. (2018). *The Platform Society: Public Values in a Connective World.* Oxford: Oxford University Press.
Wang Gang. (2018). We are Different from "wanghong" [我们和网红不一样]. *CCTV.* Retrieved from https://www.youtube.com/watch?v=iC_T6m8zWoA&t=397s
Wang, S. (2019). *Living with Censorship: The Political Economy and Cultural Politics of Chinese Gay Dating Apps* (Doctoral dissertation, Universiteit van Amsterdam).

Wang, Y. (2018) Interview Li Ziqi: Drop Out at 14 Years Old and Tuned Out to be a Widely Popular Online Vlogger [专访李子柒:14岁辍学打工, 半路出家却红遍全网的古风博主].NewRank. Retrieved from https://zhuanlan.zhihu.com/p/36134923

Xiong, Z. (2018). What Has Been Changed by Hu Ge's *A Bloody Case Caused by a Steamed Bun* [13年前胡戈神作《一个馒头引发的血案》, 到底改变了什么]. *Shengdao*. Retrieved September 30, 2020, from https://www.sohu.com/a/226532945_100121259.

Ye, F. (2016). Tao Yuanming and His Idyll. *Youlin Magazine*. Retrieved September 30, 2020, from https://www.youlinmagazine.com/story/tao-yuanming-and-his-idyll/NTc3.

Yu, H. (2007). Blogging Everyday Life in Chinese Internet Culture. *Asian Studies Review, 31*(4), 423–433.

Zhang, Y. (2006). My Camera Doesn't Lie? Truth, Subjectivity, and Audience in Chinese Independent Film and Video. In P. Pickowicz & Y. Zhang (Eds.), *From Underground to Independent: Alternative Film Culture in Contemporary China* (pp. 23–46). Rowman & Littlefield.

Zhu, B. (2019). Interview Shougong Geng: My Works are Not "useless", But Simple and Crude [采访微博网红手工耿:我的作品不是"没用", 而是真的简单粗暴]. *Guancha*. Retrieved September 30, 2020, from https://www.guancha.cn/culture/2019_08_05_512381.shtml.

CHAPTER 6

Global Wanghong

The wanghong industry comprises a media ecology operating within China separate from the otherwise global-scaling social media entertainment industry carried on United States platforms. Wanghong's "parallel universe" is not isolated from the conditions of digital and platform capitalism (Srnicek 2017; Hong 2017; Schiller 1999), although we have observed that the wanghong industry lives in a platform environment that is in general more competitive and collaborative than classic accounts of Western platform capitalism would allow. As a leading edge of China's transition to a digital economy, wanghong shares both continuities and discontinuities with other "platform societies" (van Djick et al. 2018). While autarkic in development, more recently elements in the wanghong industry have begun to exert greater influence on the global stage, whether through state-based imperatives or capitalist demands for growth.

In this chapter, we consider the rise of "global wanghong", with reference to the regional and global extension of platforms, creator practices, and wanghong culture. Gathering up our cultural, creative, and social themes, global wanghong is considered across the perspectives of governance, platforms, creators, and culture. Like Jeroen de Kloet, Thomas Poell, Zeng Guohua and Chow Yiu Fai's (2019) account of "China as method", we approach global wanghong "in order to interrogate, complicate, and complement current research on the global rise of platform societies" (p. 250).

We write amidst the backlash to the rise of global China. China's pursuit of cybersovereignty and their own internet (Hong and Goodnight 2020) has itself been a response to United States-led platform imperialism and repeated attempts to dominate every market (Jin 2013). Rising platform nationalism, fueled in part by Sinophobia, may be the leading edge of a major pivot away from multilateralism, globalization, and historically high levels of global trade. The larger consequence of what we are experiencing in 2020 may prove to be a planet separated by multiple firewalls, a balkanized internet, and "tech-tonic" clashes between nations over political, economic, and socio-cultural power.

Global Wanghong Governance Mandates

Chapter 2 focused on the way Chinese tech and platform policy and regulation incubates, protects, as well as censors the wanghong industry. Consistent with Chinese party-state practice, top-down policies feature prominently in the nation's advance towards a digital economy. These policies fostered tech and platform national champions (the BATs) that, as described in Chap. 3, proved vital to investments in fostering a competitive and collaborative platform landscape. In turn, these platforms operate as proxies for the state, charged with social governance, as evidenced by increasing commitments to content moderation, admonitions, and censorship, to prevent users, creators, and firms violating regularly calibrated cultural norms.

Policy directives advancing Mass Entrepreneurship and Innovation incentivize not only platforms and businesses, but also wanghong creators and MCN firms, to build brands and careers. It is important to distinguish the outworking of mass entrepreneurship policies in the wanghong industry from merely the further advance of gig labor. Low margin platformed service-based labor, like food delivery and car sharing services, in China as much as anywhere else, involves a "third kind of worker" marked by diminished benefits, job protections, and employee rights, even dehumanization (Lu and Chen 2020).

Even though it is riddled with inequality and precarity, the wanghong industry is different. It occurs on a different array of platforms. Rather than service-based, this industry is co-dependent on creator entrepreneurialism and innovation, where value inheres in their individual or group brand ownership and development. The wide divergences of outcome for wanghong testify that value lies in entrepreneurial endeavor rather than in a single, supervening platform-tech business model. Wanghong can succeed whether operating in the tier one cities or located in the "grassroots" where pig farmers like Liu Mama can "live-stream her life and make a fortune" (Liu 2018). Such enterprising creators emerged against the backdrop of earlier social policy that contributed to gender divides and economic policy that contributed to migration from countryside to city.

Chinese media policy now promotes universal high-speed internet access and smartphone usage, platform and app development, and online shopping and mobile banking. All the while, tech policy directed that great firewalls locked out competition. Initially engaging in "edge-ball" tactics that embodied vulgar and offensive violations of cultural norms, as the wanghong industry matured, so have creators. Pivoting to a "social-benefit" model, wanghong creators are the new national champions, building sustainable careers while trying to avoid state and platform scrutiny, and garnering the admiration of their followers as well as their sustaining support.

Chinese governance within the Great Firewall may have birthed an autarkic wanghong industry but, now in its adolescence, state policies are directing it over the wall. Chapter 3 noted the range of instruments for and instances of platform investment from abroad, such as United States-based Sequoia Capital, that continues to underwrite Chinese platforms. Since the late 1990s, this strategy of "attracting-in" (引进来 yin jinlai) also featured a "going-out" (走出去 zou chuqu) strategy, encouraging Chinese companies to look globally for investment opportunities and export (mostly manufacturing) products (Huang 2016). In the ICT sectors, the state encouraged Chinese internet companies to "go out" through "overseas mergers and acquisitions, joint ventures, opening overseas branches" and through "providing internet services including industrial Cloud, supply chain management and big data analysis", for the aim of incubating "Chinese Internet+ platforms with global influence" (The State Council 2015).

The ambition of China's going-out strategy was first introduced by former president Jiang Zemin in 1999 and later articulated by former president Hu Jintao in 2007, which not only focused on international economic and business activities, but also included the aim of promoting the going-out of cultural products and presenting Chinese culture to the world (Li 2016). Officially named as "Cultural Going-out" (文化走出去 wenhua zou chuqu), the aim of this policy was to enhance Chinese "soft power" (软实力 ruan shili) globally—to increase the influence and appeal of China through "persuasion and attraction" instead of coercion (Nye 2012). As Aynne Kokas (2017) and Weiying Peng and Michael Keane (2019) detailed, these initiatives sparked co-production and co-financing initiatives with Hollywood in the 2010s. However, the tactic of investing financially in Hollywood projects while also trying to intervene in storylines and character portrayals that where not sufficiently positive about China largely failed. The pathway of advocating for modern China to global audiences through Western narratives has been replaced by China's film industry turning inward, producing Hollywood-style genre movies like action films *Wolf Warrior 2* and sci-fi space operas *The Wandering Earth*. While these franchises secure massive box office returns domestically, emulating if also supplanting the mythmaking and nation-building once dominated by the United States "dream factory", these cultural products barely register abroad outside of Chinese expatriates.

Of potentially much greater import is China pivoting towards a tech and platform-forward export strategy traced back to the launch of its "Belt and Road Initiatives" (BRI) in 2013. According to the Chinese authorities, the BRI aims to establish a comprehensive economic architecture that promises to mutually benefit all the regions and countries participating in the initiative (The State Council 2015; Huang 2016). This classically loose and highly flexible policy framework represents a fundamental shift from the previous bring-in and going-out strategies that predominantly focuses on export of manufacturing industry and foreign direct investment (FDI) from and to the developed economies (Huang 2016, p. 315). Within a few years of its launch, stage 2.0 of BRI shifted to include high-tech, high-value-added sectors along with low-value-added and labor-intensive manufacturing industries. The goal remained the same—to establish a more favorable international economic architecture that allows China to exert greater influence in global economic governance (Huang 2020).

The "digital silk road" (DSR) marks the next phase of BRI, predicated on the expansion of the material infrastructure of Chinese telecommunication and the "Chinese" internet across the targeted BRI regions. Within its own borders, Chinese tech has become an indispensable part of modern infrastructure of the digital economy, facilitating the international trade of goods and equipment. Now the mandate is to expand beyond their borders. As Hong Shen (2018, p. 2689) described, the Chinese state "encourages its homegrown internet companies to complement other team members in conquering foreign markets" and the Chinese internet industry in this process has identified themselves as a "boat to help other

Chinese companies when they venture out". Outbound Chinese platforms like Alibaba and ByteDance are advancing a "digital empire in the making" (Keane and Yu 2019) and, along with it, components of the wanghong industry are beginning to encroach into the territory of the global-scaling social media entertainment industry controlled by United States-owned platforms.

Inside the Firewall, and in the context of domestic tech policy, Chinese platforms have avoided accountability for violating user privacy and civil rights. Derived from Western liberal societies, these are international norms missing from the Chinese internet policy agenda. Instead, datafication becomes more than a fundamental mechanism for platform business, but also a crucial tool for social and cultural governance. This tool is best demonstrated by state investment in the social credit system: a "punishment/reward system based on credit scores that will determine whether citizens and organizations are able to access things like education, markets, and tax deductions" (Liang et al. 2018).

Outside the firewall, wanghong creators' content and communication, poised to go out, face "cultural discount". This notion is well theorized in studies of global audiovisual trade: in addition to language differences, cultural products are "rooted in one culture and thus attractive in that environment, will have diminished appeal elsewhere as viewers find it difficult to identify with the styles, values, beliefs, institutions and behavioral patterns of the material in question" (Hoskins et al. 1994, p. 367). For those projects inhibited by "narrowly nationalistic and realistic stories" (Mirrlees 2013, p. 3) are often "valued less by foreign viewers, who lack the cultural background needed to understand the product" (p. 181).

But the challenge extends beyond the cultural and linguistic to the demands by the state for creators to propagandize the virtues of China. "Tell good stories about China to the world" is a refrain oft repeated by President Xi Jinping (Xinhua 2016). Overtly nationalistic proselytization has rarely proven viable in any entertainment industry. But in the wanghong industry such demands are in direct violation of the normative appeals towards authenticity by creators that drive community engagement.

This deviation from the international norm of internet governance has posed challenges for the global operation of Chinese internet and platform companies. Despite the constant efforts in expanding their overseas business, none of Baidu, Alibaba and Tencent (BAT) has managed to achieve significant growth among international users and the majority of their online traffic remains from either the domestic Chinese market or overseas

Chinese communities (Negro 2017). The "Chineseness brand" intrinsic to these companies means that when it comes to political controversies (such as Xinjiang and Hong Kong), these companies ostensibly need to show their allegiance to the Chinese party state and "stereotypes and negative Western media coverage of Chinese issues like censorship" make it even harder for Chinese platforms to maintain a positive image among their international users (Negro 2017, p. 185).

As we will see in the next section, one path to secure wider success of Chinese platform companies has been to decouple from the purported "Chineseness brand". Through a combination of parallel platforms and localization strategies, Chinese social media platforms have a proven ability to compete, even to surpass their United States competition, in tech and platform performance, but not in global competition with Western narratives formats and genres of culture and entertainment. Chinese ceding the popular culture field to Hollywood may be the price for a larger prize—supremacy in data, information, or surveillance capitalism.

Yet this strategy diverges from the tenet of "cultural going-out" and "soft power", as advocated for decades by the Chinese state, and underlines the challenging conditions for any advance on that ambition. Chinese tech is now in direct competition with Silicon Valley. But the key cultural output of the two tech systems—the wanghong and SME industries—exist in starkly different operating environments. As we see in the next two sections, wanghong platforms have adopted parallel platform strategies, with creator-first localization and regionalization strategies. The consequence is creator segregation, preventing Chinese creators from going beyond the wall on Chinese-owned platforms. However, some Chinese and non-Chinese creators have developed cross-border, cross-platform strategies. These creator voices, despite increasing challenges, advance intercultural communication through shared affinities while seeking to overcome cultural discount and linguistic divides.

Global Wanghong Platform Strategies

In Chap. 3, we saw how the wanghong platform landscape operates at the vanguard of the transformation of China's digital economy. More technologically advanced than the SME platform landscape, we also described a more competitive and collaborative system that differs in key respects from central tenets of United States-driven digital and platform capitalism.

China's well-tended tech garden is outgrowing its borders. The national champions like Tencent and Alibaba, along with second generation platform firms like ByteDance, are ambitiously expanding their overseas empires. These private platform companies together with their unique platform affordances appear to have gained more credibility and "communication capacity" (Sun 2010) than the traditional media organizations like CCTV (China Central Television) and People's Daily in the process of cultural "going-out". With Tencent and Alibaba mainly target overseas Chinese population, the second-generation platforms like TikTok and Kwai aspire to expand their user base beyond the "Chinese-speaking" communities. However, these outsized successes have provoked anxieties in response to the expansion of Chinese platform power. Chinese tech has adopted a parallel platform strategy to address these anxieties and further expansion. But these strategies decouple "Chineseness", potentially violating the state's mandate for cultural "going out".

The response by Chinese wanghong platforms to the political unrest in Hong Kong illustrates the challenges they face. On 30 June 2020, the Standing Committee of the National People's Congress of China enacted the Hong Kong national security law. One week later, Bytedance announced that it would pull TikTok out of that market. According to prior official statements, the platform did not store user data in China or follow Chinese government regulations to censor content. Nonetheless with passage of the national security law, the platform was perceived to be under complete surveillance by Beijing and would be forced to submit user data to the Chinese government (Haldane 2020). In its stead, however, some journalists speculated that in the future Bytedance will probably turn on Douyin, its domestic, more technologically advanced, version of TikTok in Hong Kong (AFP 2020).

Whereas Google, Facebook and Twitter continue to operate in Hong Kong and comply with Chinese state and Hong Kong police (Haldane 2020), TikTok's departure epitomizes the complex global strategies adopted by Chinese social media platforms. By blocking access from Hong Kong users, TikTok signaled that they place user privacy and security alongside their own commercial interest while being unwilling to compromise their autonomy and independence in data management for a sustained Hong Kong market. But the increasing political strife in Hong Kong may still place ByteDance in an untenable situation. How might TikTok respond to Chinese government demands for the user data of Hong Kong activists or removal of anti-Chinese content? In this regard, replacing TikTok with Douyin appears to be a "win-win" for ByteDance.

Corporate Discourses

One strategy of decoupling starts with public-facing corporate discourses. On their international webpages, China-based platforms such as Alibaba, TikTok and Kwai identify themselves as global platforms, like their American counterparts Facebook and YouTube. Alibaba defines its mission as "to make it easy to do business anywhere". TikTok sees itself as "the leading destination for short-form mobile video" while emphasizing they have "global offices including Los Angeles, New York, London, Paris, Berlin, Dubai, Mumbai, Singapore, Jakarta, Seoul, and Tokyo". Kwai claims to have "over 700 million users worldwide", while without mentioning the majority of them are located in Mainland China.

This discourse is complimented by a display of visual images of international creators on their webpages (see Fig. 6.1). In a recent study of Alibaba's electronic World Trade Platform, or eWTP, Alibaba features language combined with images that appeal to Westernized ideals of diversity, multiculturalism, and marginalized identities. These strategies help to deflect a focus on Alibaba's eWTP ownership and participation within a China-centered, private-led digital trade regime (Seoane 2020).

In July 2020, TikTok published an update of its "Global Transparency Report", which discloses the number of requests the platform has received from governments around the world for user information and content removal between July and December 2019. The report claims the platform follows the localized legal and professional procedures in dealing with these requests and provides detailed statistics and technical protocols surrounding content moderation. However, the list of countries in this and prior reports omitted any reference to China or the Chinese people.

By publishing the report, TikTok aspires to be known as a "global platform" not subject to the statutes of an authoritarian, illiberal, government. As promoted in the report, the platform features "thousands of people across the markets where TikTok operates working to maintain a safe and secure app environment for everyone" (TikTok 2020). This report also echoes earlier company statements that they "store all TikTok US user data in the United States, with backup redundancy in Singapore". Reinforcing their autonomy from the Chinese state, the report claims that they do not "remove content based on sensitivities related to China" and "[have] never been asked by the Chinese government to remove any content and … would not do so if asked" (TikTok 2019).

Fig. 6.1 Webpages of TikTok and Kwai (captured on 13-July-2020)

Parallel Platforms

In addition to these corporate discourses decoupling from domestic governance regimes, Chinese platforms have pursued a dual platform strategy, launching international versions with similar, but not identical functions to their domestic apps. These include ecommerce platforms like Alibaba's Aliexpress, and social video and social streaming platforms owned by Bytedance, Kuaishou, and Tencent. ByteDance and Kuaishou have adopted a similar strategy by launching Chinese and international versions. By renaming Douyin as TikTok, Kuaishou as Kwai, the international versions of these apps are only accessible in mobile app stores when users are outside China. Like their domestic counterparts, these platforms have advanced the affordances of social presence (see Chap. 3). Whether through social streaming or social video, a mobile-first user-interface with in-app editing features, a voluble music library, and discovery algorithms, as of mid-2020, these apps have proven state-of-the-art and globally popular. Unlike their domestic counterparts, these platforms cannot emulate the same conditions and platform strategies of hyperplatformization and interplatformization including near frictionless interoperability across ecommerce platforms coupled with online mobile payment systems.

Beyond their socio-technological features and affordances, Douyin and Kuaishou's international apps promote more liberalized platform practices, governance, and control. Both apps claim to have separate servers mostly located outside China and allow users to sign up through their American social media accounts such as Facebook and Google. Curiously, the sign-up pages of Douyin and Kuaishou also include these western social media plug-ins, but Chinese social media like WeChat and QQ are placed in more central positions. With regard to content moderation, these firms block outside content from coming into China but do not share or promote Chinese content across these platforms. Alongside the content, search and hashtags are completely different as are algorithmically-driven recommendations and discovery. As further discussed below, these are based on localized interests and appeal.

While censorship and propaganda are prevalent on Douyin and Kuaishou, TikTok and Kwai appear to be more lenient and even active in allowing and facilitating certain forms of online activism. For example, TikTok allows hashtags under its discover tab like #blacklivesmatter, #MyEarthHour, and #Forclimate, featuring critical socio-cultural issues in the West regarding racism, animal abuse and climate change. After TikTok's apology for deleting a video about Uyghur education camps in Xinjiang, at least as of mid-2020, users can search and find content critical of the Chinese government, whether searching "Hong Kong" or "Uyghurs".

But Fergus Ryan, Audrey Fritz, and Daria Impiombata (2020) qualify this, claiming they discovered "an algorithm with CCP characteristics" in which most of the content "glosses over the human rights tragedy unfolding there and instead provides a more politically convenient version for the CCP, replete with smiling and dancing Uyghurs" (p. 17). These developments may align with earlier proclamations by the platform, including Bytedance CEO Zhang Yiming, that the firm will continue to promote state interests, suggesting that these firms "can't outrun Beijing's shadow"

(Spence 2019). Despite the concern surrounding political discourses and control, these platforms are nonetheless generating growth in creator economies through a mix of creator-first, localization, and regional strategies.

Localization: Creator-First and Regional Strategies

Platforms like TikTok have also pursued "localization done at a global scale" (Tirosh 2019). Described as "parallel platformization" (Kaye et al. 2020), the co-evolution of different versions of these platforms comprise a "new paradigm of global platform expansion that differs from strategies of regionalization adopted by previous major social media platforms" (p. 1). Like their United States counterparts YouTube, Facebook, and Instagram, these platforms use algorithms to feed user-generated content to online audiences based on their geo-locational and online behavioral data, stimulating online interactions among local users. These comprise a marked departure from the ethnocentric strategy by traditional media platforms whose audiences are comprised of overseas Chinese already familiar with the content (Keane and Chen 2017, p. 70).

Unlike their Western counterparts, however, Kwai and TikTok have pursued a "creator-first" strategy, localized within each market. Western platforms position their creators as minor stakeholders in their growth, relying more on digital advertising through ad-tech stacks in an increasingly monopolized landscape. Catapulted to compete globally outside of China, these platforms optimize native platform entrepreneurs for growth. TikTok recruits local wanghong creators, often through contests and challenges, enticing them and their fan communities on to these platforms, followed in rapid succession by advertisers and brands. In Australia, for example, former YouTube and Google executives have been hired to run TikTok offices and "oversee the creator and community ecosystem across the regions, which will involve developing creator opportunities and building support for communities across key verticals including LGBTQIA, sports, fashion, and education and science" (Cheik-Hussein 2020).

The combination of parallel platform and creator-first localization strategies have proven remarkable at driving scale and growth outside the country. In 2020, despite—or because of—the global pandemic, TikTok had a "monster year" (Newton 2020). This expansion is not uniform globally. Rather than compete with United States platforms in the Euro-American markets, these firms have focused on emerging social media markets including India, Southeast Asia, Brazil, Russia, and Africa. The large populations and the underdeveloped internet and social media economy in those regions have provided great opportunities for Chinese wanghong platform companies, with less competition from their international rivals. This platform strategy follows a similar route mapped by China's agenda with its Belt and Road Initiatives.

These developments have been followed by a wave of Chinese firms emulating these international platform strategies, whether launching their own or acquiring platforms. Before India shut them down in 2020, 6 of the top 10 most downloaded apps in that country were Chinese-owned (Business Insider 2019). Aside from TikTok (at the top on the list), Likee (by JOYY), Helo (ByteDance) and Vmate (by Alibaba) are Chinese social media platforms developed exclusively for overseas markets. Bytedance's closest domestic competitor, Kuaishou, developed Uvideo for India, LOLita for Egypt, Vistatus for Brazil, and Snack Video for Indonesia and Vietnam. Bigo Live, a leading livestreaming platform in Southeast Asia, was originally a start-up company based in Singapore. In 2019, the platform was merged by JOYY, a NASDAQ listed Chinese platform company, which owns the popular Chinese livestreaming platforms YY and Huya. Like TikTok and Kwai, these apps were developed for specific regions and target markets, while adopting localized aesthetics, languages and habits in affordances and marketing, and competing for local creators.

If the dominance of the big five American platforms, the GAFAM (Google, Apple, Facebook, Amazon, and Microsoft), has resulted in the "platformization" of the web and social-economic infrastructures and the "infrastructuralization of platforms" (Helmond 2015; Plantin et al. 2018; Nieborg and Poell 2018), then within the global "platform society" (van Djick et al. 2018) now there is also a trend we term "platformization from China". The platform logics that have been largely developed in the technopolitical economy of contemporary China have penetrated well beyond.

Bytedance, in particular, has proven formidable in its global expansion, taking "Asia by storm" (Keane and Yu 2019), becoming the "China's first global app" (Li 2020). According to the industry-site Business of Apps (2020), as of January 2020, TikTok was one of the most downloaded apps in the world with over 800 million monthly average users (MAUs), available in 150 markets and 39 languages, while turning Bytedance into "the world's most highly valued private startup". The firm flexed its global muscle by hiring prominent Disney executive, Kevin Mayer, to run their American operations (Isaac 2020). But all that changed a few months later.

International Backlash

2019–2020 has seen what may be the start of a major pivot in the global digital economy. There were already key drivers of a retreat from globalization: the rise of right-wing populism in the United States, the United Kingdom, Eastern and Central Europe, and Brazil, major cybersecurity concerns based around global Chinese tech infrastructure players (Huawei and LTE) and roll outs of the BRI and aggressive Chinese "wolf warrior" diplomacy. COVID-19's planetary restrictions on movement and its triggering deep global recession accelerated that pivot. Wanghong platforms Bytedance and TikTok have come to take center stage in these dramatic reversals. Enjoying huge growth in this period, they have been charged of infringement of copyright and user privacy as well as online discrimination against vulnerable minorities, in violation of the norms of platform governance (Hern 2020). Malaysia, Bangladesh, Pakistan, and Egypt have either banned the platform, insisted that users secure local licenses to post content (Shukry 2020), demanded that the platform remove offensive content (Ahmed 2020), and/or arrested citizens for posting content critical of the government or "violating family values" (Walsh 2020).

India has gone a lot further, signaling a rising tide of platform nationalism pitted against Chinese platform power. Chris Stokel-Walker (2021) points out that TikTok was "banking on India for its future", targeting the entire country with an advertising blitz while offering thousands of dollars in payments for leading Instagram creators to join its platform. However, in mid-2020, India banned 50 Chinese apps, including WeChat and TikTok, the latter losing 300 million subscribers, claiming a "security issue". It then banned more than 100 Chinese apps, including popular video game PUBG, Baidu's search engine, and the online mobile payment system Alipay (Kastrenakes 2020). These developments were, in some regards, a consequence of rising border tensions between the countries, although they have exposed larger cultural tensions as well. Indian Youtubers launched a "boycott China" campaign, giving millions of one-star ratings to Chinese TikTok that drove down its rankings in the Indian app market (Kumar 2020). These tensions reflect how "ordinary Indians couldn't help feel that they were seeing a cultural invasion alongside a nascent physical one on their borders" (Stokel-Walker 2021).

Accompanying these bans, there was a rapid expansion of Indian-owned direct emulators of TikTok's short video user-interface and functions: Mitron, Chingari, and Bolo Indya. The emulation extended to creator-driven strategy. Bolo Indya's founder openly invited "all the TikTok stars from India to be a part of the fast-growing growing Bolo Indya community" that claims to be committed to "the government's guidelines for user-generated content platforms and data security" (Singh 2020).

The backlash pattern has been repeated in the United States, although in some respects the damage has been self-inflicted, reflecting poor, culturally naïve, Chinese platform management. In 2020, Kuaishou launched Zynn to complete against Bytedance's TikTok, only specifically "tailor-made" for the United States market (Zhang 2020). Zynn emulated TikTok's features—short social video featuring a mobile-first in-app user interface and a deep music library made available in international app stores. However, Zynn committed a massive misstep by allowing creators to "freeload" stolen content from other platforms, namely TikTok. In addition, the platform offered to pay users to download the app. After scaling rapidly to first place in the United States app market, the platform was banned from United States app stores (Matsakis 2020). United States Senator Josh Hawley, a critic of both United States and Chinese tech industry practices, called for a government inquiry into Zynn, claiming the platform's practices "smacks of a textbook predatory-pricing scheme, one calculated to attain immediate market dominance for Zynn by driving competitors out of the market" (McGill 2020).

Platform malfeasance and mismanagement was met by an upswell of United States platform nationalism. In mid-2020, the Trump administration threatened bans of WeChat and announced a forced divestment of TikTok by its Chinese owners (Perez 2020; Nicas et al. 2019). Typically couched as cybersecurity issues, they signaled a "proxy battle in the United States China tech war" (Marks 2020). These moves may have been a case of cynical electioneering—pure optics by Trump in his bid to win a second Presidential election. Trump appeals to his base by not only standing up to Chinese tech and platform power but playing into Sinophobic fears arising from the coronavirus that first appeared in Wuhan. These may also be efforts to deflect from his own mismanagement of the epidemic—"a China quagmire of his own making" (McGraw 2020).

This United States attack on TikTok is, at time of writing, still playing out. Oracle, a United States cloud-based data management tech behemoth, partnered with Walmart to enter into a "platform partnership" with a minor stake in the United States portion of TikTok. This offer "falls short", with no genuine intention of resolving United States security concerns (Overly 2020). However, the underlying motivations for said deal prove dubious. As we noted in Chap. 3, United States venture capital firm Sequoia Capital is a major investor in Bytedance. They are also an investor in Oracle, and have been accused of possibly being the driving the bid for TikTok (Winkler et al. 2020). There are potential synergies between TikTok's creator-driven consumer base, Oracle's aspirations to compete in cloud-based computing, and Walmart's efforts to compete with Amazon through e-commerce. In addition, the scions of Oracle's owner operate two leading Hollywood production companies, Skydance Media and Annapurna, and they may see opportunities for entertainment IP-exploitation (Stokel-Walker 2020).

In other words, Trump's political ploy may still be part of a larger effort by Silicon Valley to emulate China's wanghong economy. In late 2019, Facebook CEO Mark Zuckerberg delivered a speech calling for Chinese platforms to be banned or restricted. Zuckerberg claimed platforms like TikTok censor democratic-led protests and failed to protect user privacy. He further "cited data localization as a major concern as it could help authoritarian governments improperly access user data" (Bell 2019). Zuckerberg's stance, bordering on Sinophobia, was also, at the least, self-serving. In 2019, the European Union introduced the General Data Protection Regulation (GPDR) specifically in response to the lack of adequate privacy protections by United States platforms, including Facebook and Instagram (Solon 2018).

Zuckerberg's alarmist speech failed to mention that Facebook-owned Instagram was launching Reels, a competitor for TikTok, in India and Brazil, and later in the United States. Emulating Zynn, Instagram is buying TikTok creators to grow Reels, offering "financial incentives to TikTok users with millions of followers to persuade them to use a new competing service, an escalation in a high-stakes showdown between the two social-media giants" (Choi 2020). Similarly, YouTube has launched Shorts, a short video formed deemed a TikTok-like platform, even if it lacks all the state-of-the-art socio-technical architecture of Chinese apps described in Chap. 3.

The United States platforms are attempting to emulate the interplatformization and social commerce strategies of the wanghong industry, whether by connecting to outside ecommerce platforms or by introducing ecommerce "markets" across their own. In 2017, Amazon launched Amazon associates designed for Twitch streamers to "provide a seamless way for audiences to buy select products" (Krefetz 2017). Instagram's

Marketplace allows companies and brands to sell products and services on the platform, including a "Shopping from Creators" feature launched in 2019. In mid-2020, YouTube announced a new eCommerce feature, awkwardly referred to as "products you see in the video", in which any brand featured in a video can be purchased. Creators "would be able to earn revenue from product placements in a much bigger way all in all, as it would be more likely that users would click on suggestions given right then and there rather than relying on them searching for a product that has been marketed to them" (Muhammed 2010).

This widespread atmosphere of profound uncertainty raises questions about the experience of individual creators in the globalization of the wanghong economy. As the previous chapters have shown, the wanghong economy forms a complex ecology in which state power interacts with capital, technology, and most importantly individual creators. We finally turn to the way globalization of the wanghong economy not only plays out in the dynamics of policy, capital, and platforms, but also through the cross-border practices of wanghong and SME practitioners, their creativity and culture.

Global Wanghong Creators and Culture

In Chap. 4, we traced the evolution of wanghong creators—from the rise of KOL (key opinion leaders) crafting online IP and extending their cultural value to online communities, to native mostly amateur wanghong going professional and in some instances, securing Big-V status through their online entrepreneurialism. We also distinguished social creators, more often livestreaming zhubo or showroom hosts, whose revenue streams are reliant less upon specific knowledge and DIY skills than upon their ability for online socialization, converting attention, engagement, and play into commercial value.

The "Big V" creators secure vast remuneration from social+ business models like social tipping and social commerce. Wanghong creators are the stars of China's globally advanced games and esports industry. Livestreaming zhubo are influencing the sale of everything from lipstick to rocket systems. An industry of "virtual girlfriends" converts lonely guys into paying customers in exchange for online intimacy otherwise denied to millions of lonely souls floating over China's bustling megalopolises. These same conditions have afforded a class of "unlikely creators" to secure greater social mobility across the platforms. Tens of thousands of wanghong firms, coined "MCNs", operate as management intermediaries between platforms, creators, brands, and services. Whereas these firms were "synonymous with failure" (Rapp 2019) in the SME industry, Chinese MCNs have flourished. With more diverse types and practice than their SME counterparts, and the assistance of MCNs, wanghong creators have become "gateways to Chinese consumers" (Fan and Backaler 2018) and vital facilitators of China's digital economy. Media accounts suggest that Chinese creators "yield much better returns than their Western counterparts" (WalktheChat 2019) and provide "lessons we can learn from the Chinese influencer ecosystem" (Schwarz 2020).

Even as Chinese platforms have scaled globally, their hyper and inter-platformization strategies in China have proven less viable outside, where national industries in retail, marketing, banking, credit, and advertising are more mature and influential and are aided by protectionist government regulations eager to thwart Chinese competition. For example, Alibaba's international platform is AliExpress, which operates in direct competition with Amazon but lacks the advantages of its China-only consumer-to-consumer (C2C) Taobao stores. As we saw in Chap. 3, wanghong creators not only thrive from selling e-commerce through their Taobao stores linked across all their platforms and channels, but Taobao has incorporated livestreaming functions for wanghong creators directly on the platform. As Zhang Dayi, once the most prominent wanghong creator in China, described, extending her online brand and business abroad has proven challenging. This is due to the difference in ecommerce infrastructure and retail buying patterns: "They are not used to buying things on Taobao, so it takes time. But now we're focusing on growing followers on social media and will work on getting to the transaction later" (Pan 2017).

In Chap. 5, we explored how wanghong creators, once held in contempt, have secured greater cultural value, whether through appeals to vernacular or traditional Chinese culture or by symbolizing the rise of modern Chinese cosmopolitanism. This radical shift in cultural value is epitomized by the extent to which established media celebrities now plan to extend their profile (and income) by engaging with and through the wanghong ecology. But the significance of wanghong culture, we argue, is captured best by the rise of the "unlikely" social class of rural creators, emerging out of agrarian, manufacturing, and service-based economies as platformed labor and entrepreneurs. The bucolic everydayness of their content proves to be intrinsic to their success and sustainability, part of a longer tradition in Chinese popular culture that values rurality and authenticity.

But, where creative impulses meet platformed economic and cultural power, so does exposure and political precarity. Most notably, social creators risk backlash and censorship from the very same state-based policies and the platforms that empowered them. Driven towards ever-increasing practices of commercialization, and comparable to Western critiques of "aspirational" creator labor (Duffy 2017), Chinese creators progress towards the performance of personality, or *renshe*, for greater profit. Yet, in the poetics of lighthearted resistance in wanghong culture, we also witness often contradictory dimensions of modern Chinese culture. Wanghong creators may adhere to hyperconsumerism and the commodification of the social. But they have also been afforded the means for both greater social mobility and self-representation. Further contrast from the conditions within established media industries, wanghong culture may also comprise a break from the normative patterns of China's traditional hierarchical society, as outlined in Chap. 5.

This includes the most unlikely of classes, creators operating at the grassroots level, some of whom have also transformed into commercially successful YouTubers. As cited in earlier chapters, rural creators like Li Ziqi (Fig. 6.2) and Dianxi Xiaoge have become successful at promoting traditional and rural Chinese culture and lifestyles across wanghong

Fig. 6.2 Li Ziqi making food in her video

platforms. They have also emerged across SME platforms to secure millions of subscribers and views. People's Daily, the official newspaper of the Chinese Communist Party (Li 2020, Jan 1), praises creators like Li Ziqi for "opening a new window to let the world see the beauty of China" and their success serves as "a valuable model to study Chinese international cultural communication". The vernacular and performed "authenticity" of these wanghong culture seems to not only resonate with the everyday life experiences of domestic Chinese population but also holds great appeal to the international audiences.

How are these creators understood by international audiences? Who are their followers on YouTube—Chinese expats, cosmopolitan foodies, and cultural tourists? As compared to culturally affirmative Chinese domestic blockbusters like *Wolf Warrior 2* and *The Wandering Earth*, are these creators consumed as yet another instance of Western Orientalism in the sense elaborated by Edward Said (1978)? If so, how does this align with the cultural soft power ambitions of the state to promote a modern China?

Witness these tensions in a 2020 scandal regarding estimates of Li Ziqi's fortune. When a tech blogger claimed in a viral video that Li Ziqi makes USD 24 million from YouTube, the news stirred a backlash in China. Li Ziqi quickly dismissed the claims, perhaps out of fear of state retribution which had previously praised her for "promoting traditional Chinese to an international audience". However, Li Ziqi's parent company claimed to have secured a million dollars from YouTube advertising, and USD 50 million from the sales of her branded products on Alibaba's Tmall ecommerce platform (Yan 2020).

Other factors such as cultural discount, particularly around language, may still play a factor in the success of wanghong creators abroad. Whereas English-speaking gameplayers like Ninja, Markiplier, and Pewdiepie dominate global scaling SME, Chinese gameplayers are trapped within their Mandarin commentary systems. Yet, these gameplayers have little cause to go out while rising up the ranks of China's game and esports industry (which is the biggest national industry in the world) and securing lucrative salaries on competing gameplay platforms like Huya and Douyu. As mentioned in Chap. 5, gameplayer Buquiren has half a million followers on YouTube in addition to eleven million on Huya.

Other Chinese verticals and classes of wanghong creators see little opportunity, or need, to compete against SME creators or to demand a position in the competition between these industries. Chinese travel wanghong, for example, deliver their virtual postcards directly on wanghong platforms available from abroad, although most can only be downloaded through Chinese app stores. Cross-border practices between SME and wanghong creators have more readily flowed in the opposite direction. Western creators, like Israeli entrepreneur Raz Gavin or 9-year-old American Gavin Thomas, are "riding China's e-celebrity wave" (Yu 2020), claiming millions of followers on Chinese platforms. However, these accounts, featuring prominently in state-run media such as China Daily and CGTN, may be as much propaganda as profiteering. But the United States media, like CNN, which claimed that the infant Thomas had "struck a chord with millions of Chinese internet users" (Wang and Kleinhenz 2018), have been happy enough to go along.

Rather, the demand is from outside China, with commercial interests looking to use wanghong creators' profiles to tap into China's rising middle class. In 2018, Japanese department store Matsuya Ginza hired Candy Lian, a Chinese lifestyle creator, to livestream on Weibo and WeChat from within Tokyo's upscale shopping district. The result was a 20-fold increase in subscribers on Ginza's online shopping site designated solely for Chinese consumers (Yoshizawa 2018). While conducting interviews with the United States-born CEO of Parklu, a Chinese MCN based in Hong Kong and Shanghai, we witnessed a Taiwanese creator livestream simultaneously for an hour across six Chinese platforms at a makeup counter, selling out the latest brand of perfume from a French supplier.

Wanghong Futures

China displays a bedrock adherence to the depth of its culture that is expressed through consistent deployment of cultural industries frameworks. It has been investing hugely in reforms to oversee the growth of especially the digital creative industries. And it arguably has led the world in what we have called social industries. Drawing these themes together, we have sought to provide a critical media industries account of the rise of this creator and platform-driven industry. Through cultural, creative, and social policies, the wanghong industry has been protected, incubated, and controlled, before extending out beyond the wall. The rise of Chinese platform and portal power includes the accelerated advance towards the affordances of social presence that feature social+ business models commercially empowering wanghong creators and management firms. Wanghong culture has emerged even under ever-increasing state and platform-based scrutiny and surveillance to include "unlikely" creativity from the rural margins of Chinese society, and to be called on by the authorities to discharge responsibility for generating work and careers amongst those marginalized. It also increasingly sits centrally in the advancement of China's tech innovation and leadership and the stimulation of its consumer economy.

We write at a time—late 2020—which is witnessing rising tensions that are far deeper than the concerns raised about media globalization. The backlash towards—potentially escalating to attempted banishment from certain jurisdictions of—Chinese tech, platforms, and apps, including consumer technology and telecommunications firms like Xiaomi and Huawei, has focused notably around the global success and data management of Bytedance-owned platform, TikTok. Such extreme backlash is usually couched as threats to national security and cybersovereignty. It is also motivated by emerging forms of platform nationalism that trigger less free trade and less open borders. In seeking to limit Chinese going-out, the ironic result may be the beginnings of other national, regional, or alliance-based "firewalls". There is already firm prognostication of two internets—by ex Google CEO Eric Schmidt—and a "splinternet" (Wright 2019). We are cognizant of and not unsympathetic to the forces questioning the claims of unalloyed benefit heralded by globalization that have resulted in the rise of right-wing populism and authoritarianism in many countries in recent years. But the major infrastructural underpinning for global, bottom-up, popular cultural communication is threatened by the balkanization of the internet and with it, diminished hope for the liberalization of cultures and communities. It is the wanghong industry, having produced a successful proof of concept for Chinese cultural going out, that now sits at the leading edge of concerns for the future prospects of globalizing popular culture.

REFERENCES

AFP. (2020). TikTok's Hong Kong Exit a 'Win-Win' Business Move. *Gadgets 360*, 9 July. Retrieved October 8, 2020, from https://gadgets.ndtv.com/apps/features/tiktoks-hong-kong-exit-a-win-win-business-move-2259798.

Ahmed, A. (2020). TikTok's content moderation report shows it deleted over 100 million videos in the first half of 2020. *DigitalInformationWorld.com*. 24 September. Retrieved from https://www.digitalinformationworld.com/2020/09/tiktok-deleted-over-100-million-videos-in-the-first-half-of-2020.html.

Bell, K. (2019). Mark Zuckerberg Says the Real Threat is TikTok and China. *Mashable Australia*, 17 October. Retrieved October 8, 2020, from https://mashable.com/article/mark-zuckerberg-tik-tok-china/.

Business Insider. (2019). Top Ten Most Downloaded Apps in India. *Business Insider*, 27 December. Retrieved October 7, 2020, from https://www.businessinsider.in/slideshows/top-ten-most-downloaded-apps-in-india/slidelist/72977234.cms.

Cheik-Hussein, M. (2020). TikTok Continues Local Expansion with Key Hires to Its Content Division. *AdNews*, 14 September. Retrieved October 8, 2020, from https://www.adnews.com.au/news/tiktok-continues-local-expansion-with-key-hires-to-its-content-division.

Choi, E. (2020). Facebook Offers Money to Reel in TikTok Creators. *The Wall Street Journal*, 28 July. Retrieved October 8, 2020, from https://www.wsj.com/articles/facebook-seeks-to-reel-in-tiktok-creators-raising-stakes-in-social-media-rivalry-11595928600.

de Kloet, J., Poell, T., Guohua, Z., & Yiu Fai, C. (2019). The Platformization of Chinese Society: Infrastructure, Governance, and Practice. *Chinese Journal of Communication*, *12*(3), 249–256.

Duffy, B. (2017). *(Not) Getting Paid to Do What You Love: Gender, Social Media, and Aspirational Work*. New Haven, CT: Yale University Press.

Fan, Z., & Backaler, J. (2018). Five Trends Shaping the Future of E-Commerce in China. *World Economic Forum, Annual Meeting of the New Champions*, 17 September. Retrieved October 8, 2020, from https://www.weforum.org/agenda/2018/09/five-trends-shaping-the-future-of-e-commerce-in-china/.

Haldane, M. (2020). TikTok Has Officially Pulled Out of Hong Kong, But You Can Still Use It if You Try. *South China Morning Post*, 11 July. Retrieved October 8, 2020, from https://www.scmp.com/abacus/tech/article/3092574/tiktok-has-officially-pulled-out-hong-kong-you-can-still-use-it-if-you.

Helmond, A. (2015). The Platformization of the Web: Making Web Data Platform Ready. *Social Media+ Society*, *1*(2). https://doi.org/10.1177/2056305115603080.

Hern, A. (2020). TikTok 'Tried to Filter Out Videos from Ugly, Poor Or Disabled Users'. *The Guardian*, 18 March. Retrieved October 8, 2020, from https://www.theguardian.com/technology/2020/mar/17/tiktok-tried-to-filter-out-videos-from-ugly-poor-or-disabled-users.

Hong, Y. (2017). Pivot to Internet Plus: Modeling China's Digital Economy for Economic Restructuring? *International Journal of Communication*, *11*, 1486–1506.

Hong, Y., & Goodnight, T. G. (2020). How to Think about Cyber Sovereignty: The Case of China. *Chinese Journal of Communication*, *13*(1), 8–26.

Hoskins, C., McFayden, S., & Finn, A. (1994). *Global Television and Film: An Introduction to the Economics of the Business.* Oxford: Clarendon Press.

Huang, P. (2016). Our Sense of Problem: Rethinking China Studies in the United States. *Modern China, 42*(2), 115–161.

Huang, A. (2020). Who is Millionaire Li Jiaqi, China's 'Lipstick King' Who Raised More than US$145 Million in Sales on Singles' Day? *South China Morning Post,* March 9. Retrieved October 8, 2020, from https://www.scmp.com/magazines/style/news-trends/article/3074253/who-millionaire-li-jiaqi-chinas-lipstick-king-who.

Isaac, M. (2020). TikTok chief executive Kevin Mayer resigns. *The New York Times.* 28 August. Retrieved from https://www.nytimes.com/2020/08/27/technology/tiktok-kevin-mayer-resign.html.

Jin, D. Y. (2013). The Construction of Platform Imperialism in the Globalization Era. *Triple C: Journal for a Sustainable Information Society, 11*(1), 145–172.

Kastrenakes, J. (2020). India Bans PUBG Mobile, Alipay, Baidu, and More Chinese Apps. *The Verge,* 2 September. Retrieved October 8, 2020, from https://www.theverge.com/2020/9/2/21418120/pubg-mobile-india-ban-118-apps-china-alipay-baidu.

Kaye, D. B., Chen, X., & Zhang, J. (2020). The co-evolution of Two Chinese Mobile Short Video Apps: Parallel Platformization of Douyin and TikTok. *Mobile Media & Communication.* https://doi.org/10.1177/2050157920952120.

Keane, M., & Chen, Y. (2017). Digital China: From Cultural Presence to Innovative Nation. *Asiascape: Digital Asia, 4*(1–2), 52–75.

Keane, M., & Yu, H. (2019). A Digital Empire in the Making: China's Outbound Digital Platforms. *International Journal of Communication, 13,* 4624–4641.

Kokas, A. (2017). *Hollywood Made in China.* Oakland. University of California Press.

Krefetz, N. (2017). Twitch Embraces Ecommerce with Amazon Associates. *Streaming Media,* 31 August. Retrieved October 8, 2020, from https://www.streamingmedia.com/Articles/ReadArticle.aspx?ArticleID=120260.

Kumar, A. (2020). TikTok, Some Other Chinese Apps Slip in App Store Rankings in Last Month in India. *India Today,* 3 June. Retrieved October 8, 2020, from https://www.indiatoday.in/technology/news/story/tiktok-some-other-chinese-apps-slip-in-app-store-rankings-in-last-month-in-india-1685101-2020-06-03.

Li, H. (2016). Chinese Culture "Going Out": An Overview of Government Policies and an Analysis of Challenges and Opportunities for International Collaboration. In M. Keane (Ed.), *Handbook of Cultural and Creative Industries in China.* Edward Elgar Publishing.

Li, J. (2020). How TikTok became China's First Global App. *Quartz,* 24 February. Retrieved October 8, 2020, from https://qz.com/1796676/how-bytedance-made-tiktok-chinas-first-global-app/.

Liang, F., Das, V., Kostyuk, N., & Hussain, M. (2018). Constructing a Data-Driven Society: China's Social Credit System as a State Surveillance Infrastructure. *Policy & Internet*, *10*(4), 415–453.

Liu, Y. (2018). The Chinese Farmer Who Live-Streamed Her Life and Made a Fortune. *The New Yorker*, 29 October. Retrieved July 3, 2020, from https://www.newyorker.com/culture/culture-desk/the-chinese-farmer-who-live-streamed-her-life-and-made-a-fortune.

Lu, H., & Chen, Y. (2020). The Protection of the "Third Kind of Workers" in Gig Economy from the Perspective of Social Rights. *China Human Rights*, *19*(1). 27 July. Retrieved October 8, 2020, from http://www.chinahumanrights.org/html/2020/MAGAZINES_0727/15397.html.

Marks, J. (2020). The Cybersecurity 202: The TikTok Ban is Just a Proxy Battle in the U.S.-China Tech War. *The Washington Post*, 13 August. Retrieved October 8, 2020, from https://www.washingtonpost.com/politics/2020/08/13/cybersecurity-202-tiktok-ban-is-just-proxy-battle-us-china-tech-war/.

Matsakis, L. (2020). Zynn, the Hot New Video App, Is Full of Stolen Content. *Wired*, 6 August. Retrieved October 8, 2020, from https://www.wired.com/story/zynn-hot-new-video-app-stolen-content/.

McGill, M. (2020). Hawley Calls for FTC Inquiry into New TikTok Rival. *Axios*, 10 June. Retrieved October 8, 2020, from https://www.axios.com/zynn-tiktok-hawley-ftc-61acef45-f01c-4493-8bf8-b1264d124a5e.html.

McGraw, M. (2020). Trump's First TikTok Move: A China Quagmire of His Own Making. *Politico*, 11 September. Retrieved October 8, 2020, from https://www.politico.com/news/2020/09/11/trumps-tiktok-china-412053.

Mirrlees, T. (2013). *Global Entertainment Media*. New York: Routledge.

Muhammed, Z. (2010). YouTube Ventures into eCommerce with New Feature. *Digital Information World*, 1 May. Retrieved October 8, 2020, from https://www.digitalinformationworld.com/2020/05/youtube-ventures-into-ecommerce-with-new-feature.html.

Negro, G. (2017). Chinese Internet Companies Go Global: Online Traffic, Framing and Open Issues. In M. Kent, K. Ellis, & J. Xu (Eds.), *Chinese Social Media* (pp. 175–190). London: Routledge.

Newton, C. (2020). TikTok is Having a Monster 2020. *The Verge*, 10 June. Retrieved October 8, 2020, from https://www.theverge.com/interface/2020/6/10/21285309/tiktok-2020-user-numbers-revenue-smash-hit-mea-culpa.

Nicas, J., Isaac, M., & Swanson, A. (2019). TikTok Said to Be Under National Security Review. *The New York Times*, 1 November. Retrieved October 8, 2020, from https://www.nytimes.com/2019/11/01/technology/tiktok-national-security-review.html.

Nieborg, D., & Poell, T. (2018). The Platformization of Cultural Production: Theorizing the Contingent Cultural Commodity. *New Media & Society, 20*(11), 4275–4292.

Nye, J. (2012). China and Soft Power. *South African Journal of International Affairs, 19*(2), 151–155.

Overly, S. (2020). Trump's TikTok Power Play May Fall Short. *Politico*, 14 September. Retrieved October 8, 2020, from https://www.politico.com/news/2020/09/14/trump-tiktok-sale-china-414724.

Pan, Y. (2017). Top Web Celebrity Zhang Dayi Reveals the Key to Her Business Success. *Jing Daily*, 19 July. Retrieved October 8, 2020, from https://jingdaily.com/uncovering-business-secrets-chinas-top-web-celebrity-zhang-dayi/.

Peng, W., & Keane, M. (2019). China's Soft Power Conundrum, Film Coproduction, and Visions of Shared Prosperity. *International Journal of Cultural Policy, 7*(3), 904–914.

Perez, S. (2020). Shady TikTok Clone Zynn Finally Removed from the App Store. *TechCrunch*, 16 June. Retrieved October 8, 2020, from https://techcrunch.com/2020/06/16/shady-tiktok-clone-zynn-finally-removed-from-the-app-store/.

Plantin, J., Lagoze, C., Edwards, P., & Sandvig, C. (2018). Infrastructure Studies Meet Platform Studies in the Age of Google and Facebook. *New Media & Society, 20*(1), 293–310.

Rapp, J. (2019). How do multi-channel networks (MCNs) work in China? *Parklu.com*. 29 March. Retrieved from https://www.parklu.com/multi-channel-networks-mcns-china/.

Ryan, F., Fritz, A, & Impiombata, D. (2020). TikTok and WeChat: Curating and Controlling Global Information Flows. *Australian Strategic Policy Institute*, 8 September. Retrieved October 8, 2020, from https://www.aspi.org.au/report/tiktok-and-wechat.

Said, E. (1978). *Orientalism*. New York: Pantheon Books.

Schiller, D. (1999). Digital Capitalism: Networking the Global Market System. *Education for Information, 17*(3), 268–270.

Schwarz, R. (2020). What We Can Learn From The Chinese Influencer Ecosystem. *Forbes*, 7 January. Retrieved October 8, 2020, from https://www.forbes.com/sites/forbescommunicationscouncil/2020/01/07/what-we-can-learn-from-the-chinese-influencer-ecosystem.

Seoane, M. (2020). Alibaba's Discourse for the Digital Silk Road: The Electronic World Trade Platform and 'Inclusive Globalization'. *Chinese Journal of Communication, 13*(1), 68–83.

Shen, H. (2018). Building a Digital Silk Road? Situating the Internet in China's Belt and Road Initiative. *International Journal of Communication, 12*(2018), 2683–2701.

Shukry, A. (2020). Malaysia Clamps Down on Film-Making With TikTok in The Fray. *Bloomberg*, 23 July. Retrieved October 8, 2020, from https://www.bloomberg.com/news/articles/2020-07-23/malaysia-clamps-down-on-film-making-with-tiktok-in-the-fray.

Singh, J. (2020). What are India's Biggest TikTok Competitors Saying about the China App Ban? *Gadgets360*, 30 June. Retrieved October 8, 2020, from https://gadgets.ndtv.com/apps/news/tiktok-ban-india-competitors-mitron-chingari-china-app-2254578.

Solon, O. (2018). How Europe's 'Breakthrough' Privacy Law Takes on Facebook and Google. 19 April. Retrieved October 8, 2020, from https://www.theguardian.com/technology/2018/apr/19/gdpr-facebook-google-amazon-data-privacy-regulation.

Spence, P. (2019). ByteDance Can't Outrun Beijing's Shadow. *Foreign Policy*, 16 January. Retrieved October 8, 2020, from https://foreignpolicy.com/2019/01/16/bytedance-cant-outrun-beijings-shadow/.

Srnicek, N. (2017). *Platform Capitalism*. Oxford: Polity Press.

Stokel-Walker, C. (2020). Experts Think TikTok's Tie-Up with Oracle and Walmart Gives it a Route into Film, TV, books, and Merch. *Business Insider*, 22 September. Retrieved October 8, 2020, from https://www.businessinsider.com/tiktok-oracle-tv-shows-books-merchandise-2020-9.

Stokel-Walker, C. (2021). *TikTok, China and the Superpower Battle for Social Media*. Surry: Canbury Press.

Sun, W. (2010). Narrating Translocality: Dagong Poetry and the Subaltern Imagination. *Mobilities*, 5(3), 291–309.

The State Council. (2015). *Instructions on Promoting 'Internet +'* [国务院关于积极推进'互联网+'行动的指导意见]. State Council Bulletin No. 53 of 2015. Retrieved October 8, 2020, from http://www.gov.cn/zhengce/content/2015-07/04/content_10002.htm.

TikTok. (2019). Statement on TikTok's Content Moderation and Data Security Practices. *TikTok Newsroom*, 24 October. Retrieved October 8, 2020, from https://newsroom.tiktok.com/en-us/statement-on-tiktoks-content-moderation-and-data-security-practices.

TikTok. (2020). TikTok Transparency Report 2019 H2. *TikTok Newsroom*, 9 July. Retrieved October 8, 2020, from https://www.tiktok.com/safety/resources/transparency-report.

Tirosh, O. (2019). What is TikTok?: Localization done Right at a Global Scale. *Tomedes*, 14 November. Retrieved October 8, 2020, from https://www.tomedes.com/tomedes-insider/what-is-tik-tok.php.

van Djick, J., de Waal, M., & Poell, T. (2018). *The Platform Society: Public Values in a Connective World*. Oxford: Oxford University Press.

WalktheChat. (2019). How Much Money Do Influencers Earn in China vs. Elsewhere? *Jing Daily*, 15 February. Retrieved October 8, 2020, from https://jingdaily.com/influencers-china-elsewhere/.

Walsh, D. (2020). Egypt Sentences Women to 2 Years in Prison for TikTok Videos. *The New York Times*, 28 July. Retrieved October 8, 2020, from https://www.nytimes.com/2020/07/28/world/middleeast/egypt-women-tiktok-prison.html.

Wang, S., & Kleinhenz, J. (2018). How an Eight-Year-Old American Boy became a Viral Sensation in China. *CNN*, 9 November. Retrieved October 8, 2020, from https://edition.cnn.com/2018/11/08/china/gavin-meme-kid-china-intl/index.html.

Winkler, R., Gottfried, M., & Lombardo, C. (2020). General Atlantic, Sequoia Capital are Key Drivers in Oracle Bid for TikTok. *The Wall Street Journal*, 24 August. Retrieved October 8, 2020, from https://www.wsj.com/articles/general-atlantic-sequoia-capital-are-key-drivers-in-oracle-bid-for-tiktok-11598310734.

Wright, K. (2019). The 'Splinternet' is Already Here. *Techcrunch*, 13 March. Retrieved October 8, 2020, from https://techcrunch.com/2019/03/13/the-splinternet-is-already-here/.

Xinhua. (2016). President Xi Urges New Media Outlet to "Tell China Stories Well". *Global Times*, 31 December. Retrieved October 8, 2020, from https://www.globaltimes.cn/content/1026592.shtml.

Yan, A. (2020). Chinese YouTube Star Li Ziqi Dismisses Claim She Makes US$24 Million a Year. *South China Morning Post*, 10 January. Retrieved October 8, 2020, from https://www.scmp.com/news/china/society/article/3045620/chinese-youtube-star-li-ziqi-dismisses-claim-she-makes-us24m, date accessed 8 October 2020.

Yoshizawa, K. (2018). Cosmetics Influencer Demonstrates Clout of Chinese Social Media. *Japan Times*, 2 March. Retrieved October 8, 2020, from https://www.japantimes.co.jp/news/2018/03/02/business/chinese-social-media-clout/.

Yu, C. (2020). Foreigners Ride China's E-Celebrity Wave. *China Daily*, 11 February. Retrieved October 8, 2020, from https://global.chinadaily.com.cn/a/202002/11/WS5e41eaeea310128217276761.html.

Zhang, Y. (2020). Chinese Rival Launches U.S. App to Challenge TikTok. *The Information*, 28 May. Retrieved October 8, 2020, from https://www.theinformation.com/articles/chinese-rival-launches-u-s-app-to-challenge-tiktok.

Index[1]

A
Adaptability, 20, 44
Affective labor, 90, 109, 118
Affective platform economies, 82
Affinities, 11, 16, 20, 80, 86, 110, 166
Affordances, 17, 19, 20, 35, 39, 40, 46, 49, 60, 62, 63, 70, 72, 75, 77–79, 81–84, 89–92, 107–109, 114, 116, 120, 122, 145, 151, 156, 167, 170, 172, 180
Agency, 7, 9, 10, 33, 40, 41, 45, 50, 76, 80, 107, 110, 115, 121, 124, 125, 128, 153
Algorithms, 6, 85, 107, 171
   with CCP characteristics, 170
Alibaba, 4, 5, 38, 48, 50, 61, 66, 68–71, 73–75, 89, 91, 125, 165–169, 172, 177, 179
Amateur production, 113
Ambivalences, 9, 146
Anti-hegemonic struggles, 141

App-centric ecology, 71
App factory, 85
Artificial Intelligence (AI), 32, 41, 59, 85, 86
Aspirational labor, 90, 106
Aspirations, 18, 85, 106, 175
Authenticity, 10, 11, 21, 112, 126, 129, 137, 141–146, 151, 153, 155, 165, 177, 179

B
Baidu, Alibaba, Tencent (BAT), 61, 62, 66–69, 75, 85, 162, 165
Balkanization of the internet, 181
Beauty blogging, 154, 155
Be creative, 108, 150
Belt and Road Initiatives (BRI), 164, 172, 173
Better self, 107, 119
Bigo, 118, 172

---

[1] Note: Page numbers followed by 'n' refer to notes.

Big V, 20, 110, 112, 116, 121, 176
Bilibili, 59, 62, 75–79, 88, 112, 113, 121, 137, 138, 141, 146, 147, 150, 152–154
Blued, 59, 62, 82, 156
Boredom creativity, 140, 150, 151
Boredom culture, 140
Brand culture, 10, 126, 129, 140
Bytedance, 5, 6, 38, 62, 66, 68, 77, 85, 86, 88, 120, 121, 165, 167, 169, 170, 172–175

C

Celebrification, 2, 3
Censorship, 35, 43, 51, 74, 79, 105, 109, 117, 118, 129, 150, 156, 162, 166, 170, 178
China as method, 161
China Central Television (CCTV), 110, 118, 135–137, 149, 151, 167
Chinese Communist Party, 30, 179
Chinese cosmopolitanism, 177
Chinese internet, 4, 19, 44, 65, 66, 68, 138, 163–165, 180
Chineseness brand, 166
Chinese popular culture, 144, 148, 150, 155, 177
Chinese rural, 38, 50
Chinese socialist cultural development, 31
Chinese traditional idyll, 143
Clean Plate campaign, 122
Command economy, 46
Commercial viability, 11
Commodified culture, 10
Commodified entertainment, 21, 136
Community engagement, 11, 73, 108, 165
Confucian value, 136
Connectivity, 16, 36, 77, 118

Consumer economy, 21, 181
Consumerist culture, 10
Content genre, 8, 47, 114
Contradictory interests, 45
"Convergence" culture, 37, 140, 148
Copyright, 42, 173
Cosmopolitan, 5, 86, 88, 109, 112, 156, 179
COVID-19, 4, 40, 46, 82, 92, 122, 173
Created in China, 14, 31
Creative clusters, 35
Creative destruction, 32, 33
Creative industries, 11, 13–14, 19, 29, 31–35, 39, 40, 42, 51, 80, 106, 109, 180
Creative labor, 14, 106, 107, 150
Creative wanghong, 20, 110, 112–116, 121, 139, 154
Creator Culture, 3
Creator-first, localization, 166, 171–172
Creator-first strategy, 171
Creator labor, 17, 60, 78, 81, 107, 108, 151, 178
Creator marketplace, 121
Creators, 2, 3, 5, 7, 8, 10, 11, 14, 16–18, 20, 21, 29, 30, 35, 39–44, 46–48, 50, 51, 59, 60, 63, 64, 70–78, 80–84, 86–92, 105–129, 137, 139–143, 145–154, 157, 161–163, 165, 166, 168, 171–180
Creator segregation, 166
Critical media industry studies (CMIS), 9, 10
Cross-border practices, 176, 180
Cross-platform integration, 70
Cultural and media creativity, 31
Cultural capital, 112, 114, 126
Cultural commodities, 40
Cultural dilemma, 136

Cultural discount, 165, 166, 179
Cultural disruptions, 35, 49–50
Cultural economy, 32–34, 150
Cultural export, 34
Cultural going-out, 21, 32, 163, 166, 181
The Cultural Industries, 9, 11–12
Cultural politics, 7, 30, 145, 146, 156
The Cultural Revolution, 20, 136
Cultural security, 34
Cultural value, 39, 176, 177
Cultural wanghong, 20, 110, 112–114, 116, 139, 148
Culture, 6, 7, 9–14, 17, 18, 20, 21, 31–35, 39–41, 45, 49, 60, 72, 75, 77, 80, 87, 88, 92, 109, 112, 113, 115–117, 126, 129, 135–157, 161, 163, 165, 166, 176–181
Culturization, 13
Cybersovereignty, 162, 181
The Cyberspace Administration, 6, 44, 45

D
Danmaku, 75, 78, 79
Da shang, 89, 121
Datafication, 16, 152, 165
Data localization, 175
Decouple "Chineseness," 167
Decoupling, 71, 168, 169
Depoliticization, 33
Dianxi Xiaoge, 142, 178
Digital China, 30
Digital creative industries, 11, 29–35, 40, 180
Digital economy, 7, 8, 14, 16, 21, 30, 31, 36–38, 42, 44, 47, 59–62, 64–66, 68, 71, 72, 90, 116, 120, 123, 125, 127, 136, 161, 162, 164, 166, 173, 177

Digital payments revolution, 69
Digital silk road (DSR), 164
Digital technologies, 37, 39
Dissidence hypothesis, 156
Do-It-Yourself (DIY), 75, 138, 139, 149, 154, 155, 176
Double responsibilities, 150
Douyin, 5, 20, 49, 59, 62, 66, 67, 83–88, 112, 113, 118, 120–122, 128, 138, 143, 147–150, 153, 155, 167, 169, 170
Douyu, 5, 47–49, 59, 67, 77, 80, 81, 122, 138, 153, 179
Dual platform strategy, 169
Dynamism, 20

E
E-commerce, 4, 5, 16, 17, 37–40, 49, 50, 60, 62, 63, 66, 69–71, 80, 89, 91, 122, 123, 125, 126, 140, 149, 153, 175, 177
Economic restructuring, 36, 50
Economy, 2–4, 7–14, 16–19, 21, 30–47, 49, 51, 59–66, 68, 69, 71, 72, 78, 80, 82, 89, 90, 106, 108, 115–117, 120, 123, 125, 127, 129, 136, 137, 140, 145, 146, 150, 152, 156, 161, 162, 164, 166, 171–173, 175–177, 181
Edge-ball, 45, 49, 122, 127, 163
Emerging industries, 1, 34
Employment, 6, 18, 36–38, 40, 49, 50, 126, 136, 157
Entertainment IP-exploitation, 175
Entrepreneurial agency, 80, 115
Entrepreneurial creators, 18
Entrepreneurialism, 72, 78, 90, 92, 105, 107–109, 116, 120, 123, 124, 162, 176
eWTP, 168

F

Fan base, 4, 128
Fan communities, 7, 8, 11, 72, 74, 75, 77, 79, 82, 88, 105, 107, 114, 120, 122, 171
Fashionable lifestyles, 86
Fishing, 113, 121, 140, 142, 152
5G, 5, 61
Flying geese models, 74
Food vlogger, 154
Fragmented authoritarianism, 45

G

GDP growth, 46, 65
General Data Protection Regulation (GPDR), 175
Gig economy, 43
Gig labor, 162
Global China, 162
Global wanghong, 161–181
Going out, 8, 21, 32, 34, 35, 44, 163, 164, 166, 167, 181
Gonghui, 126
Governance, 6, 17–19, 21, 29–51, 59, 61, 63, 105, 108, 109, 117, 127, 129, 135, 145, 161–166, 169, 170, 173
The governance of China, 18
Grassrootedness, 112
Grassroots, 3, 5, 10, 36, 39, 60, 88, 89, 109, 112, 136, 137, 148, 150, 163, 178
Great firewalls, 66, 163
Grindr, 82
Guerrilla policy-making, 46
Guichu, 137
Guild, 43, 116, 126, 127

H

Hands-off approach, 40, 41
"Hooligan" novels, 137
Huanjushidai, 80
Huanong Brothers, 140, 141, 143
Huawei, 59, 173, 181
Huoshan, 62, 85, 86, 88, 119
Hyperconsumerism, 178
Hyperplatformization, 19, 60, 63–72, 92, 121, 128, 170

I

Ideological character, 32, 33
iGet, 111
Indie rock, 137
Individualism, 14, 21, 32, 33, 107, 136, 137, 155
Industry ecology, 7
Information and communication technology (ICT), 13, 19, 36, 59, 63, 68, 163
Infrastructuralization of platforms, 172
In Real Life (IRL), 81, 191
Intensified play, 86
Interfaces, 17, 74, 77, 84, 86, 87, 107, 122, 124, 174
Intermediaries, 2, 7, 20, 29, 38, 73, 105, 110, 112, 123–125, 176
Internet +, 36–40, 50, 89
Internet celebrities, 3, 4, 116
Internet celebrity economy, 4
Internet infrastructure, 38
Interplatformization, 19, 60, 63–72, 75, 91, 92, 121, 123, 170, 175, 177
Intersectionalities, 106
Intersubjective relations, 135
IP platform strategies, 74
Irreducible core, 13

J
Jiediqi, 154
Joyful playground, 141

K
Key opinion leader (KOLs), 2, 20, 76, 108, 110, 112, 128, 176
KOL management, 76
Kuaishou, 5, 37, 39, 49, 50, 59, 62, 66, 68, 77, 83, 85–88, 110, 117, 118, 121, 122, 138, 146, 147, 149, 150, 153, 169, 170, 172, 174

L
Labor practice, 39, 51, 116
Laotie, 88
Leapfrogging, 68, 69
Legacy media, 7, 20, 29, 34, 35, 39, 41, 60, 63, 73, 74, 83, 110, 116, 124
LGBTQ dating apps, 82
Light-hearted resistance, 21, 137, 140, 156, 178
Li Jiaqi, 86, 87, 91, 140, 149, 155, 156
Lite apps, 71
Little Red Book, 91, 153
Live clubbing, 92
Live gaming, 77, 79–81, 83, 121, 122
Live + miniseries, 83, 89
Livestreamers, 2, 5, 8, 46, 47, 90, 108, 114–119, 121, 127, 152, 155
Livestreaming, 6
  affordances, 49
  platforms, 39, 49, 50, 59, 67, 70, 80, 81, 114, 118, 121, 122, 127, 172
Live streaming +, 89

Li Ziqi, 35, 140, 143, 178, 179
Lonely leftover men, 49, 115

M
Machine learning, 117
Mainstream, 116, 120, 137, 139, 145, 148, 149, 156
Manufacturing labor, 44
Mass entrepreneurship, 18, 36–40, 50, 151, 162
Mass Entrepreneurship and Innovation, 36, 38, 151, 162
Materialistic values, 136
MCN management, 126
Micro-platformization, 153
Mini-programs, 71
Modularity, 71
Mo lei tau, 146
Monetization, 41, 42, 74, 120–123, 153
Multichannel networks (MCNs), 20, 46, 75, 76, 88, 105, 112–114, 116, 120, 121, 123–129, 153, 162, 176, 177, 180
Multilateralism, 162
Multisided markets, 38, 40

N
National characteristics, 32
Nationalism, 11, 19, 21, 67, 72, 82, 152, 156, 162, 173, 174, 181
National unity, 34, 45
Native creators, 11, 76, 77, 83
Network publics, 78
New Year's Eve Spring Festival gala, 76
NoCal, 60, 72
Non-mainstream (feizhuliu) culture, 116
Non-state capital, 33

O

One-child policy, 49, 115, 137
One night stand app, 81
Online culture, 35, 40, 141, 156
Orientalism, 179

P

Panda TV, 81
Papi Jiang, 4, 74, 75, 113, 116, 143
PapiTube, 75, 114
Paradoxical co-creation, 141
Parallel platformization, 171
Parallel platforms, 6, 66, 166, 167, 169–171
Parallel universe, 7, 61, 161
Participatory culture, 10, 17, 80, 137
Participatory viewing, 79
Party-state, 6, 8, 10, 12, 21, 32, 34, 44, 45, 108, 136, 162, 166
Performance of personality, 152, 178
Performative labor, 82
Permanent beta, 60
PGC, 128
Pinduoduo, 40, 49, 50, 66, 69, 88, 89, 91, 123
Platform, 5, 8, 179, 180
  capitalism, 51, 60–62, 81, 106, 157, 161, 166
  companies, 39, 40, 51, 85, 106, 121, 165–167, 172
  dynamics, 107
  economy, 12, 19, 36–41, 44, 51, 62, 63, 66, 82, 89, 106, 140, 156
  evolution, 19
  imperialism, 64, 162
  labor, 106, 108, 121
  moderation, 79
  nationalism, 21, 67, 72, 82, 162, 173, 174, 181
  pillarization, 86, 88
  power, 41, 42, 69, 167, 173, 174
  society, 16, 63, 86, 106, 161, 172
  strategies, 60, 68, 70, 74, 75, 81, 85, 166–176
Platformativity, 116
Platform-dominated network system, 40
Platformization, 16, 19, 29, 38, 39, 60, 63, 71, 106, 148, 153
  from China, 172
Plusification of internet technologies, 89
Policy, 3, 6–9, 11–14, 17–19, 21, 29–51, 59, 61, 62, 80, 89, 106, 115, 117, 118, 127, 137, 162–165, 176, 178, 180
Policy incentivization, 62
Political agenda, 32
Popular culture, 9, 10, 12, 21, 34, 140, 144, 148, 150, 155, 157, 166, 177, 181
Populism, 145, 173, 181
Porn 2.0, 47
Porn industry, 47
Portalization, 19, 60, 63, 72–77, 82, 83, 88, 92, 121
Portals, 7, 16, 19, 63, 72–75, 128, 148, 180
Positive values, 139, 150
Poverty alleviation, 18, 40, 50
Precarious management, 105, 126
Private and social capital, 38
Produsers, 17
Professionalization, 74, 107, 116
Professional video content, 19
Programmability, 16, 71
Propaganda, 4, 14, 30, 31, 145, 150, 170, 180
Prosumers, 79, 106
Pseudo-synchronicity, 79

R
Regionally decentralized authoritarian (RDA) regime, 45–46
Relational labor, 14, 107–109, 119
"Relationship-based" platform, 88
Renshe, 153, 155, 178
Restructuring, 32, 36, 50, 108, 136
Ruhan, 125, 126
Rural life, 142

S
SARFFT, 117, 127
Self-censorship, 109, 117, 129
Self-governance, 109, 117
Self-regulation, 29, 41, 47, 105
Self-representation, 118, 123, 178
Shopping from Creators, 176
Short video, 37, 39, 49, 50, 67, 70, 83–86, 113, 120, 138, 142, 143, 149, 150, 153, 173, 175
Showroom hosts, 2, 80, 108, 114, 176
Sinking market, 50
Sinophobia, 162, 175
Skepticism, 136
Smartphone penetration, 64
SoCal, 60, 72
Social affordances, 79, 107
Social amelioration, 19, 21, 29, 50
"Social-benefit" approach, 32, 49
Social business models, 16, 17, 78
"Social+" business model, 20, 77, 80, 89–92, 176, 180
Social commentary, 20, 77–83, 92
Social commerce, 17, 20, 77, 88–92, 108, 109, 118, 120–123, 125, 175, 176
Social content, 17, 83, 92, 140
Social credit system, 40, 165
Social dimension, 9, 17, 18, 145
The social dis-dance, 92
Social eating, 47, 114
Social games, 15
Social governance, 17, 32, 36–40, 162
Social industries, 11, 14–18, 20, 39, 72, 90, 180
Socialist advanced culture, 32
Sociality culture, 146
Social journalism, 15
Social media entrepreneurs, 2, 108
Social media platforms, 1, 7, 8, 15–17, 20, 59, 60, 63, 68, 72, 73, 75, 77, 80, 91, 106, 109, 109n1, 110, 112n2, 117, 122, 123, 128, 147–149, 166, 167, 171, 172
Social plus, 17
Social presence, 17, 19, 20, 60, 62, 63, 77–92, 105, 108, 109, 114, 116, 119, 121, 122, 151, 170, 180
Social production, 17
Social streaming, 20, 77–83, 92, 110, 169, 170
Social tipping, 17, 20, 77, 81, 88–90, 92, 108, 109, 118, 120–122, 125, 127, 176
Social video, 15, 17, 20, 59, 77, 83–89, 92, 110, 169, 170, 174
Social wanghong, 20, 105, 110, 114–116, 126–128, 139, 152, 154
Socio-technical innovation, 105
Soft power, 34, 35, 44, 163, 166, 179
Splinternet, 82, 181
Stakeholders, 29, 38, 40, 42, 43, 61, 68, 71, 76, 105, 120, 129, 171
STAR, 67, 68
Star-Station TV, 128
State, 6, 8, 12, 18–20, 29, 30, 32, 33, 35, 36, 38–41, 43–46, 49–51, 59–61, 74, 79, 86, 89, 105, 108, 117–119, 127, 129, 136–138, 141, 145, 146, 149–151, 156, 157, 162–168, 170, 176, 179, 180

State apparatus, 33
State-control, 62
State discursive formation, 33
State policy, 18, 29, 41, 44, 118, 163
State surveillance, 20, 46, 79
State-owned cultural entities, 31
State-owned television, 118, 150
State-platform-capitalism complex, 157
Streamers, 48, 49, 70, 80, 81, 89, 90, 115, 119, 122, 127, 152, 156, 175
Streaming wars, 73
Stream queens, 49
Structural changes, 13, 31
Subcultural sell-out, 88
Subculture, 76, 148
Subjective formation, 157
Subscription revenue, 120
Sustainability, 41, 42, 77, 78, 85, 107, 120, 121, 177

T
Taobao, 5, 37, 38, 40, 48–50, 60, 62, 69–71, 86, 91, 113, 123, 125, 126, 149, 155, 177
Taxonomy of Wanghong labor, 108–116, 138
Tech conglomerates, 6, 60, 66
Techlash, 41, 42
Tech marketplace, 67
Technological innovation, 20, 31, 47, 68, 77, 92
"Tech-tonic" clashes, 73, 162
Tech war, 174
Tencent, 6, 19, 38, 49, 50, 61, 67–73, 75, 77, 81, 84, 85, 91, 148, 165–167, 169
Third kind of worker, 162

Thirteenth 5-year Plan, 29, 34
Tier 1 cities, 113
TikTok, 5–7, 21, 35, 39, 62, 66–68, 70, 72, 85, 118, 120, 128, 167–175, 181
Top-down governance, 42
Toutiao, 38, 62, 66, 85, 121
Traditional media, 16, 17, 39, 43, 73, 75, 76, 167, 171

U
Unicorns, 66, 68
Unlikely aesthetics, 18, 21, 148
Unlikely creative class, 18, 147, 148
Unlikely creative workers, 109
Unlikely creativity, 146, 147, 153, 181
Unlikely creators, 5, 18, 146–151, 176
Up zhu, 76
Urban culture, 148
User-Generated Content (UGC), 39, 73, 112, 137, 171, 174

V
Venture capital (VC), 66–68, 75, 91, 175
Vernacular creativity, 17, 21, 140, 142, 150
Verticals, 47, 73, 74, 79, 80, 83, 112, 114, 120, 122, 138, 154, 171, 179
Viability, 11, 20, 51, 72, 75, 77, 80, 89, 91, 109, 121, 124
Virtual girlfriends, 2, 49, 81, 108, 114, 115, 176
Virtual liveness, 79
Virtual tipping, 48, 80
Visibility labor, 106
Viya, 91, 123, 155

W

Walled garden, 70, 72
Wang Shuo, 137
Wanghong, 2–11, 16–21, 29, 30, 35, 39–48, 50, 51, 59, 60, 62–64, 66–68, 70–72, 74, 75, 77, 78, 80–86, 88, 90–92, 105–129, 135–157, 161–181
Wanghong economy, 2–4, 17–19, 30, 35, 39, 40, 45, 46, 68, 117, 125, 129, 145, 146, 150, 152, 175, 176
Wanghong entrepreneurialism, 72, 92, 109, 124
Wanghong incubators, 125
Wanghongization, 148
Wanghong labor, 20, 105–116
Wanghong management, 118, 123–129
Wanghong-style, 148
WeChat, 1, 6, 7, 16, 37, 38, 59, 69–72, 75, 91, 109, 110, 112, 117, 138, 154, 170, 173, 174, 180
WeChat Public Account, 109, 110
WeChat Wallet, 70
Weibo, 59, 62, 70–72, 90, 112, 113, 117, 118, 125, 128, 129, 138, 146, 152–154, 180
Weishi, 84, 85, 153

Wenhua zou chuqu, 163
Western centrism, 9
"Wolf warrior" diplomacy, 173

X

Xianchang, 144, 145
Xiaodian, 71
Xiaohongshu, 91
Xigua, 62, 77, 113, 121, 122, 138, 141
Xinpianchang, 128

Y

Yin jinlai, 163
Youku, 59, 62, 72–77, 80, 92, 110, 128, 148
Youth culture, 137, 140, 141, 148, 155
YY festival, 82
YY Live, 80, 81

Z

Zhang Dayi, 8, 113, 116, 126, 177
Zhenyu, 110
Zhubo, 2, 48, 80, 81, 91, 108, 114, 115, 118, 126, 127, 152, 176
Zou chuqu, 163
Zuckerberg, Mark, 48, 175

CPSIA information can be obtained
at www.ICGtesting.com
Printed in the USA
LVHW082218270221
680126LV00005B/79